TRANCE-MIGR∤

TRANCE-MIGRATIONS

Stories of India, Tales of Hypnosis

LEE SIEGEL

THE UNIVERSITY OF CHICAGO PRESS · CHICAGO AND LONDON

LEE SIEGEL is professor of religious studies at the University of Hawaii. He is the author of many books, including *Love in a Dead Language*, *Who Wrote the Book of Love?*, and *Love and the Incredibly Old Man*, all published by the University of Chicago Press.

The University of Chicago Press, Chicago 60637
The University of Chicago Press, Ltd., London
© 2014 by The University of Chicago
All rights reserved. Published 2014.
Printed in the United States of America
23 22 21 20 19 18 17 16 15 14   1 2 3 4 5

ISBN-13: 978-0-226-18529-3   (cloth)
ISBN-13: 978-0-226-18532-3   (paper)
ISBN-13: 978-0-226-18546-0   (e-book)

DOI: 10.7208/chicago/9780226185460.001.0001

LIBRARY OF CONGRESS CATALOGING-IN-PUBLICATION DATA
Siegel, Lee, 1945– author.
    Trance-migrations : stories of Indea, tales of hypnosis / Lee Siegel.
        pages cm
    Includes bibliographical references.
    ISBN 978-0-226-18529-3 (cloth : alk. paper) —ISBN 978-0-226-18532-3 (pbk. : alk.
paper)—ISBN 978-0-22618546-0 (e-book) 1. Hypnotism—Fiction. 2. India—Fiction. 3.
Hypnotism. I. Title.
    PS3569.I377T735 2014
    813'.54—dc23
                                                                            2014008395

FOR REEN,
*who was hypnotized by a Hindu fakir and
read stories to me as a child*

CONTENTS

IN[TRO]DUCTION
Reading, Listening, and Hypnosis

The good subject [or listener] accepts the hypnotist's [or reader's] words as true statements; he perceives and conceives reality as the operator [or writer] defines it.

THEODOR XENOPHON BARBER, *HYPNOSIS: A SCIENTIFIC APPROACH* (1969)

"Now Rann the Kite brings home the night, that Mang the Bat sets free," so long ago she softly read to me. "The herds," I heard her words, "are shut in byre and hut, for loosed till dawn are we." Rhythmic phrases read in bed soothed senses, heavied eyelids, made me yawn and blink, yawn, yawn again, and, as eyes closed, my bedroom was slowly, slowly trance-formed into a lair somewhere in a moonlit Indian jungle. The bed was earth, a flannel blanket the fur of nestling cubs warming Mowgli as a hypnotic flutter of words configured a family of wolves. "He came naked, by night," the wolf-mother whispered, "alone and very hungry; yet he was not afraid!"

Language lullabied me deeper and deeper into lush and languid epiphanies. Listening to bedtime stories read by my mother was initiation into the sublime transports of literature.

Soon, however, I was expected to be able to read to myself. Learning to do so in the first grade was a daunting, arduous, and frustrating task. Struggling to master the ways in which twenty-six letters, variantly capital or small, roman or cursive, of an alphabet we had been trained to recognize by strenuous drill could form sounds in our minds, which in turn could be construed as words arranged and punctuated in such a way that we, by scrutinizing clusters of black ciphers on the page of a book, could decode the knowledge that Spot was the name of a dog. Once upon a time reading stories about Dick and Jane at play was, as perhaps you remember, hard work.

I imagine that our teacher must have appreciated the struggle, because after each tedious lesson she'd invite us to lay our books aside and rest our heads on arms crossed on little desks that in those days still had inkwells. And then she'd grant us the comfort of listening, welcome rest from the laborious exercise of reading. "By the shores of

Gitche Gumee," she began, "by the shining Big-Sea-Water, stood the wigwam of Nokomis, daughter of the Moon, Nokomis."

Eyelids became heavy, heavier and heavier, soon to close, as we, floating adrift in the gently rippling currents of her melodic voice, were entranced by words that enabled us to hear "the whispering of the pine trees, the lapping of the waters, sounds of music, words of wonder," and to see the Indian boy going "forth into the forest straightway, all alone walked Hiawatha."

The inevitable harsh ringing of a mechanized bell would suddenly disrupt reverie, bringing me out of a shadowy wigwam wherein the daughter of the Moon taught Hiawatha "of the stars that shine in heaven, how the beavers built their lodges, and why the rabbit was so timid," and back into a stark classroom.

Once upon a time, listening to stories was easy enchantment, gentle transport, and sweet dream. In retrospect I wonder if perhaps, deep down, I then feared that once I was able to read on my own, women might no longer read to me.

The pleasure of listening to a story is a regressive one, personally a return to childhood and collectively a retrogression to a time before Gutenberg and widespread literacy when stories were, by most people most often, heard rather than read.

For me the pleasure has also been a digressive one, experienced in an Indian excursus, an exploration of an extraordinarily bountiful tradition of enchanting narratives in India—erotic, heroic, religious, comic—all meant to be recited again and again by itinerant bards, human vessels of fluid fables, to be heard again and again in delight by people highly adept at listening. The pleasure of reading them is in imagining what it must be like to hear them.

With a conviction that the experience of listening to a story can be quite literally a hypnotic one, and that the relationship between a reader and listener is analogous to that between a hypnotist and subject, I have, with the intent of exploring the psychological dynamics and esthetic implications of that analogy, written eight tales to be read aloud to a willing listener about hypnosis and its erotic, religious, and political dimensions. The stories are about hypnosis inasmuch as hypnosis is, by its very nature, about the power of stories.

This book is an experiment in a sort of Pavlovian project to test my hypothesis that a story, by being heard in a certain context and particular way, in a state at least akin to hypnotic trance, can become more believably real than the same tale as it was mutely written and is silently read. What is heard, I would suggest, has the potential to be more absorbing and luminous, more vividly imagined, viscerally experienced, and unquestionably believed than what is read.

The fictional tales about hypnosis ("For the Listener") are juxta-posed with eight nonfictional stories ("For the Reader"), which, like this introduction, are meant to be read silently by you. As the passive, silent reader of these words, you are, by continuing to read, agreeing to a relationship with me, the active, silent writer of these words—a relationship intended to provide you, as an active, voicing reader, with words to be read aloud to a passive, silent listener, who, in listening to those words, will be consenting to a relationship with you, which will, in turn, provide him or her with an opportunity to experience and understand the tales in this book differently, perhaps more vividly, than they are by either you, the reader, or me, the writer.

My tales "for the listener," are meant to generate fluidly various meanings as determined by whatever relationship they establish between a writer (me), reader (you), and listener (him or her). Those meanings are to be sequentially modulated by our senses in their transmission from the mind of the writer by means of typing fingers into the mind of a reader, in through reading eyes and out through a speaking mouth into the mind of a listener through hearing ears.

These tales have been composed to be what hypnotherapists re-fer to as induction scripts. To the degree that a subject concentrates on the semantic suggestions of the hypnotist, an induction script stimulates a progressive detachment from all sensory input from the immediate environment other than the voice of the hypnotist. An effective script instigates a dissociation from the phenomenal world, an isolation of immediate cognitive and sensory functions, and a concentrated state of mind in which the subject allows hypnotic ut-terance to fabricate realities out of illusions. In the hypnotic state the subcortical structures of the brain cease to differentiate between verbally suggested experiences and actual ones. Hypnosis allows the imagination and memory of the subject, as stimulated by the hyp-notist's speech, to construct subjective scenarios in which illusions seem empirically real. Hypnosis blurs distinctions between fiction and nonfiction.

In reading these words you are constrained to hold this book in your hands, to turn its pages, to keep your eyes open, focused, and busily moving back and forth across this page. These conditions and distractions, slight as they may be, limit the dissociation from reality that hypnosis sponsors and that listening to my tales is intended to encourage. A listener can relax more than any reader. Eyes can rest, eyelids can close, and slowly, slowly, the listener's attention can become more focused than yours, their concentration more intense and credulity more expansive. There's nothing that demands to be heard other than your voice, nothing to be seen other than what my words suggest, nothing to be felt other than whatever feelings the tales evoke in your listener.

In our silence there is, right now, a distance and distinction between us, you the passive, present reader of these words and me the active, past, and absent writer. But your physical presence and the sound of your voice as you read the tales to a willing listener should allow for the sort of rapport that favors induction into a hypnotic state of consciousness in which you and I, as well as your listener and mine, become indistinguishable from one another.

While you, for whatever reason, have chosen to read this, I did not choose for you to do so. While you do not need me, I do need you. I cannot control whether you read on or decide to close this book and put it aside. Our relationship is literally in your hands. Your relationship with a consenting listener being, on the other hand, a mutually chosen, agreed upon, and sustained collaboration, should engender an intimacy that will serve hypnotic induction.

The vocabulary, rhetoric, and style of hypnotic induction scripts have dictated the language of the listener's tales. They are trance-scripts—thus there are rhythmic cadences, run-on sentences, euphonic constructions, incantatory monotonies, dissociative comments, counting forward and backward, anaphoric and epistrophic repetitions, punning for embedded suggestion ("go to the *en-trance*"), a reiteration of—and stress on—key words (*heavy, relaxed, calm, deep, deeper, slowly, softly*), combinations of ideomotor ("with every *breath* you take") and ideosensory suggestions ("you can *smell* the incense"), and frequent reassurances (*"yes, yes"*). The second person singular pronoun is used in a permissive and invitational present tense ("you can, *if you wish*, allow yourself to imagine a pipal tree in a village in India") and in an encouraging future tense ("you *will be able to see* a man sitting beneath it"), as well as in an authoritarian and commanding imperative tense (*"imagine it," "picture* him," and *"listen"*).

In a psychoanalytic understanding of hypnosis as a process that reactivates or recapitulates the parent-child experience, the direct authoritarian and indirect permissive modes of induction are characterized as "father hypnosis" and "mother hypnosis," respectively. I've alternated between these modes in the tales for the listener.

The fictions are meant to be performative, read slowly, gently, as when reading to a child, calmly in a soothing, sonorous voice, modulated in response to your listener's responses, paced to deepen trance. The depth of hypnotic immersion can be evaluated by changes in the eyes (blinking, rolling, eyelids trembling, closing), movements of the head (rolling sideways, falling backward or forward, jaw loosening), breathing (slowing and deepening from diaphragmatic to rhythmic abdominal breathing), and by a limpness of the limbs.

While empirical hypnotic susceptibility scales indicate a very wide range in the degrees of the depth of trance that are reached by clinical subjects, in general those scales suggest that practically all mentally functional individuals are, so far as they are able and willing to relax, concentrate, play along, and imagine, susceptible to some degree of odylic persuasion. Most of us want to be enchanted. We know the potential pleasures of surrender and joys of illusion.

Hypnotic practice has demonstrated that the susceptibility of the hypnosand is enhanced by the ritualization of the inductions. Your readings should likewise be ritualized, performed under the same conditions, in the same place, at about the same time of day or night.

It is conventional in hypnotic practice for the hypnotist to prepare the subject for hypnosis with a preinductional talk. The stories designated for the reader in this book are meant to provide orientational information which you may or may not, to whatever extent, depending on the interest or curiosity of your listener, chose to relate as a means of establishing a context and mood for each reading.

During hypnosis, a subject is learning how to be hypnotized and so does, with each subsequent induction over a period of time, become reliably and more rapidly relaxed, more able to actively imagine and effectively concentrate. There is an intensification of the rapport with the hypnotist, a greater susceptibility, vulnerability to suggestion, and willingness to surrender. Likewise, while hearing the fictional narratives in this book, the listener should be learning how to listen to them and should become progressively more conditioned to concentrate with exponentially greater focus on what is suggested by the reading. With each reading, disbelief should be more rapidly and substantially suspended.

The first inductional narrative to be read aloud, "The Storyteller's Tale," is not so much expected to sponsor deep trance as it is intended to prepare and condition the listener for incrementally more profound states of absorption to be induced during the reading of each subsequent trance-script. The second narrative, "The Magician's Tale," invokes what has been imagined during the first reading to encourage greater narrative immersion. The third reading, "The Translator's Tale," is modeled on the "fractionational" technique of induction, a procedure whereby trance is significantly deepened by a process of hypnotizing, dehypnotizing, rehypnotizing, dehypnotizing again, and again rehypnotizing the subject in a single session.

To the degree that your listener is willing to relax, trust us, play along, and concentrate on what is verbally suggested, he or she should be able gain access to a cognitive and sensory engrossment in which each of the ensuing tales becomes more and more intensely envisioned so that by the last narrative, "The Mesmerist's Tale," the listener might be able to imagine, at least momentarily, that the events in the story have actually been witnessed and that the characters are intimately known.

At that point, this book, as an external object containing white pages of paper imprinted with black letters that form words, sentences, and paragraphs, vanishes into thin air.

And it will reappear in your hands only when the story is over and the eyes of listener open to look at the real world once more.

Mayavati's Spell

INDIA, STORIES, AND HYPNOSIS

The object of literature is to put to sleep the active or rather resistant powers of our personality, and thus to bring us into a state of perfect responsiveness, in which we realize the idea that is suggested to us and sympathize with the feeling that is expressed. In the processes of the literary arts we shall find, in a weakened form, a refined and in some measure spiritualized version of the processes commonly used to induce the state of hypnosis.

HENRI BERGSON, *TIME AND FREE WILL* (1889)

part one

FOR THE READER

Two Stories to be Read Silently

India is the hallowed home of Hypnosis.
Since time immemorial Hindu Yogis in India
have practiced the secret science of Maya,
what scholars, doctors, and psychologists in
the modern West call Mesmerism, Animal
Magnetism, or Hypnotism. Using the
power of Maya the Adept can cause you to
believe that imaginary things are real.

SADHU SATISH KUMAR,
ORIENTAL HYPNOTISM (1958)

THE CHILD'S STORY

And now, if you dare, LOOK into the hypnotic eye!
You cannot look away! You cannot look away! You cannot look away!

THE GREAT DESMOND IN *THE HYPNOTIC EYE* (1960)

I was eight years old when my mother was hypnotized by a sinister Hindu yogi. Yes, she was entranced by him, entirely under his control, and made do things she would never have done in her normal waking state. My father wasn't there to protect her and there was nothing I, a mere child, could do about it. I vividly remember his turban and flowing robes, his strange voice, gliding gait, and those eerie eyes that widened to capture her mind. I heard his suggestive whispers—"Sleep Memsaab, sleep"—and saw his hand moving over her face in circular hypnotic passes. "Sleep, Memsaab."

It's true. I heard it with my own ears and saw it with my own eyes as I watched "The Unknown Terror," an episode of the series *Ramar of the Jungle*, on television one evening in 1953. Playing the part of a teak plantation owner in India, my mother, the actress Noreen Nash, was vulnerable to the suggestions of the Hindu hypnotist they called Catrack. "When the dawn comes," he instructed her, "You will take the rifle and go to the camp of the white Ramar. You will aim at his heart and fire."

I watched as my mother, wearing a pith helmet, bush jacket, and jodhpur pants, rose from her cot, loaded her rifle, and then trudged in a somnambulistic trance, wooden and emotionless, through the jungle to Ramar's tent. Since my mother, as far as I knew her at home, had no experience with firearms, I was not surprised that she missed her target. She dropped the rifle and disappeared back into the jungle.

Later on in the show, once again hypnotically entranced, she was led by Catrack to the edge of a cliff where the yogi declared, "We are in great danger, Memsaab. The only way to escape is to jump off this cliff." Just as my mother was about to leap to her death, Ramar arrived on the scene and fired his rifle into the air. The loud bang of the gunshot awakened her in the nick of time and caused Catrack to flee. Thanks to Ramar, my mother survived her adventures in India.

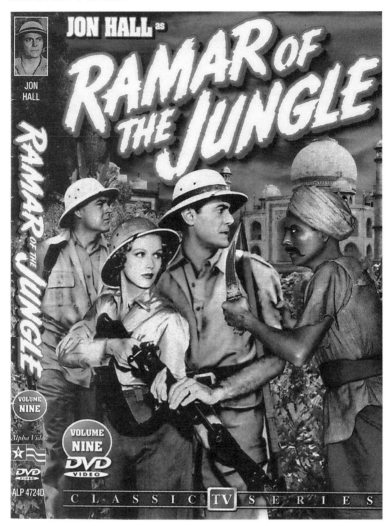

The seeds of my curiosity about hypnotism and an indelible association of it with an exotic, at once alluring and foreboding, India were
sown in front of a television. At about the same time I saw my mother
hypnotized and made to do terrible things by a yogi, I watched another
nefarious Hindu hypnotist, Swami Talpar, played by Boris Karloff in
Abbott and Costello Meet the Killer, try to take control of the feeble mind
of Lou Costello. Both India and hypnosis were dangerous.

But then another old movie, *Chandu the Magician*, assured me
that just as Indian hypnotism could be used for evil, so too it was a

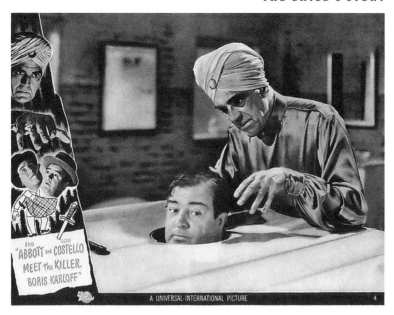

power that could be employed to overcome wickedness and serve the good of mankind. The film opened somewhere in India at night with a full moon casting eerie shadows on an ancient heathen temple as the American adventurer Frank Chandler bowed down before a dark-skinned, long-bearded Hindu priest in a white dhoti and matching turban. The Hindu swami addressed his acolyte in a deep echoic voice: "In the years that thou hast dwelt among us, thou hast conquered the Atma of the spirit and, as one of the sacred company of the Yogi, thou hast been given the name Chandu. Thou hast attained thy reward by being endowed with the ancient Oriental magical power that the doctors of thy race call hypnotism. Thou shalt look into the eyes of men and they shall be as straw in thy hand. Thou shalt cause them to see what is not there even unto a gathering of twelve by twelve. To few, indeed, of thy race have the secrets of the Yogi been revealed. The world needs thee now. Go forth in strength and conquer the evil that threatens mankind."

That India was the home of hypnotism was further confirmed by listening to my mother read Kipling to me at bedtime. We had moved on from *The Jungle Book*, read to me when I was about the same age as Mowgli, to *Kim*. And I imagined the hero of that story and I were the same age, as well. "Kim flung himself wholeheartedly upon the next turn of the wheel," my mother began. "He would be a Sahib again for a while. . . ." and soon I'd yawn, blink, blink, and yawn again, feel the heaviness of my eyelids, heavier and heavier, more and more relaxed. I'd roll over, eyes closing, and soon be able to imagine that her voice might be Kim's: "I think that Lurgan Sahib wishes to make me afraid," she'd say he said. "And I am sure that that devil's brat below the table wishes to see me afraid. This place is like a Wonder House."

I'd picture the interior of Lurgan's shop as vividly as if I were there and could see what Kim saw, focusing my attention on each of the objects, suggested one by one: "Turquoise and raw amber necklaces. Curiously packed incense-sticks in jars crusted over with raw garnets, devil-masks and a wall full of peacock-blue draperies . . . gilt figures of Buddha . . . tarnished silver belts . . . arms of all sorts and kinds . . . and a thousand other oddments."

When, as commanded, Kim pitched the porous clay water jug that was on the table there to Lurgan, I saw it "falling short and crashing into bits and pieces."

My mother reached over and lightly placed her hand on the back of my neck as Lurgan, in his attempt to hypnotize Kim, "laid one hand gently on the nape of his neck, stroked it twice or thrice, and whispered: 'Look! It shall come to life again, piece by piece. First the big piece shall join itself to two others on the right and the left. Look!' To save his life, Kim could not have turned his head. The light touch held him as in a vice, and his blood tingled pleasantly through him. There was one large piece of the jar where there had been three, and above them the shadowy outline of the entire vessel."

"Look! It is coming into shape," my mother whispered and "Look! It is coming into shape," echoed Lurgan Sahib. Yes, it was coming into shape, all the shards of clay magically reforming the previously unbroken jug. I could see it. The words my mother read aloud to me were as hypnotic as the words uttered by Lurgan.

My childhood fascination with hypnosis was sustained by a school assignment to read Edgar Allan Poe's stories, several of them—"The Facts in the Case of Mr. Valdemar," "Mesmeric Revelation," and "A Tale of the Ragged Mountains"—being about mesmerism, and the final story reaffirming an association of hypnosis with India. The main

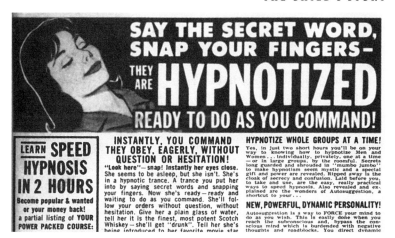

character goes into a trance in Virginia in which he has a vivid vision of Benares, a city to which he has never been, indicating that he had lived in India in a previous lifetime.

"Not only are Poe's stories about hypnosis," I grandly proclaimed in a book report I wrote in the seventh grade, "They are also written in a language that is very hypnotic, especially if they are read out loud." Little did I suspect that that homework assignment would be prolusory to a book written more than half a century later.

When subsequently in the eighth grade I was required to prepare a project for the school science fair, I was determined to do mine on hypnosis as the only science, other than reproductive biology, in which I had much interest. The science teacher warned that it was a dangerous subject: "Hypnotism is widely used in schools in the Soviet Union to brainwash children so that they believe that Communism is good and that they must do whatever their dictator, Nikita Khrushchev, commands."

Despite its abuse behind the Iron Curtain, I was determined to learn as much as I could about hypnosis. And so I ordered a book, *Home Study Way to Hypnotic Practice*, that I had seen advertised in a copy of *Twitter* magazine, a naughty-for-the-times pulp publication that I had discovered hidden in my uncle's garage.

The ad promised that a mastery of hypnotism would enable me to control the minds of others, particularly the minds, and indeed the hearts, if not some other parts, of girls: "'Look here'—Snap! Instantly her eyes close. She seems to be asleep but she isn't. She's in a hypnotic trance. A trance you put her into by saying secret words and snapping your fingers. Now she's ready—ready and waiting to do as you command. She'll follow your orders without question or hesitation. You'll have her believing anything you suggest and doing whatever you want her to do. You'll be in control of her emotions: love, hate, laughter, tears, happy, sad. She'll be as putty in your hands."

The winsome smiling girl with closed eyes in the advertisement reminded me of a classmate named Vickie Goldman, whose burgeoning breasts were often on my mind. I was naturally intrigued by the idea that by means of hypnotism those breasts might become as putty in my hands.

It was disappointing to discover in reading that book that a mastery of hypnotic techniques was much more complicated and tedious to learn than the ad for it had promised, and even more disheartening to learn that, in order to be hypnotized, Vickie would have to trust me and want to be hypnotized by me.

Another ad, in another copy of *Twitter* snatched from my uncle's collection of girlie magazines, however, suggested that, by means of various apparatuses, I would be able to take control of her mind without her consent. All I'd have to do is say, "Look at this," or "Listen to this."

So, for the sake of having both a science project and as much control over Vickie Goldman's emotions and behavior as Catrack had had over my mother's, even as much power over her as Khrushchev had over children in the Soviet Union, I ordered the products advertised by the Hypnotic Aids and Supply Company: the Electronic Hypnotism Machine, the Electronic Metronome, the folding, pocket-sized Mechanical Hypnotist, and the 78-rpm Hypnotic Record. Because I was spending more than ten dollars on these devices, I also received the Amazing Hypno-Coin at no extra charge. My mother was willing to pay for these devices since I needed them for my science project.

I also purchased the book *Oriental Hypnotism*, "written in Calcutta India with the cooperation of Sadhu Satish Kumar," because the yogi pictured in the ad reminded me of the one who had hypnotized my mother in *Ramar of the Jungle*. The text revealed that, by means of hypnosis, "the power of Maya," Hindu yogis are able to "charm serpents, control women, and win the favor of men. Self-hypnosis gives the

Hindus their amazing ability to lie down on beds of nails. And it is by means of mass hypnosis that their magicians have for thousands of years performed the legendary Indian Rope Trick." I was familiar with the rope trick from seeing Chandu use his hypnotic power to cause "a gathering of twelve by twelve" to imagine they were seeing it performed.

My science project exhibit, HYPNOTISM EAST AND WEST IN THE PAST, PRESENT AND FUTURE BY LEE SIEGEL, GRADE 8, featured a poster board mounted over a table upon which waved my Hypnotic Metronome and spun both the Hypnotic Spiral Disc of my Electronic Hypnotism Machine and side one of my Hypnotic Record. Over the eerie drone of Oriental music there was a monotonously rhythmic deep voice: "As you listen to these words your muscles will begin to relax, to become more and more relaxed, yes, very relaxed, and your eyelids will become heavy, yes, heavier and heavier, very, very heavy, very relaxed. Deeper and deeper, relaxed." The words "relaxed," "heavy," and "deeper" were repeated over and over and then there was counting backward, then imagining going down, "deeper and deeper," in an elevator, more counting backward, and finally, at the end of the record, right after "three, two, one," came the crucial the hypnotic suggestion: "The next voice you hear will have complete control over your mind."

That's when I would to take over. That's when, if the principal of our school, the judge of the projects in the fair, listened to the record, I'd command: "You will award Lee Siegel the first-place blue ribbon for his science project." And if Vickie would look and listen, that's when my interest in hypnosis would really pay off: "You will go behind the handball courts with Lee Siegel and there you will ask him to fondle your breasts."

To intensify the hypnotic mystique of my project, I placed a warning sign by the Electronic Hypnotism Machine: STARE AT THE SPIN-NING DISC AT YOUR OWN RISK. LEE SIEGEL WILL NOT BE HELD RESPONSIBLE FOR ANY ACTIONS RESULTING FROM A LOSS OF MENTAL CONTROL.

Along with all of my puchases from the Hypnotic Aids Supply Company, I placed the Westclox pocket watch on a chain that my uncle had given me for my bar mitzvah.

I livened up the poster board with a photo labeled EAST: SADHU SATISH KUMAR, HINDU YOGI HYPNOTIST, cut from *Oriental Hypnotism* side by side with a picture labeled WEST: DR. FRANZ MESMER, FATHER OF ANIMAL MAGNETISM, that I had clipped from the *World Book Encyclopedia*.

There was also a timeline beginning in 3000 BC (as estimated by Sadhu Satish Kumar) with "Indian Fakirs and Yogis" and ending

"Sometime in the Future" with "Lee Siegel who has learned so much for this science fair project that he plans to become a professional hypnotist. After graduating from high school and college he will go both to India to study hypnotism with yogis and to Oxford University to study it with science professors."

In between the ancient Hindu hypnotists and my future self were luminaries in the history of hypnosis as enumerated in the *World Book Encyclopedia*: Franz Mesmer (1734–1815), the Marquis de Puységur (1751–1825), Abbé Faria (1756–1819), John Elliotson (1791–1868), James Braid (1795–1860), James Esdaile (1808–1859), Ivan Pavlov (1849–1936), and Sigmund Freud (1856–1936). In order to make the list more acknowledging of India's contributions to hypnosis I added Swami Catrack (1919–1953), Frank Chandler, a.k.a. Chandu (1932–), and Sadhu Satish Kumar (1928–). I also included The Amazing Kreskin (1935–) and William Kroger (1906——), because, other than Catrack, Swami Talpar, Chandu, Lurgan, Satish Kumar, Nikita Khrushchev, and Sigmund Freud, they were the only hypnotists I had ever heard of. I knew that Sigmund Freud was a psychiatrist who thought that little boys were in love with their mother and that little girls wished they had a penis. I included Kroger, a gynecologist, avid proponent of medical hypnotherapeutics, and a friend my parents who occasionally visited our home, in the hope that he might, once I had shown him my science project, write a note on the official stationery of the International Society for Clinical and Experimental Hypnosis of which he was president, something to be framed and included in my display, something like "Lee Siegel's science project deserves a blue ribbon and should be sent on to the national competition, which it will certainly win."

All he wrote, however, was: "Young Siegel has done a good job in presenting a subject that deserves wider recognition and acceptance."

Not having been awarded the first-place blue ribbon—or a ribbon of any other color, for that matter—for my science project, nor having been able to successfully use my hypnotic aids to turn Vickie—or any other girl—into putty in my hands, ready to follow my orders without question, my interest in hypnotism waned.

I don't think I thought about hypnosis very much until a couple of years later when, in 1960, I happened see a horror film, *The Hypnotic Eye*, the movie, according to publicity posters, "that introduces Hyp-

noMagic, the thrill you SEE and FEEL! It's the amazing new audience sensation that makes YOU part of the show!" There were warnings that HypnoMagic could cause viewers of the film to actually become hypnotized: "WATCH AT YOUR OWN RISK!"

The movie was about a mysterious series of gruesome acts of self-mutilation by beautiful women, none of whom were able to remember why or how they had disfigured themselves, and all of whom, a detective, the hero of the film, discovered, just happened to have gone to a theater to see the stage hypnosis show of The Great Desmond. That each of them had been hypnotized during one of his performances caused the detective to suspect that the hypnotist might have been involved in the crimes. Consulting a criminal psychologist, he learned that, "Yes, posthypnotic suggestion could indeed cause a woman to do things she would not otherwise consider doing."

At one point in the film, during a performance of his stage show, the despotic Desmond held up something meant to resemble an eyeball flashing with light—the titular Hypnotic Eye! After daring his audience to stare into it, he turned to the camera and dared us, the audience in the movie theater, to do the same. The camera moved in closer and closer on the pulsating orb as, "deeper and deeper" was repeated again and again until soon, as commanded by the diabolical hypnotist, the members of his audience were lifting their arms and then lowering them. And then Desmond stared straight at us again and commanded us to do the same, and soon, together with the audience *in* the movie, we, the audience *of* the movie, were lifting our arms, then lowering them, again and again, until Desmond finally ordered us to stop and then, after counting from one to three, he snapped, "Wake up!"

Although I don't think I was actually hypnotized by the Great Desmond and don't know how many members of the movie audience were, I felt compelled to go along with the show, to act as if I was in a trance, and do as I was told. That, I would suggest, is in and of itself a kind of hypnosis. Hypnosis, like listening intently to a story, is playing along with words.

At the very end of the movie, after the crimes had been solved and the evil hypnotist apprehended, the criminal psychologist addressed the viewers of the movie: "Hypnotism can be a valuable tool, helping humanity in many ways. But, just as it can be used to do good, so too,

in the hands of unscrupulous practitioners, it can be used to perpe-
trate evil. We must be wary to maintain our safety because they can
catch us anywhere, and at anytime." He paused as the camera moved in
for a close-up: "Yes, even during a motion picture in a movie theater."
He winked, then smiled, and the screen faded to black.

I didn't think much about the film until recently, when I began writing about hypnosis. I confess, although I should probably be ashamed
to admit it, that this text has been stylistically inspired by the B movie
gimmick. In the spirit of *The Hypnotic Eye*, the tales in this book that
are meant to be read aloud to a cooperative listener are written with
HypnoMagic, the thrill you SEE and FEEL! It's the amazing literary
sensation that makes the listener part of the story! But beware! HypnoMagic could cause listeners to actually become hypnotized and actually imagine that they are participants in the tales they hear.

THE HYPNOGRAPHER'S STORY

*All world travelers are familiar with the Hindus, Fakirs, Yogis, snake charmers,
and Eastern magicians who induced themselves and others in cataleptic states by
eye fixation and other mesmeric techniques, and were able to perform unusual
physical feats and eliminate pain.*

WILLIAM J. BRYAN, "HISTORY OF HYPNOSIS" (1958)

James Braid (1795–1860), the Scottish physician credited with the introduction of the word "hypnotism" into the English language, believed
the term defined a traditional Indian practice. In his *Witchcraft, Animal
Magnetism, Hypnotism, and Electro-Biology*, he stated: "Last May [1843],
a gentleman residing in Edinburgh, who had long resided in India, fa-
voured me with a letter expressing his approbation of the views which
I had published on the nature and causes of hypnotic and mesmeric
phenomena. In corroboration of my views, he referred to what he had
previously witnessed in oriental regions, and recommended me to
look into the *Dabistan*, a book lately published, for additional proof
to the same effect. On much recommendation I immediately sent for a
copy of the *Dabistan* in which I found many statements corroborative
of the fact that the eastern saints are all self-hypnotisers, adopting

means essentially the same as those which I had recommended for similar purposes."

The proposition in 1894 of the German physician, psychiatrist, and psychic researcher, Baron Albert von Shrenck-Notzing, that yoga is fundamentally autogenic hypnosis remains a widespread assumption in hypnological literature. William Kroger, the physician who was no help to me in getting a blue ribbon for my eighth-grade science project on hypnotism, typically observed in his book *Experimental Hypnosis in Medicine, Dentistry and Psychology* that "the fundamental principles of Yoga are similar to those of hypnosis. The goal in Yoga of ultimate reality or nirvana, the state of complete liberation, is strikingly similar to depersonalization and to other dissociative state characteristic of hypnosis."

Yogic procedures and hypnotic inductions obviously have much in common—eye fixation, regulation of and concentration on breathing, a focus of perception on various parts of the body, a dissociation of awareness of sense data from the external world, an absorption in suggested images and emotions, all culminating in a trance state. These similarities encouraged Russian occultist Madame Blavatsky (1831–1891) in her *Modern Panarion* to construe "hypnotism as naught but the Trâtaka of the Yogî, the act of concentrating his mind on the tip of the nose, or on the spot between the eyebrows. It was known and practised by the ascetics in order to produce the final Samâdhi, or temporary deliverance of the soul from the body; a complete disenthralment of the spiritual man from the slavery of the physical with its gross senses. It is being practised unto the present day."

With an impulse to demonstrate that hypnosis was well understood thousands of years before Mesmer made it known in the west, the *Yogasutras* of Patanjali are frequently submitted as evidence. An article in the *Indian Streams Research Journal* written by Shitika Chowdhary and Jini K Gopinath, professors in the Department of Psychology of Christ University in Bangalore, typically maintains that "there are similarities between the trance in hypnosis and the trance in Patanjali's yoga sutras, in the induction and deepening of the trance states in hypnosis and that of Samadhi, the phenomena present in hypnosis and the kinds of siddhis that are obtained through Samadhi, and the therapeutic techniques in Patanjali's yoga sutras and hypnosis."

While hypnosis is often invoked to validate a scientific basis of yoga, so yoga is frequently invoked to postulate spiritual benefits of hypnotherapy.

On many Indian hypnotherapy Internet sites potential clients are assured that hypnosis is an ancient, and therefore hallowed, Indian tradition. The site of Dr. V. Nagesh, a clinical hypnotherapist in Hyderabad, certifies that he has received "formal training in hypnotism in the United States," that he is "featured in America's *Who's Who*," that he holds a *Limca Book of Records* citation for a thirty-six-hour nonstop demonstration of hypnotism, and that he has "hypnotised many terrorists and elicited valuable information from them for many Intelligence Agencies." While proclaiming his mastery of modern Western scientific skills, Nagesh sanctifies his practice by grounding it in the Veda. "I am introducing a new concept of Vedic Hypnosis after doing a thorough research in the Vedic literature. Our rishis and Hindu sages attained absolute control over their sense and mind. That made them to achieve ultimate happiness." Nagesh explained Vedic Hypnosis in an article about him in *The Hindu*: "Rishis used hypnosis or 'Sammohana' in ancient ages as a passive form of meditation and by combining Vedic hymns and hypnosis, one can achieve greater results of relaxing and soothing the mind, purging negative emotions, improving concentration and revitalising the bio-magnetic field (aura) around an individual."

Hypnosis and yoga have long and repeatedly been invoked together out of an impulse to reconcile so-called Western empirical science and mystified Eastern contemplative religions. Scientifically inspired studies of religious adepts were frequently conducted by the British in India during the nineteenth century. Imagining that the "buried alive" illusion was performed without deception, James Braid attributed its success to a Hindu mastery of hypnotic methods. In *Observations on Trance or Human Hibernation* (1850), Braid related a report made in 1837 by the British resident at the court of the Maharaja Runjeet Singh of Lahore detailing the burial of a yogi named Haridas. "He remained underground, without air, water, or food for six weeks."

The stunt, one of the conventional illusions in the traditional repertoire of Indian conjurers, became emblematically representative of the magical prowess of Hindu adepts. "Girl Buried Alive" was a headline in the *New York Times* on August 9, 1908: "When the town clock at Cedar Point strikes 9 tomorrow night Florence Gibson of Washington D.C. will be resurrected from her grave and carried to the Opera House, when she will be returned to her normal condition. At least that is the schedule arranged by Bunda Kupparow, a Hindu hypnotist who eight days ago placed the young girl in a state of hypnosis, and, after putting her in a coffin, had buried her in a vacant lot in the town six feet under the earth."

A subsequent article in the *Times*, dated March 6, 1910, epitomized the assumptions inherent in an association of hypnotism with occult Indian practices: "Mesmerism and hypnotism were practiced for centuries in the Orient before they ever made their way to Europe or America and have been developed in India to an extent that savors of the supernatural and which nevertheless is wholly within the laws of nature. . . . Nature has shown herself less secretive to people of dusky hue than to the white races and there is no doubt that in India natives have succeeded in mastering some of those mysteries which were described by Lord Salisbury as the riddles of nature."

There were reports from India in the seventeenth century, quoted in Edward Claflin's *Street Magic*, that a group of workmen digging outside the city of Amritsar uncovered the body of a yogi who informed the men that his name was Ramaswamy and he had been buried for more than a hundred years. Ramaswamy, according to one account, "did indeed seem to have a remarkable knowledge of events that occurred a century before."

A credulous Thomas Frost, in his nineteenth-century chronicle of wonders and enchantments, *Lives of the Conjurers*, relates a fantastic story of a yogi buried alive in India: "The man is said, by long practice, to have acquired the art of holding his breath by closing his mouth and stopping the interior opening of the nostrils with his tongue." After being exhumed from his grave several weeks later the yogi "conversed with us in a low, gentle tone of voice, saying we might bury him again for a twelvemonth if we pleased."

In *Hypnotism and Mysticism of India*, a report on his visit to the mystic East to learn Oriental hypnotism, Ormund McGill (1935–2005), a magician and stage hypnotist, in describing a performance of the buried alive trick, asserted that "there is no trickery in the demonstration. A trance state is induced and the breathing and body functions reduced to a low ebb which makes it possible to survive for a surprisingly long time in the burial situation."

McGill also claimed to have seen a presentation of the Indian rope trick and reported having asked an Indian magician-hypnotist if it had been accomplished by mass hypnosis. "Parimal Bandu nodded slowly and said, 'Yes, it is hypnotism of an Oriental kind, but it is quite different from the psychological hypnotism you know in the West. In India it is what we call Maya.'"

Adopting the stage name Dr. Zomb, McGill included demonstrations of hypnosis in his magic shows and later magic in his hypnosis shows. In both he would inform audiences that he, like Chandu the Magician, had been taught Oriental methods of hypnotism by fakirs in India. As an entertainer, McGill understood the efficacy of fraudulence. Both magic and hypnosis rely upon the deception of the spectator or subject. With what I suspect to be the sham sincerity of a true showman, McGill professed a belief that the performances of levitation he had witnessed in India were real and could be explained in terms of self-hypnosis. "The phenomenon is produced by creating a strong mental picture of one's body (or the body of another) rising in the air, then projecting a strong current of prana in such a way as to neutralize the pull of gravitation."

The fourteenth-century traveler Ibn Battuta, in the company of the sultan Muhammad bin Tughluq and his entourage, watched the same performance that McGill witnessed some five hundred years later. A yogi seated on the ground before them began to rise from the earth, and ascend higher and higher until he came to rest hovering above them.

In the early nineteenth century there were accounts in the European press of a yogi named Sheshal, the South Indian "Brahmin of the Air," of how, deep in hypnotic trance, he would float up off the ground and remain suspended in midair. Thomas Frost attributed the feat to yogic practice: "It was effected, by holding the breath, clearing the tubular organs, and a peculiar mode of respiration."

Levitation was, as a formulaic spectacle in the golden age of theatrical magic, conventionally associated with India. The magician Alfred Sylvester (1813–1886), billing himself as the Fakir of Oolu, dressed as a maharajah to perform a levitation on a set with an Oriental back-drop. In another version of the sensational "floating lady" illusion, the renowned magician Howard Thurston (1869–1936) would remark that he had learned the art of levitation on a tour of India. That patter invested the act with an exotic allure. Costumed as the Fakir of Ava, the magician Kellar (1849–1922) called his rendition of the trick "The Levitation of Princess Karnac," and, in publicity posters for it, Indian fakirs would bow reverentially before him. Like Thurston, he claimed to have learned levitation in India.

Playing on a public assumption that hypnosis was the secret method for levitation, the magician who defined modern Indian stage magic and established most of its conventions, P. C. Sorcar (1913–1971), costumed as the Maharaja of Magic, would wave his hands over the girl he was about the levitate in emulation of hypnotic passes. "Your body is becoming lighter, lighter," he would say with patter imitating a formulaic hypnotic induction, "so light that you are beginning to float up, off the table, and into the air. Yes, floating up higher, lighter and lighter, higher and higher."

In *India's Hood Unveiled*, a book purporting to be a manual for Hindu hypnosis and attributed to "a native Hindu of South India," there are instructions for using hypnosis "to raise the body in the air without any support, a superhuman feat that is done even at the present day in India. . . . Ask your subject to lie prostrate on his back and induce as deep a hypnosis as possible. Then suggest mentally: 'Your body will become filled with air; every portion of your body is charged with air; all the heavy components of your body will become light as air.' Then think firmly that his body will rise in the air." The author advises that this should be practiced in a low-ceilinged room so that the levitated person does not float so high that, if by chance he or she wakes up, the fall will not be too dangerous. The author further suggests that before trying to levitate someone, the amateur hypnotist should try it on himself. The instruction is suggestive: it is certainly possible to imagine that in hypnotic trance one could imagine that one is levitating, and out of that trance to remember, by way of posthypnotic suggestion, the experience as if it were as real as the feelings it had evoked.

There is, in fact, a relationship between hypnosis and levitation,

a method of induction and deepening, "arm levitation," commonly described in scientific hypnotherapeutic manuals: "Now your arm is getting lighter, lighter, moving and now lifting, rising, rising, and as your arm rises you're going deeper and deeper into hypnosis."

The Indian magician who was adept at hypnotism became a stock character in circus, vaudeville, and variety theater in Europe and America in the early twentieth century. A performer who called himself Blacaman (1902–1949) and claimed to be an Indian Fakir became famous for his performance of the buried alive stunt in Europe in the 1920s. Audiences were convinced that he survived by means of the ancient Hindu technique of yogic hypnosis and that his mastery of yoga enabled him to hypnotize deadly serpents, crocodiles, tigers, lions, and other ferocious beasts from the jungles of India.

One of Blacaman's female assistants known as Koringa (1913–1976) left his troupe to perform on her own in European circuses and billed herself as the "Only Female Fakir in the World." Her publicity claimed that she had been born in India and raised there by fakirs who taught her the ancient magical art of hypnotism that gave her the power to entrance, like Blacaman, cold-blooded reptiles, particularly dangerous snakes and crocodiles. Lithe female dancers alluringly

garbed in Indian costumes performed with her and were assisted by bare-chested muscular young men in dark makeup and silk turbans. Hindu self-hypnosis gave her the ability to dance on the sharp blades of swords and then be balanced as a cataleptic human plank between two swords and endure it as the blow of a sledgehammer shattered a

27

concrete block balanced on her stomach. The fluttering of Koringa's diaphanous robes as she gracefully danced in the slithering embrace of a huge python insinuated the erotic undercurrents of Oriental hypnosis.

The performances of both Blacaman and Koringa suggested that the famed snake charmers of India enchanted their venomous serpents with hypnotism, inducing trance by swaying rhythmically to the entrancing sound of their gourd flutes.

The performative alliance of hypnotism and magic in India became apparent to me when, some years ago, while doing field research for my book *Net of Magic: Wonders and Deceptions in India*, I traveled with an itinerant magician, Naseeb Shah, whose street performances often included demonstrations of a supposed mastery of hypnotism. Inviting a volunteer from his gathered audience, he would ask him to clasp his hands together and then, once the magician muttered a hypnotic mantra, "*tantru-mantru-jalajala-tantru*," the man, much to both the amazement and amusement of the spectators, was unable to separate his hands.

Although Naseeb is not, as far as I know, aware of it, the "handclasp technique" is regularly used as a hypnotherapeutic induction and deepening procedure: "Your hands are sticking tighter and tighter together . . . your hands are now so tightly stuck together that you cannot tell your left fingers from your right. Your hands feel as though they are a solid piece of wood."

The street magician confided his method: "I whisper in his ear, 'Pretend you can't separate your hands.'" Like the theatrical hypnotist, one of Naseeb's talents is knowing how to select from volunteers one who will play along with the show. To some degree, hypnotic susceptibility is a matter of the degree to which a subject is able and willing to play along. And deep hypnosis is, I would suggest, a matter of playing along with what is suggested with enough conviction and suspension of disbelief to make it seem like not playing along.

Performing as a shill by pretending to be a tourist who has just happened to pass by, I would be hypnotized by staring into a gem in one of the magic rings that Naseeb tries to sell after his show. In what seemed to be a hypnotic trance I was able, by means of Harry Anderson's "needle-thru-arm," purchased by me for Naseeb from the Magic Depot for $34.95, to feel no pain whatsoever as the magician pushed the needle into my flesh and through my forearm, a classic demonstration of the anesthetic power of hypnotism.

On one occasion when the police arrived to arrest Naseeb for doing this to me, I insisted that it had been planned, that it was just a trick, that I was Naseeb's friend, and that he was a field informant for a book I was writing about Indian magic. One of the policemen tried to set me straight: "No, you are not his friend. He has merely hypnotized you to believe it is so. He has hypnotized you to get your money. This is a common practice with these jadugars. They use hypnosis to cheat innocent people out of their cash."

Hypnosis in India is perceived as a dangerous force often used for criminal purposes. A recent report in the *Indian Express* is typical: "Cheating senior citizens by resorting to hypnotism before making off with their money was Sonu Malik's signature style of operation for six-seven years. Luck, however, ran out for the thief when he was finally arrested by a Delhi Police team on Wednesday." An Indian friend recently told me about a Tantric sadhu who had approached her on a ghat in Varanasi. "I know he must have hypnotized me because I gave him all the money I had in my purse. And now I don't know why I did it. It must have been sammohana. I'm just lucky that all he got was my money and left me with my virtue in tact."

The insinuation that he might have used hypnotism to seduce her typifies a widespread notion in India that hypnotism often serves rape as well as theft: "Bhawani Baba, a 'tantrik' claiming to have spiritual powers, has been sentenced to seven years imprisonment by a Delhi court for raping a 28-year-old widow by hypnotizing her on pretext of solving her problems" (ZeeNews.com, December 18, 2012).

The yogi as villainous Indian hypnotist is a regular conceit in popular culture, a dangerous character in television shows like *Ramar of the Jungle*, comics like the Tintin adventures *Cigars of the Pharaoh* and *The Blue Lotus*, and more recently in Playboy Entertainment's *Temptress* (1995) a soft-core pornographic movie in which a beautiful photographer played by Kim Delaney returns from a visit to India with insatiable sexual appetites that cause her boyfriend to wonder what happened to her in the mysterious land of the *Kama Sutra*. With the help of an Indian hypnotherapist, he discovers that she had been hypnotized and that in a Tantric trance had become possessed by the goddess Kali.

Seeing *Temptress* brought Vickie Goldman, the girl I had a crush on in the eighth grade, back to mind. After graduation from high school (and I swear this is true) she had gone to India for the summer with her boyfriend, also a classmate of mine. He had returned without Vickie but with a creepy story about her. They had gone to an ashram in Banaras to hear a lecture on the *Bhagavad Gita*. "The guru singled her out immediately. He told her she had been a Hindu in her former life and that karma had brought her to him so that he could teach her yoga and experience what he called 'the supreme bliss of union with the Absolute.' He hypnotized her, I'm sure of it. Maybe he used yoga to do it, or maybe it was just the way he looked at her, or maybe it was the sound of his voice. However he did it, she was under his control. She wouldn't leave with me. She's a different person. Yeah, Victoria Goldman is now a weird Hindu guru-groupie named Chandra. She calls the guru Bhagavan. It means God. I'm sure God is fucking her and probably convincing her that it's union with the Absolute. "

When Vickie's parents went to India in a desperate attempt to bring her home, she refused to recognize them and, according to the boyfriend's account, told them, "Bhagavan is my mother and father now. Only Bhagavan can tell me what to do." They too attributed her transformation to hypnosis. The guru-disciple relationship in India is always analogous and, as in Chandra's case, often homologous, to the hypnotist-subject relationship. The story was told in the *Los Angeles Times* as a cautionary tale in a period during which Indian gurus had become alluring to American youth.

It's hard for me to imagine that the girl on the cover of a Hindi book on Tantric hypnosis, *Vashikaran Siddhiyan Sadhna Avam Prayog*, is not Vickie Goldman. The goddess Kali garlanded with human skulls, hovers above her and the Hindu holy man intimates an inscrutable dimension, a danger at once frightening and enticing, of the association of India and hypnotism. The hypnotic power of the terrifying goddess brings devotees to her and enables her to possess them not only as in such films as *Temptress* and novels as *Kalee's Shrine* by Grant Allen and Mary Cotes (1902), but also in such supposedly factual reportage as a post on Yahoo India Travel about the Kali Temple in Calcutta avowing that "pilgrims are really hypnotized once they look in the eyes of Mataji."

"She is the goddess of illusion," a pujari at the Mayavati mandir

in Hardwar told me years ago, pointing to the gaudily ornamented statue of the divinity associated with hypnotic sammohana, the tutelary deity of magician/hypnotists. "By her maya-power she appears as Lakshmi to some, Parvati to others, and Durga to many. They are all forms of her illusion."

The demon Shambara is Mayavati's lover and derives his manipulative hypnotic powers from her. "Make obeisance at the feet of Indra, after whom magic—*indrajala*, the net of Indra—gets its name, and at the feet of the Shambara, whose glory is established in generating illusions," a magician-hypnotist in Harshavardhana's romantic seventh-century Sanskrit melodrama, *Ratnavali*, recites in the court of the king of Kaushambi.

After introducing himself as Shambarasiddhi, "he who has the powers of Shambara," the enchanter asks the monarch what illusions he would like to witness: "The moon on earth? A mountain in the sky? Fire in water? Darkness at noon? Or whatever else you wish to see!" Similarly, a magician with hypnotic powers in Rajashekhara's tenth-century Prakrit play *Karpuramanjari* offers to show a king the moon brought down, the sun stopping in the sky, and the consorts of the gods and demigods dancing for him.

The hypnotist carries a garland of peacock feathers, that feather being to hypnosis in traditional India what the pocket watch on a fob is to hypnosis in the modern West. Shambarasiddhi begins to rhythmically wave the peacock feather wand before the king's eyes, back and forth to fix his gaze, to and fro to induce a trance in which hypnotic suggestions are activated: "Look! See the ruler of the heavenly pantheon, Indra and other gods as well—Brahma, Vishnu, and Shiva. See heavenly magicians, celestial bards, and enchanting apsaras dancing in paradise."

"Amazing!" the king, stepping down from his throne, exclaims, pointing at what he imagines to be real. "The Creator in a lotus, the moon-crested Destroyer, and the Preserver with a weapon in each of his four hands—a bow, sword, mace, and discus. Yes, there's Indra on his elephant, and, yes, yes, I see celestial nymphs and hear the anklets jingling on their feet."

The scene plays upon, if not parodies, the epiphanic episode in the *Bhagavad Gita* in which Krishna, addressed as Lord of Yoga (and as such, in some sense, acknowledging a command of hypnotism), having failed to convince Arjuna to fight in the great battle against the Kurus by arguing that it is his duty as a warrior to do so, seems to hypnotize Arjuna. His repetition of the second person singular imperative "See!" again and again—"See . . . See . . ."—is characteristic of hypnotic induction. "See . . . See many wonders never seen before . . . See my myriad manifestations . . . See what you wish to see!" Hypnotic suggestion induces cosmic vision. Just as the king of Kaushambi beheld the heavenly pantheon in hypnotic trance, so too does Arjuna: "Yes, I see all the gods within you," he proclaims in awe, "the Creator seated in a lotus, the holy seers and divine serpents, a multitude of arms, torsos, faces, and eyes. I see you in your divine manifestation with a crown, mace, and discus. Yes, I see a monumental all-pervasive splendor, the blazing radiance of innumerable suns." And the post-hypnotic suggestion is that Arjuna must overcome his resistance to fighting in the great battle.

It is a scene in a story heard within a story heard within a story. Vyasa's telling of the *Mahabharata* to Sanjaya in the widest narrative frame is hypnotic in the sense that it makes Sanjaya clairvoyant and clairaudient, which is to say able to actually see and hear the events in that story. And within that frame, Sanjaya's telling of the story to Dhritarashtra is hypnotic in the sense that it allows the blind king to actually see Krishna and Arjuna in their chariot on the battlefield, to actually hear Krishna's words and with Arjuna to imagine he is actually beholding the sovereign cosmic form of the deity. And bardic metrical retellings of the story for centuries to come would surely have been no less hypnotic to the degree that they enabled listeners to likewise see the blazing radiance of innumerable suns. It's a trance within a trance within a trance in a story within a story within a story. . . .

King Vipula, in that epic, endowed with hypnotic powers by a rigorous performance of penances, uses those powers to prevent his guru's wife from succumbing to the wanton advances of Indra. While sitting with her and speaking to her softly, "he directed his gaze into hers, merging the rays of light emanating from her eyes with his, and by means of this was able to enter invisibly into her, restraining every part of her body, and thus protect her from Indra." Krishna, the bucolic cowherd of later devotional texts, often invokes yogamaya, his hypnotic power to beguile his enemies and enchant his lovers. He is called Mohana—the Entrancer. Entranced by the hypnotic sound of his flute and captivated by the sight of quivering peacock feathers in his crown, each individual girl in a multitude of milkmaids, dancing around him in the forest on an autumn night, blissfully imagines in rapturous trance that he dances with her alone.

In the *Yogavashishta*, a twelfth-century collection of metaphysical parables, another itinerant magician-hypnotist, again with a peacock feather wand in hand, appears in the court of King Lavana. As he waves the feathers back and forth, the king's eyelids become heavy, heavier and heavier, and soon close as, drifting deeper and deeper into trance, he becomes more and more susceptible to the hypnotist's verbal suggestions. The cataleptic king vividly imagines a stallion entering the throne room, and, following the magician's suggestive command, he mounts the horse and rides away.

The courtiers watch over Lavana, sitting motionless and silent until, after some time, his eyes suddenly open. Emerging from hypnotic trance, trembling with fear and trying to rise, he stumbles and would have fallen had his ministers not grabbed him and helped him back to his seat. At the behest of the courtiers, the king reports what he has experienced: he rode the conjured horse from the court to a faraway tribal village where he married, fathered sons, and toiled in the fields as a poor farmer. Lavana recounts the manifold miseries suffered there on account of a devastating famine, and how, after the death of his wife and children, he had tried to put an end his sufferings by taking his own life: "As I lay down upon a funeral pyre, the heat of the crematory flames awakened me and I found myself once again here among you."

The story is framed by an epistemological elucidation of maya: what we perceive as the phenomenal world is but an evanescent illusion that we merely imagine to be substantive, palpable, and true. The cosmology is ancient: "A magician creates this world by magic," according to the brahminically authoritative *Shvetashvatara Upanishad*. "Nature is an illusion and God the illusionist."

While I imagine that to imagine imagining we only imagine reality would be unsettling, for the ecstatic medieval Hindi poet Kabir there was beatitude in supposing himself to be but "a spectator at God's uncanny magic show," hypnotized by God, subject to illusions suggested by the divine hypnotist: "The magic may be false, but the magician is true— he and he alone is real."

Through ascetic yogic magic, human beings were and are believed to be capable of attaining the faculties of gods—*siddhis*, supernatural

powers categorized in Tantric literature to include two modes of hypnotism, *vashitva* and *vashikarana*. The former is the ability to control
one's own will, thoughts, and perceptions so that, in autogenic trance,
one perceives the ultimate and veridical reality beyond the relative
illusions of the quotidian trance that ordinary people accept as empirically reliable. In mastering vashitva, the yogi is prepared to acquire
the hypnotic skill of vashikarana, the siddhi giving him the power to
control the minds of others, to make them perceive, feel, believe, and
even do whatever he commands.

While the esoteric practice of vashitva as developed in ancient
India was ideally dedicated to gaining liberation from this illusory
world, vashikarana was primarily a means of accruing power within
this world. By the magic of hypnotism—yogamaya or indrajala, sammohana or vashikarana—the adept was believed to be able to win the
favor and patronage of kings, charm serpents, tame ferocious beasts,
stupefy and subdue enemies, and bewilder and seduce women. As
such, the magician-hypnotist was and remains an object of both ven-
eration and fear.

While yogamaya and indrajala refer generally to the generation
of magical illusions, sammohana refers specifically to hypnosis, and
vashikarana (literally, "magical subjugation, fascination, bewitching,
controlling the will of another"), as a mode of sammohana, is particularly associated with the use of mantras, the repeated sound of which
induces trance. Such incantatory spells were established some three
millennia ago in the *Atharvaveda*, a Vedic text containing incantations
which, if properly intoned, were believed to, among other things, endow the reciter with the power to impassion and possess a woman:
"I pierce your flesh with the well-aimed devastating arrow of Kama,
the god of sexual desire and pleasure, the shaft of love winged with
lust and barbed with passion. I pierce your heart with the incendiary
arrow of Kama and the fire consumes you. You come to me inflamed
with a scorched heart, shameless, ardent, amorous, devoted, and you
speak tenderly to me with parched lips. I drive you from your bed, take
you from your mother and father, assume power over you, and bring
you to me. O Mitra and Varuna deprive her of her will! Let me alone
control her!"

Vashikarana as subjugation, the sorcerous capacity to control women with mantras, was subsequently developed within both Tantric texts and *Kamashastra*, the classical compendia of Indian sexology. The hypnotic spells for the activation of erotic energies are frequently addressed to Chamunda, a fearsome aspect of the primal goddess: "*Om uttishtha Chamunde jambhaya jambhaya mohaya mohaya amuka vasham anaya anaya svaha. Om!* O Chamunda, stand up, snap at her, snap at her and stupefy her, stupefy her and lead [name of the woman desired] into my dominance! Hail!"

The erotological textbooks include complementary pharmacological formulae for magical potions, powders, and pills with which to bewitch a woman. A recipe from the medieval *Anangaranga* is typical: "Take a human skull from the cremation grounds on the eighth day of the moonlit fortnight of the month of Ashvin and hold it over a flame. Collect the soot from it on a Tuesday and then, after disemboweling a blue jay, put the soot mixed with a portion of your own semen into the cavity in the bird's body. Place the bird in an earthen pot, cover it, and wrap it in cloth. Keep the pot in a solitary place for seven days and then remove the bird, dry it, pound and pulverize it into a fine powder, and then form pills of that powder. If one of these pills is swallowed by a woman, she will be utterly enamored of the man who has made the preparation and entirely submissive to his will."

Alternatively, if the powder is scattered on the ground, any woman who inadvertently walks over it will become passionately entranced and infatuated with the man who has concocted and strewn it.

Yet another option: "Remove the dirt from under your fingernails and toenails, mix it with discharge from your nose, and wrap it in a betel leaf. Give it to the woman you desire and, once she swallows it, she will be completely under your control, utterly in love with you, and ever faithful to you no matter what you do." I would add "provided you do not tell her the ingredients in the treat she just swallowed."

The same text includes a recipe for a potent unguent with which a woman can fascinate all men: "Dissolve gorochana [the gall stone of a cow] in your menstrual blood and then apply it to your forehead as a cosmetic spot. Any man who looks at that spot will become smitten, hypnotized, and entirely under your control."

Practitioners of vashikarana have traditionally sold these mantras and potions, as well as amulets, talismans, and consecrated yantras with which to hypnotically ensnare a beloved. The ancient tradition is maintained on the Internet. In addition to selling magical products (and "spiritual accessories," as one site calls them), most of the vashikarana specialists, usually astrologers, numerologists, and palm readers as well, are available for consultation by e-mail, telephone, Skype, interactive chat, or in person: "If you love someone but can't get him or her to love you now, it is possible with the help of Hypnotism or Vashikaran, the ancient secret Tantra Power by which you can definitely possess his or her whole mind absolutely as per your wishes or dreams whether you are rich or poor, educated or uneducated, tall or short, fair or dark. Whether he or she is unmarried or married, younger or elder, in India or abroad, or from any caste or religion or even hates you, he or she will become most definitely yours within a few days. He or she will get passionate in love with you and have great sex drive for you and cannot even live without you. So don't delay. Contact Shree Shree Swamiji Mohan Kamacharan, specialist in Love and other problems, gold medalist of Tantra winner, and fulfill all your Love desire today. Get your True Love now and keep him or her faithful and devoted to you as long as you like. "

There were enthusiastic testimonials on Swamiji's site: "It's a miracle," proclaimed Ravi in Lucknow: "Once there was a time when all girls always avoid me. Now I bow before respected guru Swamiji with so many pranams because now all girls love me very much and I can choose anyone to marry."

Shalini in Hyderabad avowed: "I loved a guy but he was always stepping back and refusing about marriage. I got sick and depressed. I wanted to die. Luckily, I found this holy site and contacted to Swamiji. His Powerful Tantra Vashikaran saved my life. So I purchased mantra and yantra. And now the guy is my husband and we are even soon going to USA. Swamiji is the best godman for love."

A comment posted on a site linked to Swamji's by Rahul in Baroda bore different witness: "all positive comment r posted by him to lur customers to send money this guy is fake fraud cheat liar who just wants to take ur money so don't trust him and don't believe anything he says because nothing is true."

Another site with postings on vashikarana as Tantric hypnotism by both practitioners and clients, IndiaDivine.org, includes skeptical rejoinders to the claims of the swami: "It is very absurd to propagate in public forums that by just taking recourse to vashikaran or mohan, as you wrote, one can get a girl under his charm. if this is the case, aishwarya rai and other most beautiful girls in the world must be dancing even naked before the tantriks."

In spite of Rahul in Baroda's warning, I punched the buttons on my phone of Swamiji's contact number, and, as I did so, I imagined a magician-hypnotist with serpentine locks and a matted gray beard, ashes on his bare chest, a scarlet tilak, and strings of beads and amulets around his neck, sitting cross-legged in a loincloth with a peacock feather in one hand and a ringing mobile phone in the other.

He answered: "Acharya Mohan Kamacharan speaking in person. What is your problem?"

"I'm a professor from America on sabbatical in India, and I'm writing a book about hypnosis in India, about sammohana and vashikarana, and. . . ."

"Yes, I am the expert of sammohan and vashikaran vidyas. Sammohan Tantra for all your problems on job, boss, money, education, politics, enemies, family, and black magic against you. I make vashikaran to get lost love back or attract new one and make her love you so she wants to marry, and then to make parents consent to marriage. Vashikaran is also best effective for other love problems like impotence, too soon ejaculations, too small penis, frigidity, infertility, infidelity, and whatever else you have. What, sir, is your problem?"

I tried to explain that I had not contacted him because of a personal problem but that, for the sake of research for my book, I hoped to interview practitioners of vashikarana and sammohana.

"I have done all research you require. I am number-one expert as testified by a true fact that I am currently considered for *Guinness Book of World Records* for most number of love problems solved. For your love problem today, you purchase my vashikaran mantra and yantra on my website, four hundred and ninety-nine rupees only paid by certified bank draft or PayPaisa."

"I don't really have any love problems at the moment," I insisted. "No, the only problem I'm having is with writing my book. And that's why I have telephoned you. I would like . . ."

"You are telephoning a right person for your future problem when there is no problem now. Vashikaran mantra and yantra will stop a woman you love from becoming fed up of you and will keep her faithful and obedient to you forever. And in your future if you become fed up of her, you will easily dispose of her with vashikaran tantra. You will have a big power to control any woman. Purchase my products now and you will always be happy. For your book problem Sarasvati mantra and yantra you can buy on my website for also four hundred and ninety-nine rupees. Then you will write a number-one book on hypnosis. Everyone who reads it will be hypnotized. They will tell their family, friends, and associates to purchase it and you will be very rich. If you want money and happiness buy vashikaran and Sarasvati mantra and yantra on my website now. They are number one for writing and love. Valmiki composed *Ramayana* after reciting Sarasvati mantra while gazing at yantra. Do not be fooled by other tantra sellers. Many vashikaran specialists are conmen and scam operators. They are cheating people too much. But I am a number one you can trust. My tantra is one hundred and one percent guaranteed."

I asked where in India he was located, avowing that I would like to visit him, to meet with him in person to discuss tantric hypnotism and interview him about the history and dynamics of current practices.

"After you buy my mantras and perform my yantra pujas as per se the instructions included, you will telephone again and, then we will know your sincerity so I can reveal my whereabouts and other informations you desire. I am an overoccupied man with so many devotees from all over a world, famous in politics, business, and film industry, including many famous writers of books all lining up to see me."

When placing my order for the mantras and yantras I was requested to supply astrological data—the exact time, date, and place of my birth—that would be used to personalize my products. That information would also reveal to the acharya who I was in my previous life.

The yantras that arrived, each embossed on a small copper plate, had been blessed and energized by priests under the supervision of Swamiji in a five-hour puja at the Shri Mayavati Mandir in Hardwar, or so it was claimed in the pamphlet included in my order. I had everything I needed to keep my listener faithful and loving, to make her adore me as a god, and to seduce, enchant, and captivate another woman if I were to ever tire of her. I also had what would give me the

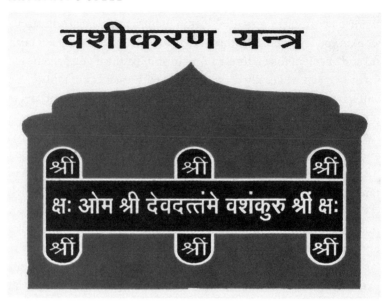

वशीकरण यन्त्र

श्रीं श्रीं श्रीं
क्षः ओम श्री देवदत्तंमे वशंकुरु श्री क्षः
श्रीं श्रीं श्रीं

magic power to write, publish, and successfully sell a book on hypnosis in India. I would have the power to hypnotize you, my reader,
yes you!

The instructions for guaranteed success were, however, somewhat
daunting: "After thoroughly bathing and applying tilak, sit private and
naked on a yellow mat facing south-east at dawn on a Tuesday. Light
a samai, perform pranayam breath control, and worship yantra with
dhoop, kumkum, sandal paste, coconut, betel nuts and leaves, white
flowers, and amrita consisting of milk, ghee, curd, honey and three
drops of the semen if you are a male while substituting the same of
the menstrual flow in a case you are a lady. With eyes focused on yantra recite mantra one hundred thousand times. Repeat puja for three
successive days and you will most definitely attain your goal."

The vashikaran mantra for love, "*Om namo Kamakshi Devi amuki me
vamsham kuru kuru svaha*," was to be recited (substituting the name
of the woman to be enchanted for the word *amuki*) while gazing at the
vashikaran yantra.

"*Om Sarasvatyai namah stotrenanena tam devim jagaddhatrim Vagdevatam ye smaranti trisandhyayam sarvam vidhyam labante te*" would insure
the success of this book if recited one hundred thousand times on
three successive mornings while staring at the Sarasvati yantra.

"I'd imagine the love spell could work," my listener reflected as she inspected the vashikaran yantra that had just arrived in the mail. "I'd think that in order to recite the mantra a hundred thousand times the man would have to believe in the magic. And that belief would give him confidence as a suitor. And women naturally respond to confidence in a man . . . just as readers respond to confidence in a writer."

I, too, suppose that the magic might work. Its potential efficacy can, I imagine, be understood in terms of the basic dynamics of hypnosis. The vashikarana practitioner, as hypnotist, provides his client with an inductional procedure for autogenic hypnotic trance that includes eye fixation, rhythmically regulated deep breathing, counting, concentration, and monotonous verbal repetition. Sitting still, gazing intently at a geometrical diagram, repeating over and over the same syllables—the name of the goddess and the beloved, and the command, *"me vam-sham kuru kuru"* (put her under my control)—while counting to one hundred thousand, instigates an incremental fading of the thought processes and a detachment of other sensory input from the immediate environment so that, at some point, only the overpowering aroma of the incense is smelled, only the flickering lamplight on the yantra is seen, and only the mantra is heard. And the posthypnotic suggestion, given prior to the induction, is that subsequent to the trance, the client will have hypnotic prowess. He does, of course, at that point, have self-hypnotic skills, proficiencies that allow and encourage him to imagine that anything he wishes to be true is true. He can imagine that he has magical powers, that he can enchant a beautiful woman or write a mesmerizing book.

"You have been cheated," Johnson Eyeroor, a convivial practicing hypnotherapist I visited in Nilambur, a town in the teak-forested Nilgiri Hills of Kerala, told me when I showed him the yantras I had purchased online from the vashikarana specialist. "But," he continued as if to console me, "even though these mantravadis are frauds, capitalizing on superstition, and even though they have no scientific understanding of hypnosis whatsoever, sometimes, maybe one time out of ten, vashikaran tantra does work. A woman hears from someone that a certain fellow is reciting mantras again and again to win her love and that he has performed all kinds of magic rituals and pujas, and paid a lot of money to a magician for her sake. That makes her curious and it appeals to her female vanity. The rumor flatters her and flattery always attracts a woman and can even make her fall in love with a man. Her parents are also impressed by his devotion and by the large sum of money he has given to the mantravadi. And so they consent to the marriage. Then the man tells everyone that the mantravadi has great power and that he has been able to win the woman of his choice on account of his tantra magic. It's possible that, when he hears about the man's success, even the mantravadi himself believes it and imagines that he actually does have some magical power. The nine men who fail to attract a woman are, of course, too ashamed to admit it. They don't want people to know about the money they wasted and all the other foolish things they did for the sake of love. So no one hears about them. People only know the success stories. If the yantras and mantras don't work, if the woman continues to ignore the fellow or reject his advances, he goes back to the mantravadi to complain and ask for his money back. The mantravadi then tells the gullible man that it's his fault, that, if the magic ritual has not produced the desired results, it is because he didn't keep correct count and repeat the mantra the exact number of times required to activate its power. Or perhaps he wasn't facing in exactly the right direction at precisely the right time, or he didn't provide exactly the right devotional offerings to the goddess of the yantra. Or perhaps he had a lustful or greedy thought. And because the poor fool has been hypnotized by the mantravadi, he believes what he is told."

There is a tenuous distinction in India between scientific and magical modes of hypnosis, between modern clinical hypnotherapy and traditional sammohana or vashikarana. Eyeroor, like most of the Indian hypnotherapists advertising their services on the Internet, adamantly disclaims and denounces practitioners of the latter as taking advantage of people by playing upon the superstitions inherent in, and propagated by, religion.

Eyeroor contends that the premises and methods of contemporary scientific hypnosis originated in India and were first proposed by an Indian living in Paris in the early nineteenth century, a Brahmin Catholic cleric from Goa named Abbé Faria. "He was the first to disprove Mesmer's theory of magnetic fluid and to scientifically demonstrate that the hypnotic state is not caused by the so-called magnetizer, but that it comes entirely from the imagination of the subject as stimulated by the hypnotist. He showed that hypnosis has nothing to do with magic but that it is a matter of suggestion and concentration."

Eyeroor told me that his parents had believed in faith healing. "Being a skeptic and a rationalist by nature, I did not believe that God was responsible for successful healings. But if not God, then who or what? That question led me to discover hypnotism and I was immediately so fascinated by it that you could even say hypnotism became my religion and so much so that I took training in clinical hypnotism and earned my hypnotherapy practitioner diploma through the National Qualification Framework of the British Government."

It has become fashionable in India for hypnotherapists to specialize in "past life regression therapy." The long-established practice of regression therapy, wherein hypnosis is used to encourage the patient to discover unconscious, early-life memories of trauma, is expanded to encompass the Indian cosmological doctrine of transmigration.

Eyeroor gave me an example: "A patient comes to the therapist with a sore neck and is hypnotized. The hypnotist takes him back to his youth, his childhood, his infancy, farther and farther, back even to a previous life. There, in his unconscious, they discover that he died by hanging. That explains the sore neck." Eyeroor laughed and shook his head disapprovingly.

"The therapist tells the hypnotized patient that he is removing the noose from his neck and then he makes the posthypnotic suggestion that, now that the noose has been taken off, he will never again feel the pain in his neck. The patient is dehypnotized and, as if by magic, the pain is gone! Yes, the patient is cured! The therapy works because the patient imagines that it works. Many of my patients ask for past life regression therapy, but I won't do it because I don't believe in reincarnation and, to be most effective, the therapist, no less than the patient, should imagine that what he says is true." Perhaps that is so for the writer, that he, no less than his reader or listener, imagines that what he has written is at least in some ways true.

"Mainly I am treating patients for lack of concentration," the hypnotherapist continued, "sleep disorders, hysteria, kleptomania, satyriasis, frigidity, impotency, homosexuality, alcoholism, and smoking. But today I will be curing a young girl of migraine headaches. Because the medicines prescribed for her by doctors proved ineffective, her parents took her to a pir whose recitations of the Koran were likewise useless. You know sometimes, however, these pir babas are successful because reciting the same Koran passage again and again can be hypnotic. They recite Surah ash-Shifa, which means 'the cure' over and over in a hypnotically rhythmic voice. That's the suggestion. And then the baba tells the hypnotized patient, 'You are cured' with the posthypnotic suggestion, 'you will no longer suffer from your problem. Bismillah!' And it can work. Yes, and neither the baba nor the patient realize that it is not because of Allah but because of hypnosis, not because of the words of God from the Koran but because of the words of the hypnotist. The baba might not even know that he is actually practicing hypnotism. And even if they are not cured, you know, the patients tell people they are because they believe that not to be cured would mean they were not good Muslims and that Allah had not been merciful with them."

I told him that my own first experience of hypnosis was for a treatment for the migraines I had as a teenager. "But it didn't work. I was not very susceptible. No, I'm not a good subject. I've gone several times to hypnotherapists in hopes that that they might be able to help me stop smoking." I lit a Gold Flake cigarette. "Allah was not merciful with me."

The girl suffering from migraines arrived with her mother and father. The father, dressed in casual Western clothes, glowered in way that suggested that this was not his idea. Because his wife and daughter were wearing niqabs, only their eyes were visible. I sat with them on the verandah outside Eyeroor's office as he explained hypnotherapy to them in Malayalam, presumably assuring them of the efficacy and safety of hypnotherapy.

Eyeroor escorted the girl into his office and closed the door behind him. When I took a pack of my cigarettes out of my pocket, the father asked for one and we smoked together while the mother stood at the door with her ear pressed against it in an effort to hear what the hypnotist was saying to her daughter. She was also, I imagined, probably worried about what he might be doing to her.

After only as long as it takes to finish a cigarette, Eyeroor opened the door and, much to my surprise, signaled for me to come in and witness the procedure. He stopped the mother from joining us. The father asked for another Gold Flake.

Imagine it: a young girl lying on a bed, only her wide-open and seemingly fearful eyes showing through the opening in her black garment, and two older men, one standing over her waving his hands around and around her face in hypnotic passes and speaking softly and soothingly in a dulcet Malayalam, and the other, a foreigner, sitting in a chair next to the bed, staring at the girl. It made me uneasy.

"*Pathu ... onpathu ... ettu,*" the hypnotist recited, counting backward from ten to one in Malayalam, "*eezhu ... aaru. ...*" and it was making my eyelids heavy, "*anchu ... naalu moonnu,*" and the girl's eyes blinked, blinked again, and again, " *randu ... onnu,*" and her eyes closed as her head fell to the side, indicating, I supposed, that she was in trance. Eyeroor's voice became more commanding and authoritarian in phrases punctuated by protracted silences.

After some fifteen minutes or so, the hypnotherapist looked at me, smiled, and nodded as if to say, "It has worked."

"*Onnu, randu, moonnu,*" he counted, "*dayavu cheythu ezhunelku.*" "One, two, three, wake up," and the girl's eyes opened and she sat up. Opening the door, Eyeroor invited the parents to come in and asked me to leave.

While I was waiting for him at his house behind the office, I was joined by R. K. Malayath, a theatrical magician who stages a hypnosis show he calls Mentarama. I told him that I had gone to several hypnosis nightclub performances in the United States, had volunteered to go on stage each time, and had consistently been rejected by the performer. "I suppose they can sense that I'm not very susceptible."

Informing me that he would be staging Mentaram the following month in Dubai, he assured me, "If you happen to be visiting the Gulf at the time you will be welcome to my show and I will invite you to come on the stage and you will definitely be hypnotized."

During the lunch that the hypnotist's wife Komalam served to her husband, Malayath, and me, Eyeroor offered to hypnotize me.

"No thank you. I'm really not a good subject. Years ago, a friend of mine, an Indian doctor who had learned hypnosis in order to use it as a surgical anesthesia tried to hypnotize me and couldn't. He said that on a hypnosis susceptibility scale from one to five, I was just a one."

"But you must try again," Malayath insisted and avowed that Eyeroor could "hypnotize anyone, even the most resistant like yourself."

"I don't understand," Eyeroor added. "You say you have never been hypnotized and that you are writing a book about hypnosis. And yet you don't want me to try to hypnotize you. It doesn't make sense."

"No it doesn't make sense," Malayath chimed in. "You can't write about something you haven't experienced. You must be hypnotized for the sake of your book."

"Yes," Komalam, setting another plate of roti on the table, concurred, "It doesn't make sense even to me. You must let him hypnotize you."

"And perhaps it will enable you to give up smoking," Eyeroor added.

It was only out of politeness as a guest in his home that, after lunch, I followed my host back to his office and consented to lie down on the couch where the Muslim girl had been hypnotized earlier that day.

"Make yourself comfortable," the hypnotist began. "And take a deep breath in through your nose, hold it for a few seconds, yes, good, and now slowly let it out through your mouth. Yes, good. Again, inhale though your nose and let go of the breath with a relaxing sigh. Do this a few times, and each time you do, let the relaxation that you are beginning to feel grow and grow, more and more relaxed, deeper and deeper relaxed. Now use your mind to scan your body for tension, starting at the top of your head and slowly working down to the soles of your feet, noticing wherever your muscles are tense. Invite those muscles to become soft and flexible, to relax, completely relax. Let your whole body settle into a position of complete relaxation. Yes, good. Deep, deep relaxation. I'm going to count backward from ten to one now and with each number you will feel more and more relaxed, deeply relaxed, completely calm and relaxed."

When he got to one, I, just as the Muslim girl had done, closed my eyes. Not to do so, I felt, would be a rude refusal to play along with the show.

"Now I want you to create in your mind an image of a beautiful place. Yes, let your mind imagine a very beautiful place, a peaceful place where you can be completely comfortable, calm and relaxed. Picture yourself in this place and, as you do, notice how calm it makes you to be there. Take a moment to imagine it. Yes, imagine it."

I imagined an Indian village, a clearing in a palm grove clustered with whitewashed huts with bright-colored cotton curtains for doors, windows that were open and dark, and umber roofs of palm thatch. I could see cows grazing, dogs lazing, and a mated pair of Brahminy kites taking roost for the warm night in a pipal tree, grander than any other tree in sight, much older, it seemed to me, than the village that had formed around it. As daylight dwindled into darkness, darker and darker, I felt more and more relaxed, calm, and drowsy. I imagined a wandering teller of tales sitting cross-legged beneath that pipal tree in that peaceful village. I imagined that he was beginning to tell a story.

And I imagined that tale.

part two

FOR THE LISTENER

Two Tales to be Read Aloud

On account of the whole preceding life
of the adult, speech can signal all of the
internal and external stimuli reaching
the cortex of the brain. Spoken words can,
therefore, call forth all those reactions of the
organism which are ordinarily determined
by the actual stimuli themselves.

IVAN PETROVITCH PAVLOV, *TWENTY YEARS OF
OBJECTIVE STUDY OF THE HIGHER NERVOUS
ACTIVITY BEHAVIOR OF ANIMALS* (1923)

THE STORYTELLER'S TALE

ॐ नमः कामदेवाय। सहकल सहद्रश सहमसह लिऐ वन्हे धुनन जनममदर्शनं
उत्कण्ठतिं कुरु कुरु दक्ष दक्षुधर कुसुमवाणेन हन हन स्वाहा ||

KAMADEVA VASHIKARANA MANTRA (A SPELL TO AROUSE SEXUAL DESIRE
AND CAUSE A PERSON TO BE ENTIRELY UNDER YOUR CONTROL)

"Let me read a story to you, a tale about hypnosis that's meant to be in some way hypnotic," the writer, sitting in the chair next to their bed, says to his listener on a warm evening in rural northern Goa. "It's about an itinerant storyteller who, on an evening long ago in a remote Indian village, tells a tale to a gathering of rice farmers who, weary from a laborious day in the paddies, are eager to be enchanted. Make yourself comfortable and let's begin."

Take a deep breath in and slowly let it out. And again, a deep relaxing breath, comfortable and satisfying . . . and as you listen to this story, doing nothing, thinking about nothing in particular, just listening, calm and comfortable . . . drifting into a very, very pleasant state of mind . . . letting your body relax, more and more relaxed . . . completely relaxed . . . and soon you may begin to feel that your eyelids are becoming heavy . . . heavier and heavier . . . until finally, whenever you wish, you can let them close . . . and when you close your eyes, you'll notice that you become even more deeply relaxed, comfortable, and calm . . . hearing only the sound of my voice, letting it take you slowly, word by word, sentence by sentence, to a village in India . . . .

Let's imagine it: a palm grove clustered with whitewashed huts with variegated cotton curtains for doors, windows that are open and dark, and umber roofs of palm thatch. Cows graze, dogs laze, and a mated pair of Brahminy kites takes roost for the warm night in a pipal tree, grander than any other tree in sight, much older than the village that has formed around it. It was beneath a majestic canopy of the leafy branches of just such a tree that, long ago, an ascetic in deep autogenic hypnotic trance became the Buddha.

The wandering teller of tales sits cross-legged on the earthen dais that has been built up around the tree. As daylight dwindles into darkness, bats stir and camphor lamps are kindled, their lambent light flickering on the old tree's gray bark and on the old man's dusky skin. Picture a wispy gray beard and thickly matted ashen locks, strings of beads around his neck, a round crimson tilak on his forehead, amulets on his wrists and upper arms, a ruby glistening in a gold ring, and an ochre lungi. Look into the glistening eyes that scan the gathering of listeners. They stop to look back at you.

There are props for the show: a peacock feather, incense sticks, a conch and damaru drum, a brightly painted wooden image of the goddess Mayavati, and a black shawl is spread out to display sheaves of palm leaves into which Sanskrit words have been etched.

The storyteller picks up the conch and blows into it, once, twice, three times, to announce the beginning of a tale and settle listeners down.

Imagine one of them, a man or a woman, young or old, someone in some way like yourself, perhaps you as you might have been if, long ago, you happened to have lived in an Indian rice farming village with a primeval pipal tree at its heart. Visualize, if you will, the smoke the listener sees billowing from the glow of the bundled sticks of sandal-scented incense the storyteller waves in circles around, around, around the goddess. Smell the heady fragrance that so pleases her, the flowery perfumes, and listen to the wondrous sounds the listener hears, the invocation inscribed on palm leaf: *Om Ma-ya-vat-yai nam-ah! Sto-tre-na-ne-na tam de-vim ja-gad-dha-trim ye sma-ran-ti tri-san-dhya-yam sar-vam vidh-yam la-ban-te te.*

Although the listener doesn't understand the incantatory words any more than we do, the ancient utterance is somehow soothing. A rhythmic rataplan of celestial Sanskrit syllables lulls the mind into trust, rocks it into surrender. It's hypnotic. As is the eye of the peacock feather the storyteller waves slowly back and forth in a silence that calms the listener. Calm, calm, be calm and relaxed.

"*Prem*," the storyteller says just loudly enough for the listener to hear it, and just softly enough to make it seem a whisper: "Love. Yes, a love story that rivals the oldest love story in the world, the amorous legend of the earthly king Pururavas and the lithe apsara Urvashi, the most voluptuously beautiful dancer in the heavenly court of Lord Indra."

As the tale begins in canorous cadences, silken and seductive, ear-opening and mind-rending, slowly, slowly, word by word, the listener is progressively distracted from all other distractions as words are fashioned into a sedate refuge from quotidian concerns by the voice of the storyteller:

In the town of Mohapur on the banks of the river Svapna, there lives a merchant, Mudadatta by name, a woefully lonely, wifeless man and childless too, well-to-do in cash but poor-to-be in spirit. Picture him, the storyteller urges, and the listener remembers someone from childhood, a family friend perhaps, or maybe an uncle once or twice removed. A figure slowly comes into shape: a balding head, scrawny limbs, slumped shoulders, and a bulging belly. All of us can remember someone who looks something like that.

Without sons to perform the crematory rituals, to offer the obsequial pinda balls of sweet rice that nourish the spirits of the deceased, Mudadatta worries about dying childless and alone. His spirit will hunger so ravenously, he reckons, that he will probably return to this world as a scavenging crow, voracious vulture, or mangy jackal. This dismal intimation of starvation in death makes him desperately gluttonous, particularly for sweets. "I'd better eat what I can," he reflects, anxiously cramming a sticky wet ladoo into his mouth, "while I still can.

What, he wonders, woefully licking sugar syrup from his fingers, could he have done in a previous life to deserve being abandoned and sonless by each of his three wives?

Before his first marriage had even been consummated, the merchant's betrothed ran off with a snake charmer who had been commissioned to entertain guests at the wedding celebration. The gourd flute that makes cobras sway in trance had, it seemed, enchanted the bride as well.

The sermon of a mendicant monk who preached that sexual intercourse, no less than drinking toddy or eating meat, onions, or garlic, was the cause of sorrow and an impediment to the bliss of liberation, inspired his second wife, after less than a month of matrimony, to shave her head and become a nun.

The third marriage lasted at least a little longer. It wasn't until after almost six months of conjugal cohabitation that Mudadatta's last wife mysteriously disappeared. While no one really knows or dares to conjecture what might have happened to her, the merchant himself imagines that, like both the beautiful Urvashi and the blessed Sita, the devoted wife of Lord Ram, so faithful and pure, she must have been abducted by a demon. But why, he does not understand since he, unlike Ram, has never, at least so far as he is aware, done anything that might offend a demon.

Because he is lonely and still harbors hopes of having sons, Mudadatta calls upon Anangdas, the ghataka who had been the broker for each of his marriages. The listener imagines a bristled chin, bony fingers, vulpine eyes, and gaps between his teeth. But imagine him as you wish—scrawny or fat, eyes squinted or bulging. It's up to you. Imagine the voice with which he informs the bereft merchant that, despite his ample pecuniary assets, it is not likely that there is another mother and father in or around Mohapur who would consider giving a daughter in marriage to a suitor with his calamitous matrimonial history.

Modulating tone of voice and pitch of speech, the storyteller mimics the merchant's whine. "Then find for me a girl without parents, an orphan, or a widow still young enough to bear me sons, or even some unfortunate lady who, like myself, has been abandoned by a heartless spouse. I am very open-minded when it comes to women. Arrange, dear Anangdas, a Gandharva love marriage with neither parents nor permissions involved, no dowry, no priests to pay, nor rites to be performed, no, no, nothing required but mutual consent. I am not excessively finicky, as you know, when it comes to love. I could love almost any woman, no matter her caste, class, ancestry, complexion, or intelligence, even a woman who cannot cook or clean, or read or write, or sing or dance. Yes, I am willing to marry almost any woman who does not have a contagious deadly disease, is not insane, and who is neither missing a limb nor having any extra ones."

The storyteller pauses to give the listener the impression that the merchant is thinking. Then: "I hope it does not seem overly particular of me to add that I would also hope that she might, if it is at all possible, be at least somewhat beautiful."

Another pause, a sigh, and then: "Oh yes, and, as I think about it now, big breasts, although not absolutely necessary, would likewise be appreciated. Yes, Anangdas, do please arrange for me a marriage to a beautiful girl with no physical or mental diseases, with the proper number of limbs, and big breasts."

The listener hears the matchmaker's voice: "The problem is that to arrange a Gandharva love marriage, I would have to find a woman who might be attracted to you in some way. And, I'm sorry to say, you are not basically the sort of man with whom a woman, particularly a beautiful woman with big breasts, would be likely to fall in love. Not unless she was blind, deaf, and anosmic."

"Why?" the earnest merchant asks. "Why would you say such a thing?"

"I must be honest with you. For one thing, your body odor, no less than your breath, is rather unpleasantly pungent. Of course you could do something about that and about your slovenly appearance as well. But there are also a few minor things beyond your power to change, traits that, for you and me as intelligent and discerning men, are rightly inconsequential, but are unjustly taken more seriously than they should be by women, small-minded as they are. Trivial things like shortness of stature, plumpness of the gut, limping gait, trembling hands, flopping jowls, grating voice, baldness, yellowish complexion, and the like. Such things tend to put women off."

Without being so cruel as to also mention the merchant's lack of learning, wit, or charm, the matchmaker tries to strike a positive note. "You do, however, have one attribute that certain women find more attractive than any other. That is your wealth. Gold, as the Vedic sages have proclaimed, has the power to win the favors of women no less than the blessings of the gods. There are voluptuous women, many of them beautiful, buxom, and bawdy to boot, in the brothels of Mohapur who vend the sorts of pleasures that could help you forget about getting married again."

"But I don't want to forget about getting married," Mudadatta protested. "I want a wife who will love me, be devoted to me, and provide me with sons. I'll settle for the woman who can't see or hear or smell as long as she is at least a little bit beautiful and has breasts that are at least a little bit big."

The sympathetic matchmaker pauses to take the distraught merchant's hand in his. "Listen to me. I am sorry. I cannot help you. But I have heard of someone who possibly can, a certain magician, Shambaraswami by name, a mantravadi who camps in the burning grounds outside the town. Knowing the secrets of sammohana, he has the power to control the minds and wills of others. He can cause a person to see, hear, smell, taste, and touch what is not, and to imagine that what they imagine is real. He can make people think or believe, and even do, whatever he commands. They say he knows the yogamaya mantras that can subdue rogue elephants in rut, charm deadly serpents, win the favor of kings, stupefy enemies, and, most pertinent to your predicament, he knows the spells with which to subjugate women. He might be convinced to teach you some vashikarana mantras with which to enchant a woman, perhaps even a beautiful one with big breasts who can see and hear and smell, and entrance her into consenting to a Gandharva love marriage with you. With the right magic, anything is possible."

Like most of us, Mudadatta would like to believe that might be true. He so eagerly hurries to the cremation grounds to find Shambaraswami that he arrives there breathless, panting, drenched in sweat, his heart wildly beating. Dogs bark, Doms cackle, corpses crackle.

Hearing the storyteller's eerie evocation of the place at sundown, the listener sees grimly smoldering cadavers and strewn charred black bones, smells putrid smoke rising in ghostly whirls and ghastly curls, hears the hungry howl of jackals, cacophonous caw of crows, and strident screech of vultures. Imagine a magician with a matted beard of serpentine tresses sitting cross-legged in twilight there, his face and chest smeared with crematory ash, a scarlet tilak on his forehead, around his neck a string of rudraksha beads and the sloughed skin of a cobra.

Reverentially prostrating himself before the mantravadi and addressing him as "Swamiji," Mudadatta beseeches him for help. After patiently listening to the merchant's pathetic lament and hearing his desperate request, Shambaraswami speaks slowly in a voice that, like his appearance, is much like that of storyteller. It's deep, calm and calming, reassuring and soft on the ear. Listen: "Yes, I can supply you with a magical unguent and teach you a bewitching mantra with which to subjugate any woman. But you must give me one hundred and one gold fanams as an offering to the goddess Mayavati. She will, I can assure you, return the money if, by any chance, the spell is not efficacious."

Excitedly rushing home to fetch the gold and racing right back to the cremation grounds in such a hurry that he stumbles in the darkness and falls no less than four times. With knees scraped and bleeding, Mudadatta is ecstatic with hopes for love. One by one he counts out the coins for the magician. Gold glistens with the reflected firelight of burning cadavers.

"One . . . two . . . three . . . ," the storyteller begins as the sorcerer slowly waves the peacock feather to and fro, "four . . . five . . . six," and, with each number up to ten, the listener becomes more calm, "seven . . . eight," more and more calm and relaxed, "nine . . . ten." The magician-hypnotist tells the merchant to take a coin and hold it between his thumb and index finger.

"Concentrate on the coin and as you do, take in a deep breath. Now slowly, slowly, let it out. And again. Once more. Concentrate on the coin and breathe in deeply again and slowly out. Yes, breathe in and out, in, out, ten times. One . . . two . . . three . . . concentrating on the coin in your hand, breathe in . . . out . . . four . . . five . . . six . . . and again, slowly breathe in . . . seven . . . and out . . . eight . . . and with each breath notice that you can, if you wish, become more and more easily calm, at ease, and relaxed. As you breathe in, you can feel the splendid golden prana pulsating in your fingertips, warm and relaxing, and as you breathe out, feel it radiating up your arm, into your shoulder, now down into your chest, infusing your heart, and from there, with each breath, it flows into the rest of your body, soothing, sedating, making you feel more and more relaxed, restful and calm, calm, calm and relaxed. Now press your thumb and finger against the coin, and as you do, you will notice that the harder you press, the more your entire body becomes relaxed, so relaxed that your thumb and finger will begin to move apart so that soon the coin will slip from your hand. And when it does, you'll feel entirely soothed, peaceful, floating as if in dream, softly, slowly drifting deeper and deeper into deep and tranquil trance. . . ."

The storyteller is silent as the listener, slowly breathing in and out, drifts deeper and deeper.

And the coin drops.

"You're floating, drifting, gliding, aware of nothing but the sound of my voice. Listen. Listen to the mantra: *Om na-mo Ma-ya-va-tyai cha-nu cha-nu Chin-na-se-na mam vash-yam ku-ru ku-ru sva-ha*. With each repetition of the mantra, you go deeper and deeper. Listen to it, syllable by syllable, one syllable at a time: *Om na mo ma ya va tyai cha nu cha nu chin na se na mam vash yam ku ru ku ru sva ha*. Deeper, still deeper: *Om na mo ma ya va tyai cha nu cha nu chin na se na mam vash yam ku ru ku ru sva ha*.

"You will recite the mantra throughout the day tomorrow and then, at dusk, as you continue to intone it, you will see in the distance a woman coming toward your home. And you will believe that the mantra is bringing her to you, pulling her to you as a magnet draws iron. I will give you an ointment. You will believe that a tilak painted on your brow with it makes you appear irresistibly handsome. Repeating the mantra, you will see that, as the woman comes closer and closer, step by step, syllable by syllable, she becomes more and more beautiful. Repeat it again. By the time she stands before you, you will imagine that she is the most beautiful woman in the world. The more often you recite the mantra, the more certain you will be that, no matter what she might say or do, this beautiful woman is enchanted and that, by the power of the mantra and the tilak, she is entirely under your control, yours to do with as you wish. No matter how she behaves, you will believe that she imagines you are handsome and loves you with all her heart, and that with each repetition of the spell she will adore you all the more. When you awaken, you will remember nothing I've told you except the mantra, and you will believe that it endows you with the magic to attract women, to infatuate, sub-jugate, and enslave them. This belief will make you very happy. You will wake up eager to follow the instructions that I will give you. You will emerge from your trance as I count to three. One, you are beginning to awaken. Two, more awake. Three, open your eyes. Wake up, yes, wide awake! Good, Mudadatta! Yes, very good."

"I am so happy!" the beaming merchant exclaims as he rubs his eyes. "I've never been happier in my entire life. How could I not be happy, now that I know the mantra that will cause women, even beautiful women with big breasts, to fall in love with me? I can hardly believe it!"

"Believe it," the hypnotist commands and gives the merchant his instructions. "Listen to me. Listen. The mantra you have learned contains the name Chinnasena, the name of a beautiful young lady in Meghanagar. Ever since a tiger ate her husband last year, she has had many suitors, including princes, military commanders, poets, and scholars—handsome, adventurous, and wealthy wooers. None of them have been successful in seducing the widow. Being as virtuous as she is beautiful, she rejects them on account of a pious devotion to her late husband. She would have thrown herself upon his funeral pyre to become a Sati if her husband's father and brothers had not forcibly prevented her from doing so. I have chosen her name for the mantra as a test of its power. If it can bring her to you all the way from Meghanagar, cause her to forget her husband, and devote herself to you, to obey your every command and wish to celebrate the Gandharva love marriage with you, it can be guaranteed to subjugate any woman whose name is substituted for hers in the mantra."

"Chinnasena!" the merchant exclaims. "I want no substitutes for her! O Chinnasena, my beloved Chinnasena! Just as Nala loved Damayanti before ever having seen her, so do I already love Chinnasena. Never will I take advantage of my absolute power over her. No, I will be ever kind and tender with her, adoring her even as much as she, on account of my mantra, adores me. O my beautiful Chinnasena!"

The magician impatiently interrupts the enchanted merchant's amorous perseveration. "Listen. You must also paint a tilak on your forehead, a magic mark that will make you appear utterly handsome to women."

The hypnotist gives his subject a clay pot of an unguent containing, he explains, the crematory ashes of a Brahmin, the urine of a king, the milk of a tiger, the pulverized testicles of a cobra, and the macerated root of a black lotus: "In order to activate it, you must mix into it three drops of your own semen. After applying the tilak to your brow tomorrow morning, recite the mantra, and continue reciting it throughout the day. Recite it no less than one hundred and one times and it will bring her to you by dusk. Repeat the mantra as soon as you see her coming toward your home, entranced and drawn to you by the power of the mystic syllables. Continue to repeat the amatory charm and, as she gets closer and closer, step by step, syllable by syllable, repeating it until she is right in front of you. Your tilak will cause her to imagine you are utterly handsome. And the beautiful Chinnasena will fall madly in love with you."

Upon arriving home, Mudadatta immediately begins the manual procedure for coming up with the three drops of the ingredient that he believes will activate his ointment. He recites his mantra then pictures Chinnasena astride him in his bed, and vividly imagines the bobbling of bounteous breasts and the ardent undulations of luscious loins, wet with sweat, her swollen ruddy lower lip, coquettish glances and quivering brow, the warmth of her fingertips and softness of her sighs. By grace of that entrancing vision the merchant churns the magic fluid from his body as the gods churned the nectar of immortality from the cosmic ocean.

First thing in the morning, Mudadatta, following the magician's instructions, paints the tilak on his forehead and recites his mantra. He reiterates the spellbinding syllables one by one as he does his ablutions, and again over his customary matutinal hot milk and sweet ladoos. He orders his elderly manservant to prepare a festive meal and strew the nuptial bed with fragrant jasmine for the celebration of his Gandharva love marriage to the beautiful Chinnasena. "And then go away," he tells the old chokra, "and don't come back until you are summoned. Newlyweds require privacy."

"Chinnasena," the merchant, one hand on his heart and the other raised in the air, cries aloud: "Chin-na-se-na! O my beloved Chinnasena, my apsara, my jewel of salvation in the ocean of samsar!"

For his midday meal he eats a yabhapupa, a cake prepared with kysoor root, licorice, jujubes, ghee, datura, and hemp following a secret recipe given to him by Anangdas before his first wedding, a confection that would, according to the testimony of the ghataka, make him as potent as Shiva on the night of that god's wedding to Parvati: "Your lingam will be no less adamantine than the Destroyer's! *Om Shiva-lingaya namah!*"

In the afternoon, after the barber has shaved and shampooed him, Mudadatta rinses his mouth with tamarind water, reddens his lips with lac, daubs his armpits with sandal paste, dons a fresh dhoti, applies a fresh splotch of magic ointment to his forehead, and then gobbles up another yabhapupa.

Anxiously pacing back and forth in front of his house, he continues to rehearse the incantation that will soon bring the beautiful Chinnasena to him and cause her to love him with all her heart: *Om na-mo Ma-ya-va-tyai cha-nu cha-nu Chin-na-se-na mam vash-yam ku-ru ku-ru sva-ha.*

Now imagine the ugliest ogress you can, a repulsive crone, filthy and coarse. Picture a hunchbacked harridan with sallow skin sagging on brittle bones. Notice the warts, moles, and the scrofulous boil on her crinkled neck, and look at the scaly scalp patched with grimy gray wisps of hair, one glaucous eye, the other bloodshot red, black broken nails on scrawny toes and crooked fingers, her few remaining teeth chipped and stained with betel. Imagine her. She is Chinnasena. The hideous hag, the storyteller divulges, was a harlot in her youth. It's difficult to imagine that the cracked, chapped lips lewdly grimacing on the timeworn creature's frightful face have ever been kissed by a lover.

Shambaraswami approaches the old whore outside the Mohapur toll and customs gate where she squats each day with her scarred and scab-encrusted hand cupped for alms, tediously bleating, "Give me something. Give me."

"*Behen chod!*" she fiercely barks, "Sister fucker!" at all who pass without making an offering.

Despite the other beggars at that gate who, believing that she gives begging a bad name, have tried to chase her off, she sticks to her post, subsisting on the scraps gatekeepers toss on the ground for her retinue of growling stray dogs. When Shambaraswami places one of Mudadatta's coins in her hand, it grips the gold as tenaciously as the claw of a vulture clamping onto a succulent morsel of fresh human flesh in the cremation grounds.

"Is that all?" Chinnasena snarls. "Stingy bastard!"

"No, there's much more," the entrancer answers as he crouches down next to the wretched woman: "Much much more, Chinnasena. A fortune, in fact. I've found a rich merchant who will, if you do as I tell you, make you his wife and lavish you in luxury."

Of course she doesn't believe it, but, leering at the coin in her hand with her one clear eye and realizing it is really gold, the greedy old crone, crooked to the core and curious, cocks her ears and listens.

Shambaraswami tells her the story of the merchant who came to him to learn a spell with which he could attract, seduce, and dominate a woman. He explains that, under the pretext of teaching him a mantra that would cause a beautiful woman to consent to a Gandharva love marriage with him, he put the man himself into a trance.

"Because no fair woman would ever consider marrying him, I thought of you, Chinnasena, and used sammohana to make him imagine, the moment he sees you, that you are the most beautiful woman in the world, a young widow, as chaste and pure as you are beautiful, and that, enchanted by his tilak, you imagine he is handsome, and that, under the sway of his mantra, you are enamored of him and wish to become his devoted wife. It will be love at first sight. He is rich and eager to marry. All you need to do to make his wealth your own is to go to his home today at dusk and play along with the story. Adoring you as a goddess, he won't have the heart to deny you anything. If it isn't so, Chinnasena, I will give you one hundred more coins like the one in your hand. But if it is true—and, believe me, it will be—you, after taking charge of his purse, must bring me one hundred and one of the same. That's what's in it for me, and that is, I can assure you, but a small fraction of the wealth you will enjoy as Mudadatta's wife."

One more glance at the gold in her hand and the hag reckons it might be worth her while to see if there really are more of such coins to be had. No less than Mudadatta, Chinnasena wants to believe that, with the right magic, anything is possible.

As the sun begins to set, Mudadatta, adorned with his magic tilak and thrilling with intimations of amorous conquest, stands outside his house reciting his mantra, waiting and waiting. Suddenly it seems to be working—yes, he can see her in the distance, a woman approaching. He resumes his recitation and with each step she takes toward him, each syllable he utters, the closer she gets and the more beautiful she becomes. Her awkward limp seems the languid swaying gait of an amorous swan, the filthy rags in which her misshapen body is coarsely wrapped appears to be a shimmering silk sari, its stains embroidered blossoms, and her scrawny limbs are tender tendrils aching to enlace him as climbing creepers do a tree. By the time she stands before him, her glum glower seems a coquettish smile revealing buds of jasmine, the broken teeth in her drooling mouth. Her rancid breath is, to his nostrils, fragrant with honey. Her bleary eyes, dribbling mucus, are lotus petals moist with dewdrops, sweet tears of love. Her grunted utterance is ambrosia trickling from a luscious lower lip, ripe-red with yearning: "I'm Chinnasena. I'm here to marry you."

This is ample proof of the mysterious power of the tilak and mantra. It is plain to see that the beautiful woman at whom he gazes is ensorcelled, enchanted, and impassioned by the ointment and the spell. And the feeling is mutual. Mudadatta loves Chinnasena as Pururavas adored Urvashi, the apsara with billowing breasts, slender waist, sumptuous buttocks, and lissome thighs. Her beauty, as far as the merchant is concerned, surpasses that of the heavenly dancer.

"I'll need one hundred and one gold fanams to buy my freedom from my in-laws." The squalid crone squawks. "And, of course, our hallowed tradition requires you tie the mangalsutra around my neck, one fashioned of gold and studded with diamonds. The diamond is my birthstone. The groom must also, in accordance with Vedic injunction, offer pudava to the bride—wedding saris embroidered with gold. To wear with them, I'll require gold earrings and nose rings, of course, gold rings for my fingers and gold for my toes, gold bracelets, armlets, and anklets, gold necklaces and gold girdles, gold, gold, gold!"

Moved by the intensity of the passion with which she articulates her desire to so adorn herself, to make herself all the more beautiful for him, Mudadatta understands her request as further testimony to the efficacy of the tilak and the mantra and the resultant boundlessness of her adoration.

"Yes," he sighs: "Yes, my beloved, oh yes, yes, my beautiful Chinnasena, you shall have all that and more."

He utters his mantra once more for good measure and it seems to make her all the more eager to celebrate the Gandharva marriage, to get on with the customary feast so that they can then proceed to the nuptial bed, for, no sooner has he intoned the syllables than she stridently snarls what seems to him a tender whimper: "Give me food. Lots of food. Food! Food! I'm starving."

The thrilled merchant leads his bride to the table for the ceremonial meal: creamy sweet curd laced with cardamom and tamarind, pumpkin flowers floating in a ghee-golden soup, saffron roasted ringdove, and minced mutton kebabs, all seasoned with masalas, dressed with pickles, garnished with pomegranate seeds and mint leaves, served with raisins, dates, and coconut chutney, and a platter plentifully piled with ladoos wrapped in shimmering silver leaf. As the exultant groom nibbles on a yabhapupa cake, the scrawny old crone guzzles cup after cup of strong arak to wash down voraciously gulped handfuls of food.

"No fried fish? What kind of wedding feast is this?" Chinnasena grumbles. "I want fried fish with garlic, lots of garlic." Mudadatta blushes with the assumption that his bride, no doubt aware of the aphrodisiacal influences of garlic, wants them both well prepared for a blissful nocturne of erotic abandon.

No sooner has he offered her postprandial paan, prepared with betel and bhang, clove, fennel, cardamom, and rose-petal jam, to freshen her mouth than she leans to the side, sneers, and loudly breaks wind. The malodorous flatulent fulmination is melodious music to Mudadatta's ear, a divine afflatus, and to his nose it seems a sandal-scented breeze has wafted up from the hills of Malabar.

Worried in his jubilation that, Mayavati forbid, the spell might wear off, that his beautiful beloved might emerge from trance and suddenly stop loving him, Mudadatta recites: *Om na-mo Ma-ya-va-tyai cha-nu cha-nu Chin-na-se-na mam vash-yam ku-ru ku-ru sva-ha.*

It works, he reckons, because she complains that she is tired, a coy way, he supposes, of hurrying them to the flower strewn altar of love upon which the Gandharva marriage will be consummated.

"I want a different bed," Chinnasena gripes as she casts off her tainted garment of tattered rags. "Something bigger and more opulent than this. And lots of down-stuffed, silk-covered pillows."

"How amorously impetuous she is," Mudadatta reflects as he gazes at his bride's nakedness, "already yearning for a plusher place for us to play in pleasure Kamadeva's wildest wanton games."

Although the hag's dangling teats resemble dry old turnips, blotched and withered, they look like mangoes to the merchant, plump, ripe, and succulent. Bowed and rickety legs seem to rival the trunks of plantains for firmness and those of elephants for pliancy. Taking no notice of the large wart and little tuft of coarse white hairs above the grayish lips sagging in the gaping arid cleft between those legs, exposed as she flops down on the bed, Mudadatta falls to his knees to piously worship what he esteems as a manifestation of the divine cosmic yoni of the goddess. Leaning forward to solemnly touch his lips to the venerable vulva in preparation for making an offering to it, he hears again the blast of wind and once more smells the fragrant breezes of Malabar.

The groom assumes that Chinnasena's sudden snore is yet another coy ploy, that, being bashful as brides so often are before first uniting with a husband, she is merely feigning sleep. Both his second and third wife had done the same. Unlike them, however, the crone continues to snore as an enraptured Mudadatta consummates the Gandharva love marriage. Unaware that an ability to sleep during sexual intercourse was a skill the debauched old whore had cultivated in her youth as a debutante prostitute, the merchant is charmed by what he interprets to be symptomatic of her innocence.

The next morning, after applying his magic tilak, he awakens his bride by whispering his mantra into her ear. With each repetition, as she becomes even more beautiful, he becomes even more convinced that she loves him even more than Urvashi loved King Pururavas or Sita adored Lord Ram.

Although she finds his monotonous recitation of the Sanskrit syllables annoying, she suffers it, aware as she is that the tedious repetition of gibberish is causing him to imagine she is beautiful, which, in turn, is causing him to love her, which will, in turn, allow her to take possession of his wealth.

After reminding the merchant of his obligation to hand over the one hundred and one gold fanums for her in-laws and of his promise to buy saris, jewelry, ornaments, and a luxurious bed for her, Mudadatta's bride sets out by bullock cart with a bag bulging with gold coins.

"And don't forget the garlic, my beloved," her groom calls out as, with tears of joy in his eyes, he watches the most beautiful woman in the world heading away in direction from which she, only the day before, had come to give herself to him in love. He tells himself that he is the happiest man in the world. He is, he realizes, so happy that he no longer cares whether or not he will ever have sons.

"Children," he reflects, "would be a distraction. Chinnasena's love would be divided between them and me. It would be painful not to have her all to myself. No, I have no need of sons, nor anything else, not so long as I have my beautiful Chinnasena."

Grudgingly placing the obligatory gold fanams at the feet of Shambaraswami, Chinnasena spits a gob of blood-red tambula and complains, "Couldn't you have entranced a husband for me who, in addition to being rich, is also handsome and intelligent, noble and strong?"

"Next time perhaps," the magician-hypnotist answers.

Nine months later, a period during which, on account of love, Mudadatta has become progressively happier and happier despite becoming poorer and poorer, Chinnasena returns to the cremation grounds. Nine months is all it has taken to squander the merchant's wealth. Bemoaning her husband's poverty, she appeals to the mantravadi. "You must help me to get rid of this wretched imbecile. He's broke—barely an anna to his name! I must liberate myself from this impoverished dotard and limp-lingammed dullard who's making my life so miserable. I deserve a younger, more handsome, virile, sophisticated, and quick-witted man of a higher caste or class, one with enough money to provide me with the luxuries to which I have become accustomed."

Months of listening to her husband tell her how ravishingly beautiful she is, has, so the storyteller suggests, encouraged the hag to imagine she is not nearly as repulsive as she really is.

"Because of the mantra you gave him, the tedious sound of those inane syllables that I've had to endure again and again, over and over, day in and

day out, from morning to night, I can't get rid of him. He refuses to believe that I don't adore him! I've tried to chase him away. I scream at him,
scold and insult him, abuse him with my foulest mouth, and he doesn't
pay attention or, if he does realize what I'm saying, he merely repeats that
stupid mantra and it causes him to imagine that I'm merely joking. He
thinks 'sister fucker' is an endearment. He interprets my nastiest assaults
on him as coquettish displays of playful pique. I've tried to run away, but
he follows me everywhere, swearing that he would pursue me even into
the realm of the dead. Sneaking here without him trailing me was a feat,
and you can be sure that he's searching for me right now and that, if I'm
not back soon, he'll somehow find me here. You must, if you have any
mercy or even just some sense of justice, teach me a mantra that I can use
to dispose of that disgusting, bankrupt, husband of mine, that burden
you inflicted upon me. Yes, you did this to me! It's all your fault. So it's
your obligation to deliver me from my misery."

It is neither out of compassion nor on account of any feeling of obligation, the storyteller explains, that the magician agrees to help the
beggar woman. It is rather for the sake of the pleasure he takes in using
his hypnotic powers to transform two pitiful creatures into enchanted
characters in a tale of love that rivals the oldest love story in the world,
the amorous legend of the king Pururavas and the apsara Urvashi.

"I will teach you the charms with which you can control him," the magician says as he begins to wave his peacock feather to and fro and, just as
he did months ago outside the Mohapur toll and customs gate, he places
a gold fanum in Chinnasena's hand. This time he instructs the crone to
hold the coin between her thumb and index finger. "Close your eyes. Concentrate on the coin and as you do, take in a deep breath. Now slowly let
it out. Concentrate on the coin and breathe in deeply again and slowly
out. Feel the golden prana circulating throughout your entire body. . . ."

As soon as the coin drops from her grip, the magician-hypnotist,
lulling her into to deeper and deeper trance, commits a mantra to her
memory: *Om na-mo Ma-ya-va-tyai Mu-da-dat-ta mam pa-ti me vash-ya
ku-ru ku-ru sva-ha.* Suggesting to her that, with each repetition of it, she
will go deeper still, "more and more calm and peaceful, floating adrift in
blissful samadhi." He asks her to repeat it again, again, and again.

"When you awaken I will apply a collyrium to your eyelids. It will
cause you, the moment you see your husband, to imagine that he is

ravishingly handsome and, with each repetition of your mantra, he will become more and more handsome and will seem sophisticated and intelligent as well. With each syllable he'll become more and more pleasing to behold, yes, so wonderful to listen to and so thrilling to the touch that you will yearn for him to embrace you with what you will imagine to be his strong arms and to kiss you with his ardent lips. Repeat the mantra again, and you will believe that he is the most handsome, kind, and virtuous man in the world. Again and you will love him with all your heart, again and you will be utterly devoted to him. Again, again, again, and you will do anything to please him. This will surprise you at first because, once you awaken from this trance you will not remember anything I have said during it, nothing except the mantra. Once I awaken you, you'll be eager to follow the instructions that I will give you. You will come out of your trance as I count to three. One, you are beginning to awaken. Two, more awake. Three, open your eyes. Wake up, yes, wide awake! Good, Chinnasena! Yes, very good.

"Now listen. Now that you know the mantra, you have the power to control his will, his perceptions, thoughts, feelings, desires, and actions."

The hypnotist gives the greedy shrew a pot of collyrium concocted, he claims, of gorochana, the gall stone of a cow, dissolved in the menstrual blood of a virgin, and spiced with the pollen of ashoka flowers and the musth of a rutting elephant.

"This kajal," he explains as he adorns her eyelids with it, "will enhance the power of your mantra, a power you can invoke to make him stop loving you, let you go, or leave you. You can, in fact, use it to make him see or hear, feel, think, or do anything you wish. Do what you will with it."

Rehearsing the magic spell and clutching the pot of magical mascara, she hurries from the grounds of the burning dead back to the home of the enamored merchant. Chinnasena is eager to use her newly acquired magic, to invoke the power of her mantra to cause her impoverished husband to forget his mantra. "Yes," she thinks, "then seeing that I am not beautiful and realizing that I do not love him, he'll leave me." "No," she thinks again. "Why diminish my beauty in anyone's eyes? Better yet, I'll order him to wander alone in the forest as Pururavas, deprived of his beloved Urvashi, did in ancient times. No, Pururavas was somehow able to reunite with Urvashi in the heavens. I don't want that. No, I'll command him to commit suicide, yes, to immolate himself. Yes, that seems the best way to dispose of an unwanted spouse."

Worried as to where his beloved might have gone, Mudadatta, with a freshly painted tilak on his brow, has been frantically pacing to and fro in front of his house, repeating his mantra over and over in hopes it would, as a magnet does lead, draw her back to him.

Suddenly it works. Seeing her appear in the distance, he waves his arms about to greet her. With the new kajal on her eyelids she seems more beautiful than ever.

As soon as she spots the merchant, Chinnasena recites aloud the spell that gives her absolute control over him: *Om na-mo Ma-ya-va-tyai Mu-da-dat-ta mam pa-ti me vash-ya ku-ru ku-ru sva-ha.* She repeats it, repeats it again, and again as she comes closer and closer to him, and then, all of a sudden, she is startled by Mudadatta's appearance. Never before has she noticed that her husband is actually not so ugly as she has imagined. As she gets closer and closer, still muttering the mantra, the merchant seems to become handsome, more and more so, and all at once, still reciting, she realizes that she is running into the seemingly muscular arms that are so eagerly outstretched to receive her.

Just as Urvashi, in the caress of Pururavas, feeling the warmth of human flesh for the first time, and hearing for the first time mortal heartbeat and breath, fell in love with the king, so Chinnasena, pressed close to Mudadatta, and feeling the pounding of his heart against her chest, the warmth of his breath on her neck, believes she is truly loved for the first time in her life and she is comforted, moved, aroused, and enchanted by that love. How or why, she wonders, could she have ever wished to be anywhere but in the merchant's embrace?

"I don't want to ever lose you," Chinnasena whimpers, begins to weep, and then, after muttering the mantra that makes her wish his command, she beseeches him never to leave her and to love her always.

"Always, yes, always my beloved, my beautiful wife," Mudadatta whispers as he leads her into the house and to the bed.

"I am sorry," Mudadatta, stroking his wife's haggard cheek, proclaims, "so sorry that my father did not work harder in his lifetime to amass a much greater fortune than the one he bequeathed to me. If only he had done so, I would still be able to give you the things you deserve."

"No," Chinnasena, gently caressing her husband's hairy bloated belly with her emaciated liver-spotted hand, answers, "No, I am sorry that I have asked for so much from you. There is nothing I desire now other than your love. I will sell all the precious things you have given me so that that we can survive."

"We do not need very much," Mudadatta adds with tears of joy streaming from his eyes as he kisses her scrawny neck and places his hand on a sagging shriveled breast. "Yes, we can live simply like Sita and Ram in the forest, subsisting on what we might gather in the wild. Love will sustain us. Love is the most precious luxury of all. It is to the sentiments what gold is among metals, diamonds among stones, the sun among the planets. Time does not tarnish love. Age does not diminish either its radiance or its value."

Chinnasena has never heard anything so exquisitely expressed. Not only is her husband handsome and strong, she realizes, he is noble, sensitive and sophisticated as well—yes, Mudadatta is a poet.

For fear that the spell inspiring him to suppose that she is beautiful might suddenly wear off, she asks him to recite his mantra. He does so not only for her sake, but for his own as well. And then she recites hers for him. And then, as his drooping lips press against her gaping, wrinkled, wizened mouth, the sound of the magic syllables, though muffled by the kiss, intensifies passion, heightens pleasure, and instigates a rapture in which their bodies, made luminous by love, seem to have been fused into one.

Each morning upon waking from their perpetually sweet dreams, Chinnasena paints the tilak on Mudadatta's forehead and Mudadatta applies the mascara to Chinnasena's eyes. They recite their respective mantras to one another throughout the day, repeating them before and after meals, while bathing together, while making love, before going to sleep, and at other times as well. Sometimes his first: *Om na-mo Ma-ya-va-tyai cha-nu cha-nu Chin-na-se-na mam vash-yam ku-ru ku-ru sva-ha.* Then hers: *Om na-mo Ma-ya-va-tyai Mu-da-dat-ta mam pa-ti me vash-ya ku-ru ku-ru sva-ha.* Sometimes the other way around. And sometimes they recite at the same time, blending their syllables into a longer and even more powerful mantra that makes each of them all the more gloriously beautiful in the eyes of the other and renders both of them confident that their love will last forever.

The storyteller takes a long pause before announcing that Muda-datta died a few years later.

Shambaraswami, once again camping in the burning grounds out-side of Mohapur, performing there the yogic practices that endow him with hypnotic powers, sitting cross-legged, breathing deeply in and slowing out, waving a peacock feather to and fro, sees the Doms place the body of the merchant, swathed in a shroud of crimson silk, on the pyre.

Although there are no sons to offer funerary pinda to the deceased, the merchant's aged wife, clad in a white sari, simple and clean, is there, watched by the magician-hypnotist as she lights the crematory fire. Gaz-ing at the flames, Chinnasena sees the radiance of innumerable suns, a monumental splendor and in it she beholds the gods—Indra on his ele-phant, the Creator seated in a lotus, the Destroyer with the moon in his hair, and the Preserver with a bow, sword, mace, and discus.

And then, smiling rapturously, she lies down next to her beloved's burning body as eagerly as she would were that pyre a bed, its flames strewn jasmine blossoms, as joyously as she would were that corpse alive and ardently aching to embrace her.

Offering herself to her lord, Mudadatta, as the oblation in a sacred sacrifice, Chinnasena becomes a Sati, a true and perfect woman. Blaz-ing with bliss, lover and beloved are entirely consumed by love.

As their bones commingle in the crematory pit, their ashes blend-ing, the magician-hypnotist sees their spirits rising together in san-dal-scented smoke and wafting away on a sublime journey toward a time and place when and where, he imagines, they will be incarnated in two new and exquisitely beautiful bodies as lovers who, though oblivious to their past lives, will be united, delighted, and exalted in perfect love once more.

"That is the story," the storyteller announces and rattles the damaru drum to open the eyes of his listeners and return them to the village in the world where they live their real lives.

And that is the story of the story.

One . . . two . . . three. Open your eyes.

And that is the story of the story of the story.

THE MAGICIAN'S TALE

Take this kiss upon the brow!
And, in parting from you now,
Thus much let me avow—
You are not wrong, who deem
That my days have been a dream;
Yet if hope has flown away
In a night, or in a day,
In a vision, or in none,
Is it therefore the less gone?
All that we see or seem
Is but a dream within a dream.

—EDGAR ALLAN POE, "A DREAM WITHIN A DREAM" (1849)

The listener wonders and asks if the writer/reader has made up the storyteller's story or if it actually is an Indian narrative, a translation or perhaps an adaptation?

"I've imagined it and imagined as I did so that it was a folktale once made up in India, a tale never written, only ever told and retold, again and again, then lost in the umbral memories of imaginary people long deceased, unknown by any real living being until I heard it recited by a spectral bard in the marvelous village of imagination. It was there that the imaginary storyteller imagined a magician/hypnotist who, in turn, imagined his creator, the storyteller who imagined him. I've composed another story in which they imagine that they are really real with such intensity, conviction, and purpose that they believe what they imagine. Let me read it to you.

Make yourself comfortable again, recalling the relaxation you felt while listening to the storyteller's tale, and allow yourself to become that at ease again. Yes, calm and comfortable again. Let your eyes close, and notice how, as they do, you begin to feel even more restful and effortlessly at ease. Now take a deep breath in through your nostrils and slowly, slowly let it out through your lips and, as you do, concentrate on your breathing. Yes, concentrate. Yes, good, and again, another deep and easy breath in and slowly out and notice how each breath encourages you to drift more and more deeply into a satisfying, pleasant state of relaxation, more and more agreeably calm and comfortably at rest.

And now let's picture again the village in a clearing in a palm grove in India where you heard the storyteller's tale of unlikely love. Recollect the whitewashed huts with bright-color-curtained doorways and umber roofs of palm thatch and remember the wandering teller of tales sitting cross-legged beneath the lushly leafed branches of the ancient pipal tree. Remember his ashen beard, his strings of beads and amulets, the crimson sectarian mark on his forehead and the glistening ruby in his ring. Look at the iridescent eye of the peacock feather in his hand waving to and fro, slowly waving back and forth and notice as you gaze at it rhythmically waving that you become more and more relaxed and the more relaxed you become the more and more vivid is the village, the tree, the storyteller, and the eye of the feather in his hand, waving, waving, slowly waving. Imagine it.

Remember the story he told about the merchant Mudadatta and the crone Chinnasena? After listening to it, the villagers, weary from their day of labor in the rice paddies, then soothed by the pleasure of hearing a tale of love's enchantments, dispersed. They are falling asleep now, resting in darkness, floating in dreams, meandering in deep, deep, soft and soothing sleep.

Imagine you are alone with the storyteller, sitting comfortably beneath the pipal tree tonight, as near to him as you are to me, listening to him as to me, hearing his voice in mine. He imagines you as you imagine him and wonders if you wonder if the story's true, if there really is or ever was such a magician-hypnotist as Shambaraswami. Listen as now he tells the tale to you.

Yes, yes, believe me, Shambaraswami is as real as you or I. I was myself amazed to discover that when he appeared here, sitting where you are now. He was just as I had envisioned him, with serpentine tresses, a face and chest smeared with crematory ash, a neck garlanded with rudraksha beads, and the sloughed skin of a cobra. Remember him.

"You must help me," he insisted. "Please help me. Listen to my story and you will understand why I have come to you and how you can help me."

So let me now tell you the tale that the magician-hypnotist told me. Listen to me as if you are listening to him, hearing his voice in mine.

Before I was given the name Shambaraswami, he began, before I was a magician, a weaver of Tantric trances and hypnotic spells, I was known as Kalpananatha the kavi, a poet weaving verbal yarn into plush narrative kinkhabs, dream fabrics elegantly embroidered with images at once erotic and divine, amatory tales relished with delight by connoisseurs of the sublime in the court of my generous patron, the Maharaja of Kashi.

In appreciation of my *Kamakelikavya*, a fable about the earthly king Pururavas and the heavenly nymph Urvashi, the maharaja crowned me his laureate and gave me a concubine, one of his nubile court dancers, the lithe and graceful Lilasena, proclaiming his certainty that the charms of the ravishing courtesan with the love-lustrous eyes of a wild forest doe would surely provide me with perpetually abundant literary inspiration.

As she danced Urvashi's trance-sporting dance, her darting glance was Kama's fiery dart, her brow the entrancing bow that fired it deep into my heart, setting me ablaze with desires fanned as flames by her waving hand into a radiantly raging fire. As if an incarnation of Mayavati, the goddess of illusion, she could, in both dance and love, be as radiant as Uma or as dark as Kali, as sweetly devoted as Sita or as fiercely independent as Durga, as chaste as Sarasvati or as wanton as Kamakshi.

In her impassioned embrace I was an oblation consumed by that fire, a sacramental offering to the god of love. The jingling of her anklet bells consonated with sibilant sighs, melodious moans, and imploring whispers echoed the ragas of celestial mansions. Making love with her was an epiphany, carnal, tumescent, and ecstatic, that I supposed surpassed the transcendental joy that the rishis imagine in their austere yogic meditations to be holy Brahman, ultimate, absolute, mysterious, and eternal. I believed that, by the grace of her love, basking in her incandescent splendor, I would be happy for the remainder of this life.

It was Arbuda who robbed me of that happiness. Arbuda raped her, seduced and possessed her, forced her to surrender, and abducted Lilasena.

I did not know at first that Arbuda was responsible for the changes in her. It began with signs of an unnatural weariness. And as tired as she was, she would toss and turn fitfully in our bed, unable to sleep. She lost her appetite and was growing gaunt. She seemed distracted and confused and began to have fainting spells, then fevers alternating with chills. I did not realize that it was because of Arbuda that she no longer took pleasure in lovemaking and asked me not to touch her. I did not understand that it was on account of Arbuda that Lilasena moaned in her dreams and wept upon awakening.

My education as a poet required study of Kamashastra, the compendia of treatises on the erotic arts and sciences, texts that enumerate those very symptoms in a woman as indicators of passionate love unrequited. And so I imagined that Lilasena had a lover.

It was the learned physician Vaidyabhatta, appointed by the maharaja to attend to Lilasena, who revealed the name of the one who had ravished her. "Arbuda," he said, "Yes *arbuda*, cancer, *yonyarbuda*, uterine cancer." An incurable tumor was growing in her womb, voraciously feeding on her flesh like a vicious fetal demon.

"I can do nothing more," the physician explained, "than to use sammohana to alleviate her pain." Vaidyabhatta asked Lilasena to stare into his eyes, take a deep breath in, and slowly let it out with a sigh.

I remember the passes and counterpasses of his hands and the words he uttered to entrance my beloved: "And another breath, and another, slowly, deeply, yes, and another, concentrating on your breathing, hearing it, feeling it, and the more intently your mind is focused on your breath, pulled deeply in and let slowly out, the less and less you will notice the pain. This is pranayama. As you inhale, feel a splendid golden prana filling your lungs, warming your chest, and as you exhale, feel it radiating into the rest of your body, infusing your limbs, soothing you with each sedating breath, in and up into your neck, your head, out and down into your spine, into your pelvis and loins, melting the pain, dissolving it, so that you feel entirely relieved and peaceful, yes, so very peaceful, easily floating and gently drifting, slowly, deeply, deeper and deeper into tranquil trance and sweetest dream."

Lilasena's facial muscles, ever strained by pain, became visibly more and more placid as her breathing slowed and deepened. Her head dropped forward, her limbs fell limp.

"Now imagine you are descending steps into a beautiful lush garden, slowly down, step after step, down, down . . . one . . . two . . . three . . . and down, yes down each step into the serene bower of samadhi, so comfortably warm, misted and fragrant with sweetly sandal-scented breezes and delicate perfumes of blossoming jasmine. Picture sinewy vines heavy with honeysuckle amorously entwining the strong trunk of a mango tree and clinging tenderly to it. There is no pain in this efflorescent garden of perfect peace, your garden, your refuge, ever open to you, always waiting to receive you. Whenever there is pain, remember this garden and return here to rest, rest peacefully. Just concentrate on your breath, close your eyes, picture the steps and come down, down, down back into your garden again. The pain is an illusion. But the garden is real as soon as you return to it."

It was in that garden of samadhi one night that, after closing her eyes and taking a deep breath in, Lilasena slowly, so slowly, breathed out the very last breath of her life with a soft, soft sigh.

If, as I had once imagined, arbuda would have actually been a man I could have been angry and energized and strengthened by that anger, furious for revenge. But I was only sad and enfeebled by sorrow, without anyone to blame and hate or anything to do about it. I was more woeful than Pururavas. His misery over the loss of his beloved Urvashi was a literary sentiment, a vatic illusion. It was imaginary. My anguish was real. And it allowed me to imagine nothing else.

I turned to Vaidyabhatta in hopes that he might use sammohana to guide me to Lilasena's garden, that I might join her there, once again smile to behold her smile, to watch her dance, listen to her whispers, and feel her body warmed by ardent embrace.

"That is her garden," the physician insisted, "for her alone, within her, and gone with her forever. But, yes," he promised, "with sammohana I might be able to redeem you from your sadness."

Just as he had done with Lilasena, Vaidyabhatta, with hands waving in passes and counterpasses around my face, invited me to gaze into his eyes as he did into mine, and to take a deep breath in and slowly let it out with a sigh.

I remember the suggestive words: "And another breath, and another, slowly, deeply, yes, and another, concentrating on your breathing, hearing and feeling it, focusing on it intently, and with each breath you become more and more calm and at ease, hearing only my voice. Let your eyes close now and listen in the darkness to the spell that removes the sorrows of love, one of the myriad mantras of Mayavati, mistress of dreams and illusions, goddess of sammohana. Listen: *Om Mayadevyai namah stotrenanena tam devim svapnadhatrim Mayavatam ye smaranti moham sarvam labante te.*"

Again and again the physician recited the vertiginous incantatory syllables and with each repetition I descended deeper and deeper into trance, darker and darker. Again, *Om Mayadevyai namah* . . . and again, *Om Mayadevyai* . . . and again, *Om* . . . again and again until suddenly in my dark enchantment the goddess appeared, her manifold undulant arms rhythmically waving, rising and falling, with ferocious skull-garlanded Kali on her left and flame-eyed Kamakhya, the gloating beloved of Kama, on her right.

I was in Mayavati's heavily incense-perfumed shrine in Haridvara amidst obeisant pilgrims, exultantly chanting *"Jaya Maye, jaya Maye, Maye jaya jaya* . . ." over and over in a surging and falling monotonous drone that, together with the heady perfume of incense that laced the heavy heated air, made my eyelids heavy, my limbs languid, and lulled me into sleep, deep and soothing sleep.

When I awakened the votaries were gone, so too were Kali and Kamakhya, and the gaudily ornamented idol. At once I recognized the face of the woman kneeling next to me, a moon radiant in the dark night of the sumptuous hair in which pearls were planets and diamonds the stars. "Lilasena!" I cried out.

"No, Lilasena is gone forever," she said in what I remembered as Lilasena's voice. "I am Mayavati, the goddess of illusion, constantly appearing in my shrine and the fantasies of zealous devotees, but transiently manifesting at my whim in displays of my uncanny powers, now and then, and here and there, in divine form as Urvashi for an ancient king, in human form as Chinnasena for an old merchant, Lilasena for a court poet, someday a woman listening to man reading this tale to her. It's the game I play for the delight of spreading love's hypnotic havoc."

She laughed as she took my hand in hers. "And now I've brought you here at the behest of my devoted acolyte and practitioner of my art, the royal physician Vaidyabhatta. I've consented to teach you what I once taught him, to initiate you into the mysteries of sammohana, to help you acquire the powers by which you can deliver yourself from your anguish over the loss of your beloved, the illusory Lilasena. First the vashitva siddhi, an unqualified control of your senses and thoughts, your mind and will, an ability to feel and think whatever and only what you wish to feel and think. You will be the master, no longer the victim, of your fears and desires, your emotions and thoughts. That power will qualify you to acquire the vashikarana siddhi, the ability to control the minds of others, to dictate their thoughts and feelings, to fascinate, beguile, and entrance anyone you wish, to make them see, hear, taste, smell, feel, and believe whatever you suggest. By means of vashikarana you will be able to subdue elephants in rut, charm venomous serpents, win the patronage of kings, stupefy enemies, subjugate women, and cause people to fall in or out of love. Love is, of course, nothing but sammohana. Yes, love without sammohana, without imagination, fantasy, or illusion, is merely copulation."

The initiation began with an oath sworn on my life never to reveal the details of the procedures for the acquisition of Mayavati's magic powers. Maintaining that vow prevents me now from divulging them to you.

With my gaze fixed upon Mayavati's secret yantra, I began, following her directions, to chant a secret mantra, then chanted it again and again, one thousand and eight times. Although my eyes had at some point I do not now remember closed, I could still vividly see the yantra. Although my lips had become sealed, I could still hear my loud recitation of the mantra. One thousand eight times again. And again. . . .

"Open your eyes," the goddess commanded and I obeyed. She smiled in recognition of my accomplishment. In yogic trance I had become master of myself. I renounced sorrow and felt released from the heavy shackles of love.

Mayavati then instructed me to retire to the cremation grounds, there to practice her secret sadhana, remaining calm in meditation, clearheaded, unafraid, focused, and concentrated amidst smoldering corpses, wild and ravenous jackals, prowling and howling hyenas, screeching vultures and cawing crows. The goddess solemnized this step in my initiation with five gifts: the skull of a child, a pouch containing the crematory ashes of a Brahmin priest, a yantra drawn with tiger blood upon a strip of desiccated human skin, a peacock feather, and a new name—Shambaraswami.

It was in the cremation grounds outside of Mohapur that, after a full month of meditation, I first demonstrated my attainment of the vashikarana siddhi by enchanting the merchant Mudadatta and then the old crone Chinnasena.

My success with them gave me such confidence as a vashikaran and so emboldened me that I resolved to test the extent of my new power by trying to charm Mayavati herself, to beguile the goddess of beguilement and cause her to love me no less than Chinnasena adored Mudadatta.

Returning to her shrine from the cremation grounds with the peacock feather in my hand, waving it slowly, slowly and, seating myself cross-legged in front of her, I invited her to gaze at it, to follow it with her eyes and to breathe deeply in and slowly out. When those eyes closed, I told her the tale of Chinnasena and Mudadatta and watched, as I did so, her limbs slowly loosen, her breathing gradually deepen, and then her head suddenly fall forward. I removed the shawl that veiled her breasts, the belt of bells that encircled her hips, took her in my arms, kissed her neck, and whispered, "Yes, sleep, my beloved, sleep, sleep in deep sleep, and dream of me, a sweet dream of me inside of you, rocking you in strong embrace, rhythmically rocking and enchanted. When you awaken from this dreamy trance you will be the beautiful Lilasena once more, grace-fully dancing in love with the poet Kalpananatha."

Awakening her, flush and naked in my arms, I smiled proudly: "I have mastered sammohana and by its power I have found you, my beloved Lilasena, made you mine again, redeemed you from death for the sake of love. I will never let you go."

"No, no," she laughed as, extricating herself from my embrace, she rose up from the bed, and wrapped her shawl around her shoulders. "I used vashikarana to cause you to imagine that you could use it on me in order to discover what you would do with your power. It was as well a test to determine whether or not you have truly mastered yourself and freed yourself from the bonds of desire. You have failed. You are still a victim of your love for Lilasena. Cultivate the magic I have taught you. Return to the cremation grounds and immerse yourself again in yogic trance there, rigorously contemplating my yantra and energetically reciting my mantra until you are entirely rid of desire and fear, impervious to sorrow and joy, and free from imagination and love."

With that the goddess vanished and, in the despair all abandoned lovers know, I followed her command and returned to the charnel grounds outside Mohapur.

Sitting cross-legged there amidst smoldering corpses and scaveng-ing nocturnal creatures, I concentrated on my breathing, focused my eyes on the yantra, and chanted the mantra, again and again, until a sudden samadhi in which the truth about illusions became clear to me. I understood that I was in a trance within a trance within a trance and realized that if I could emerge from trance to trance to trance, I could awaken in the presence of Vaidyabhatta and there demand that he revise his trance so that I could be reunited with Lilasena in the garden of her love. And if he were to deny me that, to claim that it was impossible, repeating that it was her garden alone and gone with her forever, I would use the power of vashikarana that I had learned from Mayavati to take control of his will and make him do as I commanded.

Concentrating with all my strength upon awakening, I opened my eyes, closed them, opened them again, again closed them, and again, and then commanded, "Wake up, wake up and open your eyes."

And Vaidyabhatta was facing me, poised exactly as he had been when I had last seen him. Sitting up and wide awake, I demanded that he reunite me with Lilasena.

"I wish I could help you, but I cannot, at least not on my own," Vaidyabhatta confessed. "I am, you must try to imagine, merely a character in this tale and as such I have no control over it. To change the story you must use the power of vashitva as taught to you by Mayavati to find the wandering storyteller who is telling it. You must ask him for your happy ending."

And so, believing his words, I followed his counsel and once again sat cross-legged in yogic meditation. And again I commanded myself to awaken. "Wake up, wake up, and open your eyes!"

And now the storyteller speaks to you again. "And there he was," he says, "Yes, right in front of me as you are now. Yes it was Shambaraswami, the magician-hypnotist, just as I had imagined him, with serpentine tresses, a face and chest smeared with crematory ash, wearing rudraksha beads and a sloughed cobra skin around his neck.

"You must help me," he insisted, and then proceeded to tell me the story I've just told you. "You must help me. You must change the story so that it ends with Lilasena and me united in the lush garden of perfect love."

"I can do nothing," I was sorry to inform him. "I am merely telling this story and cannot change it since I am only an imaginary character within it. Your only recourse is to find the writer of the story, someone named Lee Siegel. He transcends this illusory world of ours and manipulates it. He alone has the power to end the story in whatever way

77

he wishes. You must either lure him into this story or become liberated from it. But you must hurry because the story is almost over.

Just as the rishis perform yogic austerities to gain liberation from this phenomenal world which they imagine to be illusory, so Shambaraswami immersed himself in yogic trance to attain liberation from an illusory world which he imagined to be real.

The writer was sitting with his listener on the covered veranda of a moldering Indo-Portuguese bungalow in rural northern Goa, listening to an exorbitant nocturnal downpour of monsoon rain, gazing out at the lush, storm-shaken leaves, sipping cashew feni, and thinking about how to end the story he was writing, when he imagined Shambaraswami, the magician-hypnotist, his serpentine tresses, his face and chest smeared with crematory ash, his neck garlanded with rudraksha beads and the sloughed skin of a cobra, joining them there.

"Indian love stories must always end happily," the poet turned magician-hypnotist insisted. "Pururavas and Urvashi were, against all odds, finally reunited in heaven. And so, in keeping with that convention, you should end this story with this: 'By means of sammohana, Shambaraswami found his beloved Lilasena and joyously lived for the rest of his life with her in the magic garden of love.' Finish the story now, while that's still the last line, quickly, quickly while it's still true."

It will end, the writer writes, the reader reads, the listener hears, the moment when you, the listener, after hearing the last line ("By means of sammohana, Shambaraswami found his beloved Lilasena and joyously lived for the rest of his life with her in the magic garden of love"), open your eyes.

So, one . . . two . . . three . . . open your eyes.

Le Sommeil Lucide

RELIGION, SEX, AND HYPNOSIS

Touched by the hand of the mesmerist, the body falls into a seizure and in this state it explodes in a wild delirium of erotic or religious passion.

ROBERT D. ROMANYSHYN,
TECHNOLOGY AS SYMPTOM AND DREAM (1989)

part one

FOR THE READER

Four Stories to be Read Silently

When some people read a story they are able to enter the story in imagination so completely that it seems equivalent to living the experience itself. During the time of this fantasy the reader is completely oblivious to the true reality about him. The fantasy world is an encapsulated unit and it seems totally real. There is nothing else beyond it.

R. E. SHOR, "THE THREE-FACTOR THEORY OF HYPNOSIS AS APPLIED TO THE BOOK-READING FANTASY AND TO THE CONCEPT OF SUGGESTION" (1970)

THE ABBÉ'S STORY

The guide to the Chateau d'If told the tale from Le Comte de Monte-Cristo of Abbé Faria imprisoned there as if it was a real story. My companion, a Frenchman said, "No, it is not true. It is Alexander Dumas' imagination." I said, "We are not concerned. For us Indians legends are more important than history. History doesn't affect you unless if becomes legend."

MANOHAR SARDESSAI, INTERVIEW IN ISABEL VAS'S "IN SEARCH OF ABBE FARIA" (2006)

Sitting on the covered veranda of a moldering Indo-Portuguese bungalow in rural northern Goa with my listener, listening to an exorbitant nocturnal downpour, gazing at lush, storm-shaken leaves of plantain, palm, and mango trees, breathing in sweet-scented air, and sipping cashew feni homebrew, it's easy to imagine José Custodio de Faria as a child here.

In the more than two hundred fifty years that have elapsed since his birth, this spot hardly would have changed. There would have been the same exuberant roar of rains rustling the same expansive leaves, the same clamor of langur monkeys huddled for shelter in the treetops and distant howl of restless packs of draggled dogs. And beyond the trees, on the other side of the Chapora, the same virescent patchwork of dappled paddies would appear sunlit in the morning, inundated green stretches dotted white with egrets and black with crows, daubed with bright wet swatches, the reds, yellows, and blues of the laboring women's saris. There would be the same lugubrious meandering of dusky water buffalo, the same scent of burning palm fronds and the incense offered to the same gods.

It could be a night during the monsoon of 1755, the year Faria's mother, Rosa Maria de Souza, abandoned her family in Candolim to don the veil of a bride of Christ in Velha Goa and take refuge in penitential isolation and silence as a discalced nun in the Convento da Santa Monica. The Hindu Brahmin forebears of both the Farias and the Souzas, under Portuguese colonial rule, had converted to Catholicism in the sixteenth century.

Closing my eyes, I can imagine her sitting on the edge of the bed in our room, reading to him by votive candlelight, softly, sweetly, and surely somewhat sadly in Konkani, the mother tongue: *"Tuje bogor hanga konnach na mhonn. . . ."*

When he appears to have fallen asleep, she sets the book aside, gently strokes his face with trembling finger tips, blows out the candle, rises from his bedside, and walks away. I envision a tearful Rosa Maria stopping in the doorway to turn and look for the last time at her son. *"Deo bori rat dium,"* she whispers, "Goodnight, sleep well. Yes, sleep, sleep."

It's not hard to imagine the forsaken husband's feelings of betrayal, dismay, and an anger tempered by woe. As a pious man, Caetano Vitorino de Faria found perhaps some consolation in the Church for the loss of his wife. Leaving his son in the custody of his family in Colvale, he attended the Rachol seminary in Salcete taluka, took solemn vows, and was ordained as a Roman Catholic priest.

As I walked this morning along the muddy pathways around the glistening wet verdure of the paddies, I pictured the boy ambling ahead of me, imagined him in the rice farming village where I bought my jug of cashew feni homebrew, saw him watching smoke billow from the glow of a bundled sticks of sandal-scented incense that a storyteller, seated beneath a pipal tree, was waving in circles around and around an image of the goddess Mayavati. We listened to the wondrous words of an invocation read from the palm leaves in the storyteller's lap: *Stotrenanena tam devim jagaddhatrim vagdevatam ye smaranti trisandhyayam sarvam vidhyam labante te.*

Although the child doesn't understand the language of his Hindu ancestors any more than we do, the idolatrous Sanskrit incantation is hypnotic. As is the peacock feather wand the storyteller waves slowly, to and fro, slowly, as slowly he begins to tell his tale.

In fears of the Goan Inquisition, fiercely established to punish apostate Indian Catholics, Father Caetano Faria would not have condoned visiting the Hindu village, listening to such heathen stories, or witnessing what years later, in writing his *De la cause du sommeil lucide*, he remembered from his childhood in Goa: "The Brahmin priests were profoundly aware of the somnambulistic state and they induced it in their pagodas. In that state of trance the people would consult an oracle, an idol or a human intermediary, and imagine that they heard supernatural voices answering questions about their maladies or problems with money or love." This first exposure to hypnosis linked it with religious experience.

Father Caetano took his fifteen-year-old son from India to Lisbon and from there to Rome, where José Custudio studied and was granted a degree in theology from the Collégio de Propaganda Fide. Although he never returned to Goa, I suppose he would have felt that tenuous blend of melancholy and pleasure that is nostalgia and that, as a seminarian in Rome, later as a minor cleric in Lisbon, and finally as a hypnotist in Paris, he would surely have occasionally dreamed of monsoon rains, rice paddies, lush palm groves, fish simmered in spiced coconut milk, and that he would have remembered Brahmin priests intoning their hypnotic incantations, bright sari-clad women with pots of water balanced on their heads singing melodious Konkani songs, and wandering storytellers rhythmically waving peacock feather wands.

Abbé Faria's ecclesiastical experiences in Rome and Lisbon would certainly have prepared him for his future forays into hypnosis. The relationship between Catholic priest and worshipper of Christ, no less than Brahmin pujari and votary of Hindu idol, is analogous to that of hypnotist and hypnotized. Religious experience is hypnotic experience.

The Mass is an induction ritual. Facing east, eyes fixed on the crucifix above the altar, the celebrant is lulled by the holy monotony of enchanting chant. *Kyrie, rex genitor ingenite, vera essentia, eleison. Kyrie . . . eleison. Kyrie . . . eleison.* Bells ring, one, two, three times, as censers swing to and fro, up and down, back and forth and again, spreading a heavy heady haze of fragrant smoke in which votive candles flicker. Five signs of the cross enhance the trance. Stand, sit, genuflect, rise, sit again, kneel again. Again and again. Recitation, *credo*, repetition, *credo, credo, credo. Lex orandi, lex credendi.* Then there's silent prayer to deepen the trance, a peaceful quietude in which eyelids become heavy. Deeper, deeper. There's mental absorption and focused concentration, a calm cognitive surrender and an escalating detachment from all sense impressions other than the image of Christ on the cross, the aroma of frankincense, the sound of solemn intonations, and then the commanding suggestion of an officiating priest: *Hic est enim Calix Sanguinis mei.* Devout celebrants of the eucharistic feast are able to imagine they are in the presence of God and that in a sip of sweet wine the blood of Christ is tasted. *Credo*, they recite in unison, reiterating it again and again, *credo, credo, credo*, and, with each repetition they are taken deeper still, drawn deeply into an enchantment in which a receptivity to posthypnotic suggestion will allow the susceptible to continue, even out of trance, to believe that Jesus Christ descended from Heaven for the sake of their salvation, and to imagine that, by the virtue of their faith in Him, their sins will be forgiven and that they will be redeemed from death and granted eternal life in a world to come.

Faria would surely have recognized the similarities between these liturgical procedures and the mesmeric inductions he witnessed for the first time in Paris. Reading Mesmer's *Catéchisme du magnétisme animal*, the abbé, no doubt struck by the suggestive use of the word "catechism," would have sensed the implicit affinity of Mesmer's *fluide magnétique* to his Church's *Spiritus Sanctus*, both of them as believably real as we are willing to imagine them to be.

Although Mesmer's *magnétisme* had been officially denounced by a joint commission of the Academy of Sciences and the Royal Society of Medicine as a mere *"excitation de l'imagination"* in 1784, four years before Faria's arrival in Paris, a subversive fascination with the phenomenon persisted. In defensive reaction to the official confutation of mesmerism, Amand-Marie-Jacques de Chastenet, the Marquis de Puységur, an ardent disciple of Mesmer, established the *Société harmonique* for the study and therapeutic practice of mesmerism and gave sensational and enormously popular demonstrations of it in Paris and the provinces. Attending these demonstrations, Faria became so intrigued by the somnambulistic phenomenon that he turned to Puységur for instruction and was initiated by him into its mysteries. *De la cause du sommeil lucide* is dedicated to the marquis in gratitude for his generous tutelage.

Faria had come to Paris in the same year that ambassadors from the court of Tipu Sultan, the ruler of the Indian kingdom of Mysore, arrived there with a mandate to form an alliance with the French that would enable them to rid India of the English and Goa of the Portuguese. The sultan's majestic entourage dazzled the court of Louis XVI on the eve the Revolution. The French fancied a fantastic India, a land at once mystical and wanton, an opium dream world of ornate temples, opulent palaces, perfumed pleasure gardens, and lush jungles, a voluptuous realm of warrior gods and amorous goddesses, contemplative adepts in loincloths, ecstatic mahatmas in flowing robes, and intemperate maharajas in silk brocades, their turbans festooned with diamonds and peacock feathers, their stables stocked with lavishly caparisoned elephants, their imperial harems of scantily clad, lasciviously dancing bayaderes and demurely veiled wives who would one day ecstatically immolate themselves on their master's funeral pyre. Shawls from Kashmir, Oriental slippers, and silk turbans were all the rage with fashion-conscious Parisian ladies, aristocratic and bourgeois women who would no doubt have been intrigued by the newly arrived cleric from India who was known to be frequenting the gambling houses in the Palais Royale.

Faria was certainly in Paris during the Revolution and the Reign of Terror. He would have witnessed the storming of the Bastille, the massacre of Champ de Mars, the executions of Louis XVI and Marie Antoinette, and the self-coronation of Napoleon. According to his principal biographer, D. D. Dalgado, whose hundred-year-old *Mémoire sur la vie de l'Abbé de Faria* is the source of information for almost all other accounts of his life, Faria was "*un politician exalté*" who headed a revolutionary battalion and, after the overthrow of the monarchy, fought for the Directoire against the Convention.

The suggestion that Faria was a political revolutionary informs Mikhail Buyanov's biographical chapter on him in *Child Psychiatry and You* (1989), as researched in Goa in the 1950s. The former president of the Moscow Psychotherapeutic Academy imagined Faria as an anticlerical protocommunist commander of a detachment of sans-culottes imprisoned for his political and anticlerical activities, first in the Bastille and subsequently in the Chateau d'If, an island prison off the coast from Marseille. It was in solitary confinement there, the Soviet psychiatrist supposed, that, based on his knowledge Indian yogic meditational techniques, Faria developed procedures for autogenic trance induction that prevented him from going mad.

Buyanov's suggestion encouraged Luis Vas, in his *Abbé Faria: The Life of a Pioneer Indian Hypnotist and His Impact on Hypnosis*, to further suppose that Faria used self-hypnosis to visualize fires that kept him warm in his chilly cell and that, to keep his spirits up, "he could imagine having long lunches with his family in Goa consisting of xacuti, arroz refogado and bebinca accompanied by fascinating discussions on all possible subjects."

In perhaps the most fanciful of all the Faria biographies, *Abbe Faria, the Master Hypnotist who Charmed Napoleon*, Diogo Mesana Fernandes, a contemporary Goan journalist living in Macao, conjures up the Indian cleric as a counselor to Napoleon Bonaparte, using his clairvoyant powers to advise the French leader politically and militarily, and hypnotizing him in order to reveal celestial secrets to him and to allow him prophecies of future victories and recollections of his past lives, including his incarnations as, among others, Akhenaten and Charlemagne.

Vas believes the reiterated contention that Faria was arrested in Marseille in 1797 for conspiracy and imprisoned in the Chateau d'If, an idea that arises from a confabulation of the hypnotist from Goa with a character of the same name in Dumas's novel, *Le Comte de Monte-Cristo*. The incorporation of the fictional character into the story of the real person results in the transformation of that person into a character who is imagined to be real.

Dumas's imagined Italian Abbé Faria is a crazed and yet wise and erudite monk who befriends Edmond Dantès, the hero of the novel, in the Chateau d'If where he has been imprisoned: *"Faria était un personage de petite taille, aux cheveux blanchis . . . à l'oeil pénétrant caché sous d'epais sourcils qui grisonnait, à la barbe encore noire et descendant jusque sure sa poitrine."* That Dumas in fact was keenly interested in *le somnambulisme magnétique*, dramatically depicted in his novels *Le Collier de la reine* and *Joseph Balsamo*, would suggest that he might have been familiar with the endeavors of the hypnotist from India. While I am able to discern no similarity other than the name between the historical person and the fictional character, Dalgado insists that Dumas based his character on the person, and that the character of the character is the true character of the real person. The historian however, does admit that the illustrious author of the novel had taken *"les libertés usuelles du romancier."*

With a resurgence of interest in the occult in France after the Revolution, séances, fortunetelling, magic shows, and demonstrations of divination, clairvoyance, and somnambulism once again had become fashionable *divertissements* in aristocratic and bourgeois salons by the beginning of the nineteenth century. I imagine that, given his interest in magnetism, Faria may well have been a member of one of the many occult fraternities that were emerging in Paris at the time.

In 1802, the year, incidentally, of Dumas's birth and also the year when Mesmer, formerly discredited in France, was able to return to Paris and receive a yearly allowance of three thousand florins as compensation for the money he had lost in the Revolution, Faria, reputedly an Oriental practitioner of *le magnétisme*, was invited to entertain guests at a dinner party chez Louise-Eléanore-Mélanie de Sabran, the Marquise de Custine. "He boasted that he would kill a canary by magnetizing it," François-René de Chateaubriand recollected in his *Mémoires d'outre-tombe*: "But the canary was all the livelier for his efforts, and the Abbé, quite beside himself, was forced to leave the company for fear that the canary might kill him instead. My presence as a Christian had, I suppose, rendered the experiment vain."

I imagine that it might have been on account of his embarrassment over the circulation of the amusingly derogatory anecdote about his failed performance that evening that the Indian magnetizer left Paris that year to take a job teaching philosophy at a lycée in Marseille. Dalgado, on the other hand, imagines that this teaching appointment was arranged by an acquaintance he had made in the Palais Royal, a fellow gambler who did this as much as a favor to the gaming house as to Faria, "for his mysterious powers as a magnetizer had made him a formidable gambler."

Indulging my own imaginational configurations of him, I picture the novice hypnotist from Goa in Marseille reading to his students from Ovid's *Metamorphoses*: "*Est prope Cimmerios longo spelunca recess.*" Some of the eyelids in the classroom are closed by boredom, others because listening to the story is hypnotic. "*Mons cavus ignavi domus et penetralia Somni.*" A few of the students imagine the sanctuary of Sleep in a cave cut deep into a mountain. "Out of the stony depths flows Lethe's stream which, with its murmuring waves sliding over loose pebbles, induces drowsiness." Some of the listeners see the waters, some hear the waves, others go more and more deeply into the cave.

Experimenting with hypnosis during his ten years in the south of France, Faria, developing his own technique and theory, emphatically denounced Mesmer's explanations of somnambulistic phenomena as the result of a manipulation of a magnetic fluid, proposing instead that it was the imagination of the subject that produced hypnotic trance, what he termed *"le sommeil lucide."* Faria's theory was articulated with an original vocabulary: to hypnotize was *concentrer*, the hypnotist was *le concentrateur*, and for the hypnotized Faria invoked the mystical term *épopte*, from the Greek for an initiate into the mysteries of Eleusis.

By 1813 Faria had acquired a sufficient mastery of hypnotic methods to give him the confidence to return to the capitol and open an atelier where, on Thursday evenings, he would expound his theories and give demonstrations of *le sommeil lucide*. Publicity for the weekly event identified the hypnotist as *"un brahmine oriental, docteur en théologie et philosophie, membre de la société médicale de Marseille, etc. etc. etc. etc."*

Although he was a Roman Catholic and had left Goa over forty years earlier and never returned, Faria understood the value of his Indian origins, his allure as a representative of a romantically mysticized Orient. He invoked it in his demonstrations as well as in his book. *Le sommeil lucide*, he imagined—perhaps believed and certainly declared—was long known and persists in India: "Brahmins have a deep understanding of it and benefit from practicing it in their temples."

In his *Mémoire sur le somnambulisme et le magnétisme animal* (1854), François Noizet, a general in the French Army, recounts his attendance at one of Faria's weekly demonstrations in his studio on the rue de Clichy: *"Le prêtre indien de Goa,"* was, according to Noizet, "a tall and handsome old man, his black hair streaked with gray, his complexion dark. He had an elongated face, hooked nose, and large bulging eyes."

The audiences for these demonstrations came from Parisian high society. While some with scientific interests came to learn about somnambulism, most attended for the sake of entertainment. The majority of attendees were, in Dalgado's words, *"dames élégantes"* who flocked to Faria's studio to be amused and to experience *"nouvelles sensations."*

Clad in clerical robes, the mysterious Indian priest from Goa would enter the salon accompanied by four or five young women, his *époptes*, adept assistants accustomed to his inductions.

The spectators would inevitably become restless during the lectures that preceded the demonstrations. His long-winded elucidations of *le someil lucide* and fervent denunciations of Mesmer's theories were by all accounts tediously monotonous, utterly confused, and unintelligibly obscure, all the more so because of Faria's strong foreign accent and stumbling French. Finally, following these pompously abstruse overtures, during which the audience would be assured that neither the devil nor animal magnetism would have a part in what they were about to witness, the spectacle would begin. The hero of the dramatic show would instruct his chorus of subjects to make themselves comfortable, think about sleep, and stare at him. "Fixing his large dark eyes on the young ladies," Noizet remembered, "he asked them to gaze at the back of his hand. He then took a few steps toward them, suddenly lowered his arm, and commanded, '*Dormez!*'"

Immediately the young women would fall into a lucid sleep, a hypnotic state in which he could cause them to experience whatever pleasant or unpleasant sensation he suggested. When he gave a girl a glass of water to drink, she would, under the influence of his verbal commands, imagine it to be wine and become inebriated, or, if he suggested it, vinegar that would cause her to vomit. He would desensitize his subjects' limbs to the degree that they felt nothing when their forearms were pierced with hatpins. Some adepts, according to Faria's claims in *De la cause du sommeil lucide*, could understand and speak languages of which they were ignorant in the waking state, as well as read from books with closed eyes.

In an incredulous and scoffing account of one of Faria's demonstrations published in *L'Hermite de la Chaussée d'Antin* (1814), a satirical commentary on Parisian manners by the librettist Victor-Joseph de Juoy, who had served in the military in India, portrayed "the philosopher from the coast of Malabar with a complexion browned by the fires of the Goan Sun," as a charlatan whose endeavors he belittled as "public mystification." He reported that one of Faria's subjects "had attained the extraordinary ability in her lucid sleep to read from a book [placed between her legs under her skirt] with that part of her body from which only the first created man and woman were not brought into this world. Unfortunately, the proof of this miracle was not fit for public exhibition."

When, for the climax of his shows, Faria asked for volunteers from the audience, it was most often women who came forward, eager to be entranced by the Brahmin from Goa. Women, Faria imagined, were more susceptible to *le sommeil lucide* than men, according to the convoluted physiological theories put forth in *De la cause du sommeil lucide*, because of the greater "liquidity of their blood and mobility of their other bodily fluids." The degree of that sanguinary liquidity determines the extent of the *concentrateur*'s power over the *épopte*, which is to say the amplitude of the subject's *confiance* in the hypnotist, *confiance* being defined by Faria as a "surrender of the mind to the discretion of another."

Erotic resonances are ever embedded in hypnosis as a process of submission to the will of another. Hypnotism is an erotic act. Induction is seduction. It begins slowly and rhythmically, demanding relaxation, languor, yielding, and leading to a pleasurable absorption that culminates in surrender.

"From being in love to hypnosis is evidently only a short step," Sigmund Freud, based on his own experiments with the psychotherapeutic potential of hypnosis, observed in his *Group Psychology and the Analysis of the Ego*. "The respects in which the two agree are obvious. There is the same humble subjection, the same compliance, the same absence of criticism towards the hypnotist just as towards the loved object. There is the same absorption of one's own initiative. . . . It is only that everything is even clearer and more intense in hypnosis, so that it would be more to the point to explain being in love by means of hypnosis than the other way round. The hypnotist is the sole object, and no attention is paid to any but him."

Jean Sylvain Bailly, the French astronomer, mathematician, and litterateur who in 1784 composed the elegant and reasonable report of the joint commission of the Academy of Sciences and the Royal Society of Medicine (a committee that included Benjamin Franklin, the then American ambassador to France; Anton Lavoisier, the father of modern chemistry; and Joseph-Ignace Guillotin, the physician who invented the guillotine) that dismissed animal magnetism as a mere excitation of imagination, recognized the erotic underpinnings of mesmerism and proposed that magnetic therapy posed a threat to morality. "The knees of the man who magnetizes a woman," he informed the King, "are generally in contact with those of his subject. The lower parts of their bodies touch. The magnetizer's hand is applied to his subject's abdomen and sometimes lower down over her ovaries. Such contact with the most sensitive parts of the body brings out the full force of the attraction between the sexes."

Given the analogous, if not homologous, relationship between hypnotic and erotic experiences, as well as the popularity—particularly with women—of the Goan hypnotist's demonstrations, it is hardly surprising that gossip in Paris about Faria would be heavily spiced with lurid innuendos as to Faria's relations with the credulous and adoring women who were ever eager to be his subjects, surrender to his commands, and give him control of their will, imagination, and senses.

One evening, when, for the denouement of his performance, Faria asked for volunteers from the audience, a man whom Faria did not recognize raised his hand and was invited to come forward, take a seat, and think about sleep. When, after several passes with his hand, the hypnotist commanded, "*Dormez!*" the volunteer appeared to become cataleptic. When Faria suggested the room was becoming very cold, the man began to shiver. And when he was offered a cup of water with the suggestion that it was wine, the man exclaimed that it was the most delicious champagne he had ever tasted. When, after declaring that the man's arm was completely insensitive, Faria approached him with a hatpin, the volunteer suddenly opened his eyes, leapt to his feet, roared a laugh, and declared, "*Eh bien! Monsieur l'Abbé, si vous magnétisez tout le monde comme moi, vous ne faites pas grand'chose.*"

The exposé, reported in the press with illustrated cartoon caricatures of Faria, made such an impression on the public that, rather than attending his demonstrations in order to be amazed by the formerly charismatic cleric from India, dwindling audiences came to laugh at him.

The volunteer who had feigned lucid sleep in order to mock the abbé was an actor named Poitier who subsequently starred at the Théâtre des Variétés as the buffoonish magnetizer Soporito in Jules Vernet's satirical farce, *Le magnétismomanie* (1816). A dark-complexioned Soporito with a strong Indo-Portuguese accent wearing an abbot's robe was a recognizable lampoon of Faria. And the play was so enormously popular that Faria felt constrained to defend himself against the mockery. In his preface to *De la cause du sommeil lucide*, he proposed that he be given the opportunity to add a scene to the play in which he would appear on stage and use his hypnotic skills to put the actors to sleep and in that sleep to cause them to violently convulse and roll around on the stage disoriented.

He also defended himself in that preface against the Catholic authorities who, believing that his demonstrations were feeding the "*la monstrueuse chimère de l'athéisme*," were denouncing him as a sorcerer, magician, and satanic agent. In the *Le Mystère des Magnétiseurs et des Somnambules dévoilé aux âmes droites et vertueuses*, the influential vicar, Abbé Fustier, speaking on behalf of the Church, declared hypnosis to be the work of the Antichrist. It is, I would imagine, precisely because religion ultimately relies for its power on hypnotic states that hypnotic practices which are not serving or alligned with the Church are threatening to that institution. And I assume that the vicar, no less than Bailly or Freud, sensed the transgressive sexual power of hypnosis.

An article in *Le Moniteur Universel* referring to Faria as "Satan's hellhound," and describing his countenance as "frightening and extraordinary at the same time it compliments his magnetic stances," accused him of having caused a pregnant woman to miscarry in a lucid sleep induced by him. In order not to be associated with Faria as an object of ridicule and censure, his colleagues at the Société du Magnétisme, insisting on the scientific nature of their own endeavors, dismissed him as an impostor and a charlatan. The "*brahmine oriental, docteur en théologie et philosophie, membre de la société médicale de Marseille, etc. etc. etc. etc.*" had no choice but to close his salon and retire from hypnotic practice.

In his *Histoire du merveilleux dans les temps moderne* (1861), Louis Figuier imagined a rather sad ending to the story: "Once the jokes in the newspapers had tarnished the halo of this old-fashioned thaumaturge, the Abbé Faria hid his defeat in a girls' boarding house where he served as an almoner and recited the Mass for them. Those fingers of his that had worked so many miracles and that, for those who believed in him, could, despite the distance, have knocked over the Emperor of China, were now consecrated only to a give benedictions to young school girls." Dalgado imagined the story to be true and subsequent biographers have imagined that all that Dalgado imagined is true.

They imagine Faria writing his *De la cause du sommeil lucide* in his room at that girls' school and dying there of apoplexy. No one knows where his remains are buried.

Sitting on the covered veranda of the Indo-Portuguese bungalow we're renting in rural northern Goa, listening to rain and sipping feni, encourages me to imagine him here, closing his eyes, taking a deep breath in and slowly letting it out, and imagining that he has been able to return to Goa to die.

In a lucid sleep he vividly sees leaves of palm, mango, and plantain shaken by a susurrous downpour of monsoon rain. He smells the rich perfumes of jungle night jasmine and spicy fragrances of savory sauces simmering on the stove, and he tastes lusciously sweet dodol. Imagining his mother reading to him, he concentrates on the soft enchanting voice: *"Tuje bogor hanga konnach na mhonn. . . ."*

She closes the book and sets it aside, gently strokes the child's face, then rises from his bedside, blows out the candle, and walks away. She stops in the doorway to turn, to look for the last time at her son. *"Deo bori rat dium,"* she whispers. "Goodnight, sleep well. Yes, sleep . . . sleep. . . ."

THE SCULPTOR'S STORY

If you walk from the Panaji Secretariat along the Mandovi River, you will come across a rather strange and haunting statue in the middle of the square near the bus stop. While waiting for the bus, I couldn't take my eyes off this statue. And as dusk began to fall, it gathered an even more haunting, even evil, feel to it.

MIHIR NAYAK, MITAROY GOA HOTEL WEBSITE (2012)

The first time I stood near Ramachandra Pandurang Kamat's 1945 bronze sculpture, a statue with which I was familiar from published photographs, it was raining and, lending a watery shimmer to the monument, that downpour almost brought the man and woman to life. Rain trickled off his extended, spread fingers onto her swollen breasts, their nipples noticeably erect beneath the wet bodice. Rain streamed like sweat down his forehead, dripped from her face, across

her cheeks, purled down her neck like tears, dribbled off the fingers of her right hand and into a puddle in her lap. I approached the couple to read the plaque on the pedestal upon which they have been installed: *JOSE CUSTODIO, ABBE FARIA, FUNDADOR DO METODO DE HIP-NOSE PELA SUGESTAO.*

Contemplating the statue, it's easy to imagine the sculptor's tale, the larger dramatic narrative from which it is a climactic scene. It's natural to wonder who the woman might be. In my imagination, based on the suggestions from what I know of his life, she's an enraptured French society *belle femme*. I'll call her Seraphine Goéland in the version of the story in the tale for listeners. The image is metaphorical for sexual seduction and carnal conquest.

Suggestion and imagination have generated a wide range of narratives. "Whenever I accompanied my dad to Panjim city," the Goan writer Anzil Fernandes recollected on Goenche.com in "The Man Who Pushed the Lady Down," "I always witnessed a statue of a man staring at a falling woman with his hands stretched towards her. As a child seeing the statue, I was convinced that the man pushed the lady down and God punished him by turning him into a statue." More sinister is the story suggested to a writer of the *Lonely Planet Guide* to Goa: "In a small triangle of lawn next to the Secretariat Building is an unusual statue of a man apparently about to strangle a woman." In *Abbe Faria, the Master Hypnotist who Charmed Napoleon* Diogo Mesana Fernandes ,imagines "a lady suffering birth pangs reclining by his side as he tries to alleviate her suffering through his hypnotic powers."

The taxi driver who brought us, my listener and me, to the statue that rainy day, did not seem to know what I was talking about when I asked him to take us to the statue of Abbé Faria in Panjim. But when I explained to him that it was in the square next to the Old Secretariat Building, "Oh, him," the driver exclaimed. "Of course I am familiar with him. Everyone in Goa knows about him. You should have said 'the statue of the magician.' Yes, one of Goa's greatest celebrities, he was a magician famous in Europe for his shows." And when we arrived there, he further explained, "The magician is performing one of his greatest illusions. Levitation. Yes, he is making the woman rise up off the ground to float in midair. My grandfather saw him do the trick when he was a little boy and told me about it. I personally once saw P. C. Sorcar do the same."

I heard other projections based on what the image suggested to the imaginations of Goans. In one of them the statue was allegorical with the priest representing the Portuguese Catholic colonial government who had hypnotized the passive people of Hindu Goa, the motherland, as represented by the woman, into submission. In another contrary account still with hypnosis as a metaphor for political control, I was told that "the statue was erected during Portuguese rule under the pretense that it depicted Abbé Faria and a French woman, but the native people of Goa knew the hidden meaning and understood it as a wake-up call for independence that was to be answered sixteen years later when Indian soldiers occupied the Secretariat Building next to the statue and raised the Indian flag to mark the end of a four-hundred-and-fifty-year trance."

The statue of Faria, it would dismay many proud Goans to know, was featured in the article "The World's Ugliest Public Art" in *Travel+Leisure Magazine* in December 2011, which included it along with a polychromatic likenesses of Michael Jackson in London and Marilyn Monroe in Chicago, two bronze men pissing in Prague, and a monumental thumb in Paris: "Abbé Faria was honored in 1945 with this rather unwholesome tribute. The novelist Evelyn Waugh called the thing 'wildly vivacious,' elaborating that it captured the illustrious abbé at the 'climax of an experiment, rampant over an entranced female.' Be that as it may, it's easy to imagine that the abbé's prostrate subject wishes that she could call the whole thing off and make a run for the beach instead."

The image is iconic for many Goans. It's used on the logo for the seal of the City Council of Panjim. It's also reproduced on the label of a wine produced at Vinicola, a Goan winery in Madgao owned and operated by Dr. Ivo da Costa Azaredo. Cordially welcomed by the charming elderly gentleman into his marvelous old colonial mansion with its marble floors, crystal chandeliers, and rosewood furniture, I asked about his interest in Faria and why, in particular, he had used the image on his wine label. "It has to do with the power of suggestion in marketing," he explained. "Faria, like my wine, was from Goa and he went to France, where the wine is thought to be the best in the world. And that he was a hypnotist subconsciously suggests to people that a glass of my wine will relax them. And that he was a priest reminds people that wine is the sacred drink of Holy Communion. I've made all my money because of that. Yes, I supply the sacramental wine to every Catholic church in all of India except Kerala."

After expressing a commercial appreciation of both wine and Christianity as a businessman, he confided that he is a teetotaler and an atheist. "Quite honestly, I have never been either to France or to the office of a hypnotist."

On the wall in the office of Dr. Rajendra Hegde, a psychiatrist in Madgao, "an expert," I had been informed, "on Faria, depression, and other mental illnesses," the image, imposed in black silhouette, is

rendered so that the figures of the female subject and male hypnotist are transposed.

To what degree, I wondered, does that happen in any hypnotic session. To what extent, for that matter, and at what point are seducer and seduced analogously transposed in any love affair? And to what degree is it possible for writer and reader, reader and listener, to be transposed by and within a story?

When I asked Dr. Hegde what his version of the image suggested about hypnosis in general and about Abbé Faria in particular, he told me not to take the image so seriously. "It's just a joke," the expert on Faria, depression, and other mental illnesses, explained.

THE PSYCHIATRIST'S STORY

Abade Faria can be characterized as a precursor of psychoanalysis, psychotherapy, and dynamic psychiatry, and this by the fact of his having turned famous as the first psychological experimenter, hypnotherapist and theoretician of psychology.
HANNES STUBBE, "JOSÉ CUSTODIO DE FARIA, THE SCHOOL OF NANCY, AND SIGMUND FREUD: AN UNKNOWN GOAN SOURCE FOR PSYCHOANALYSIS" (1999)

I had seen Dr. Rajendra Hegde interviewed in Isabel Vas's *In Search of Abbe Faria*, a video documentary intended "to inspire others to take up the cause for Abbe Faria to be given his due place of prominence in Goan history." Assuming, I suppose, that I was taking up that cause by doing research for this book, the psychiatrist agreed in a muddled mobile telephone conversation to talk to me about Faria on the next Saturday in his office at "number D/F3 Pancharatna, behind Borkar Super Stores, which you cannot miss, for it is known by everyone, and once there I'll be found when you inquire as to the whereabouts of my office. I too am well-known."

The pot-holed dirt street through a bedlam dappled with refuse, plastic bags, aluminum cans, discarded rotten fruit, and rancid vegetables, was lined with stalls selling fly-swarmed sweets, chickens squawking as if aware of the immanence of slaughter, cheap sunglasses, rubber chapels, cassette tapes, and pirated DVDs, and congested with walkers and strollers, bikes with bells ringing, and Rajdoot scooters and Maruti cars with horns honking impatiently. The road gushed a haphazard, jostling, noontime crowd, lots of Gujarati hawkers and peddlers, but only a beggar or two, the usual scruffy ravening Goan street dogs and lackadaisical cud-chewing cows, old umbrella repair men and young shoeshine boys. The humid monsoon-season air was laced with the aromas of incense, kerosene, cow dung, and masala.

Without any numbers on the building I had to ask a man, sitting, smoking, unfazed by the chaos around him, comfortable and at ease in it: "Where is D/F3 Pancharatna?"

"You are looking for the travel agency?"

"No, I'm looking for Dr. Rajendra Hegde."

"Oh, yes, yes, the crazy peoples' doctor. You are seeking his help?"

"Yes. But not his medical help, no. . . ." realizing that I had no need or obligation to justify my visit to a psychiatrist to this lunchtime loafer, I stopped myself from explaining that I wanted to talk to Dr. Hegde about Abbé Faria, and asked in which building was his office.

"I do not personally know that exactly because I have never had the need to see him," he chuckled.

A shoeshine boy, assuring me that he knew where the office was because he often shined the doctor's shoes, promised to tell me how to get there on the condition that I let him shine my shoes. After over-paying him for the shine, I followed his directions, which took me to a travel agency where a receptionist gave me directions, which, much to my relief, actually got me to the office.

When, after climbing up four flights of dark stairs in the dilapi-dated concrete building, I saw the sign outside the door (DR. RAJEN-DRA HEGDE M.D. PSYCHOLOGICAL MEDICINE. KINDLY REMOVE FOOTWEAR), I added my brightly polished loafers to the pile of dirty chapels and shoddy shoes, and entered the office in my stocking feet.

The glaring bluish-white glow of fluorescent ceiling lights illumi-nated the scuffed linoleum floor and the glaucous-green painted cin-der block walls. A sneezing, nose-blowing woman in a plain blue sari, her red plastic bindi applied to her forehead off center, handed me a pencil and a form to fill out.

Insisting that that would not be necessary, I informed her that I was not there to see Dr. Hegde for medical reasons, but rather to talk to him about Abbé Faria.

"I'm sorry," she answered, "but you cannot see the doctor until you fill out this form."

"No, I've made an appointment by telephone to talk about Abbé Faria."

"Is it that Mr. Faria is the patient and you are a relative? If that is the case, and he is unable to fill out the form for himself, you, sir, may fill it out for him when you bring him in. When will that be?"

"Actually, Mr. Faria is dead."

"I am sorry to hear about it, sir, but I am certain the doctor will help you with that. But first you must fill out the form. Take a seat, please, and fill out the form."

The room was crammed with a dozen or so barefoot, depressed people. A young boy rolling on the floor was relating to a seated man, his father I imagined, in a rather simian manner, stroking him, poking him, and gazing at him with alternating grins and frowns. And the man stared sadly back at him. An old woman was pacing and counting forward and backward in Konkani. A young woman in Western clothes concealed her face and muffled her moans with her hands. An unshaven old man was grunting and scratching his arms. When I squeezed my way onto the bench between him and another man, the latter, seemingly disturbed by contact with me, rose, walked over to the wall and leaned against it with his back to me.

I filled out the form as best I could. NAME AND ADDRESS, DATE, AND PLACE OF BIRTH were easy; for NEXT OF KIN FOR EMERGENCY NOTIFICATION I listed my listener; and filled out REFERRED BY with "Isabel Santa Rita Vas." METHOD OF PAYMENT: "rupees cash." ALLER-GIES, RELATED HEALTH PROBLEMS, FAMILY HISTORY OF MENTAL ILLNESS, DRUGS YOU ARE CURRENTLY TAKING: all answered "none" (I lied about the drugs). NATURE OF ILLNESS: "an interest in Abbé Faria." SYMPTOMS: "reading books and talking to people about him." LENGTH OF TIME YOU HAVE BEEN SUFFERING: "several months." I wrote on the back of the form: "I am not actually suffering from a mental illness. I just want to talk to you about Abbé Faria because I'm writing a book on hypnosis in which he is a significant figure."

After handing the completed registration form to the receptionist, I looked through the reading material on a small table next to her: Satya Sai Baba newsletters, the *Marga Bulletin* (a publication for Goan traffic police), copies of the Konkani newspaper *Ayatar*, and a Konkani children's book, which, I deduced from the illustrations, was about a naughty monkey who learns a lesson about getting along with other animals in the jungle.

After the scratching man seated next to me was called in to see the doctor, the woman who covered her face was called, and then, after almost an hour of waiting, the receptionist finally announced that it was my turn.

A very cheerful Dr. Hegde, apparently not remembering our telephone conversation and not having seen my registration form, asked, "What exactly is your problem?"

"As I explained to you on the phone and on the back of your medical form, I'm interested in Abbé Faria."

He smiled to assure me that this was nothing to worry about, that he too was interested in Faria. "As a tourist you have no doubt seen the bronze statue of him in Panjim. It is natural and normal for you to wonder who was Abbe Faria and what did he do to deserve such a monument."

"I am working on a book about him," I said to indicate that I did know something about him.

When he asked "which book?" I realized that he assumed that by "working on a book" I had meant working on reading one rather than writing one.

"Luis Vas," he continued before I could answer, "has just published his excellent *Abbe Faria: The Life of a Pioneer Indian Hypnotist and His Impact on Hypnosis*, readily available at the Broadway Book Centre in Panjim. You should also consult the Internet for the Abbe Faria website, www.abbefaria.com. You will find there all you need to know, unless you know French, in which case you must read Dr. Dalgado's exhaustive biography and, of course, Abbe Faria's own brilliant tome *De la cause du sommeil lucide*, which means 'on the cause of lucid sleep,' which means 'on the cause of hypnosis.' If you know Portuguese by any chance, you could read the masterpiece of Dr. Moniz on Abade Faria. It was the Konkani translation of that book that first aroused my own interest in Faria and inspired me to become a psychiatrist. Dr. Moniz won the Nobel Prize for inventing frontal lobotomies. And if you don't know Russian you must read the English version of Dr. Buyanov's detailed biography of Faria, *A Man Ahead of his Time*."

"Yes," I interrupted, "I'm familiar with these books and the website. I'm trying to write my own book about Faria and hypnosis in India."

"That is excellent. By publishing your book in America, you will have the opportunity to make Abbé Faria as famous and justly appreciated there as he became, thanks to Dr. Buyanov's monograph, in the Soviet Union. It will please every Goan to know that Faria has captured the attention and garnered the popularity he deserves in the United States of America. But, I must inform you in regards to your proposed volume, that actually Faria did not practice hypnosis in India. No, he practiced it only in France."

"Yes, I know."

"But he was born here in India."

"Yes, I know."

"In Candolim, which is in the north of Goa."

"Yes, I know."

"And his father took him to Portugal when he was a teenager."

"Yes, I know."

Despite my punctuation of each of his statements about Faria with another "Yes, I know," Dr. Hegde enthusiastically reiterated all of the biographical information on Faria that passes for truth on Wikipedia. He told me a story I had read in every biography and heard from practically everyone in Goa who talked to me about Faria, a yarn which, in their minds, is crucial to understanding the man they consider the Father of Hypnosis.

"After being ordained in Rome, being awarded a PhD there for his erudite dissertation in which he irrefutably proved the existence of God, and being lavishly lauded by no less a religious figure than the pope, he returned to Lisbon with his father and was invited there by no less a political figure than Her Majesty the Queen of Portugal to deliver a sermon in the chapel of the royal palace. On that occasion he was so overcome with stage fright that he could not speak. His father, who was sitting near the pulpit, sensed the cause of his silence and whispered to him in Konkani, the language of Goa: 'Hi sogli baji. Kator re bhaji!' which in English means, 'They're all just vegetables, so chop the vegetables.' Upon hearing these words, young Faria immediately became confident and gave the most eloquent and inspiring sermon the queen had ever heard. And it was that experience that enabled him to formulate his scientifically correct theory of hypnosis."

"Yes, I know," I said yet again. "I know that story, but I don't really understand how it pertains to his experiences as a hypnotist. "

"It gave him the idea that hypnotism is based not on Mesmer's magnetic fluid but on the power of verbal suggestion. And Faria responded to his father's command just as his subjects would, years later, respond to his command of '*dormez*.' In French, the word '*dormez*' means 'sleep.'"

"Yes, I know. But I'd like to ask you, as a psychiatrist, if you think that the reason so many of Faria's subjects were women might have had to do with the fact that he was abandoned by his mother at an early age. Did that abandonment perhaps impel him to use hypnotism to try to take control of women later in his life?"

"That I cannot say for I am not a Freudian, although it is true that Sigmund Freud was greatly influenced and inspired by Abbé Faria. As a psychiatrist, I too have been inspired by Abbé Faria. He is not only the father of scientific hypnotism but he is also the father of modern psychiatry. Before him psychiatry was just religion mixed with a little science. By rejecting Mesmer he made a science of hypnotism, and by rejecting religious superstitions he made a science of psychiatry. The psychiatric hospital in Altinho was called Hospital Abade Faria until it was moved to Bambolim."

"Do you practice hypnotherapy?"

"Sometimes I tell my Konkani speaking patients that if they are having problems with their relatives or customers or fellow workers, to think of them as vegetables and then to give themselves the command, '*Kator re bhaji!*' But, frankly, I do not myself actually practice hypnosis, per se. If, however, you are in need of hypnotherapy, I will happily refer you to Dr. Patanjali Mishra, a hypnotherapist in Panjim with an excellent record of results using hypnotism to cure headache, insomnia, bladder irritability, constipation, smoking, alcoholism, drug addiction, frigidity, nymphomania, satyriasis, impotence, premature ejaculation, and practically all the phobias that effect so many people in modern times. What is particularly is your problem?"

"I don't really have a problem," I insisted.

"Yes, I know," he said.

He hesitated then leaned across his desk toward me to speak through an ingratiating smile in a lowered reassuring tone of voice: "But you can tell me. Do not be embarrassed or ashamed. I am a doctor and have heard every problem you can imagine. I can refer you to Dr.

Mishra, or if you are reluctant to be hypnotized, I might, if you tell me your problem, prescribe some medications that might help you."

Insisting that I was fine, and feeling rather guilty that, being so fine, I was taking up so much of his time while the not-so-fine schizophrenic child was probably still rolling around on the dirty linoleum floor of the waiting room, I thanked him for his time and rose to leave. That's when I noticed the black silhouette on the mirror on his wall and asked what he thought the image suggested about hypnosis in general and about Abbé Faria in particular.

After being advised by him not to take things so seriously, I thanked him, left his office, retrieved my brightly shined shoes from the pile of footwear in the hall, and went to search for my listener in the Borkar market, where she said she would be waiting for me among the spice stalls.

"How did it go?" she asked.

"He convinced me not to take Abbé Faria so seriously."

THE SCREENWRITER'S STORY

When people die, we feel a grief because their minds are lost to us. How fortunate am I . . . I leave my mind behind in your possession; it is part of yours.
ABBÉ FARIA IN KEVIN REYNOLDS'S FILM, *THE COUNT OF MONTE CRISTO* (2002)

I had agreed to give at talk on Abbé Faria and Indian hypnotism at the annual Casa de Moeda Festival in Panjim. The other featured speaker was Isabel Santa Rita Vas, the woman who made the video *In Search of Abbé Faria* and had written a dramatization of the life of Faria, *Kator Re Bhaji*, for the celebration of the two hundred and fiftieth anniversary of Faria's birth in Candolim in 2006. Understanding that for Ms. Vas and many other Goans, Faria, glorified as "arguably the greatest Goan ever," the Father of Hypnotism, the Father of Psychiatry, not to mention the inventor of the one hundred square game of checkers, is egregiously undervenerated for his contributions to civilization, I realized that my lecture had to be cautiously respectful, something that does not come naturally to me.

In order to avoid offending anyone with my skepticism over the hagiographical accounts of Faria's accomplishments or with my Oedipal theories as to why his subjects were predominately women, I talked mostly about the Orientalist appeal of Faria in Paris at the beginning of the nineteenth century, invoking him as an object of romantic Gallic fantasies, using his story to epitomize and elucidate the psychological and political dynamics of a fascination with an exotic Orient. I juxtaposed the story of Faria with that of James Esdaile, a surgeon for the British East India Company posted at the Hooghly Native Hospital, "who," I said even though I didn't imagine it was true, "was profoundly influenced by and indebted to Abbé Faria when he began to experiment with the use of mesmerism as a surgical analgesic in 1845. While the Indian cleric's subjects were mostly bourgeois or aristocratic French women, the Scottish physician's were destitute Bengali peasants, washermen, rickshaw wallahs, and convicted criminals. The interactions between both Faria and his subjects and Esdaile and his patients were historically significant social behaviors illuminating the role of fascination and trance in a wide and divers range of social relationships as defined by culture, class, and gender."

I ended my lecture with a presentation of several of Faria's demonstrations of *le sommeil lucide*. When I asked for a volunteer, my listener, pretending not to know me, eagerly raised her hand as planned and was chosen to come forward, be seated, and gaze into my eyes. After a few moments of silence and stillness, taking a step toward her, in imitation of Abbé Faria I commanded, "*Dormez!* Sleep! *Dormez!*" And her head fell forward, her arms loose. After we reenacted the water tasting like wine routine, I demonstrated the human plank phenomenon, what Faria's Russian biographer, the psychiatrist Mikhail Buyanov, called the "cataleptic bridge," an easily accomplished but seemingly spectacular feat that has long been a regular feature in the repertoire of stage hypnotists.

After directing my *épopte* to recline on the floor, I suggested that her body was becoming rigid: "Imagine that your body is a wooden plank, solid and unbendable." Then, with the assistance of two young men from the audience, my listener was lifted and suspended between two chairs, her feet on one, her head on the other. I seated myself on her stomach, pretending to be resting my entire weight on her while actually keeping my feet firmly on the floor. When I claimed that Abbé Faria would often do this at his demonstrations, my thoroughly amazed audience seemed to imagine it was true.

In order to avert any suspicion that she was a shill, my human plank left the Casa de Moeda and waited for me at the Down the Road Bar on the nearby Old Patto Bridge corner.

"That was great," one of the young men who had helped to lift my listener onto the chairs exclaimed with exuberant smile after the lecture. Introducing himself as Mohan Shenoy, a postgraduate student in the History Department of Goa University, he announced that he had written a screenplay called *Sammohan* based on his master's degree thesis. "It's a biopic about Abbé Faria and, thanks to what I learned from your lecture, I'm going to add a scene showing him doing that cool human plank thing. Since you are a professor and an expert on Faria, it would obviously mean a lot to me if I could get your feedback on my script."

I told him I'd be delighted to read it, but then, being informed by him that it was in Hindi and confessing to him that I didn't know the language well enough to read a script written in it, we arranged to meet the next weekend at Curlie's, a bar on Anjuna beach where, he promised, he would describe it to me in detail. "I wrote it at Curlie's. Curlie's is my office."

The sprawling huge beach shack was packed with characters from another era, American and European men with long, gray pony tails who had been stoned in Goa since the seventies, bleary-eyed expat women with sun-roughened skin, scruffy kids running wild, Nigerians who were either professional soccer players or drug dealers, intoxicated Israelis fresh out of the army blowing off steam, Russian prostitutes attired for the kind of dinner that would never be served in a beach shack, and tourists who I imagined had been lured there by the review on TripAdviser, which noted that "if you like trance music, chilling out, and getting stoned, Curlies is the place to go." There were a few Indian families complaining about the service and a rakish pack of young Goan men drinking, smoking, playing pool or backgammon, cultivating a global hipness, gawking and cruising with heads bobbing to the blaring synthesized psychedelic 4/4 rhythms of the Cosmic Jokers' "Galactic Supermarket."

"Goa trance, body music," Mohan Shenoy said. "Of course trance music would originate here in the land of Abbé Faria. Where else? Curlie's a friend of mine, you know, and I've told him all about Abbé Faria, and together we came up with a special cocktail made out of cashew feni, rum, lime, coconut milk, and honey. We've called it 'Faria Trance, the hypnodrink.'"

Insisting on buying that cocktail for me and passing what he was smoking my way, he proudly showed me a copy of the script that had been bound as if a published work with the word सम्मोहन embossed on the cover.

"It's beautiful, isn't it? It makes you want to read it," he sighed with proud delight. "I attended a 'How to Sell Your Script in Bollywood' seminar last month in Mumbai and that's where I learned that if you want your script to get read, you must, absolutely must, submit it nicely bound with a professional-looking cover. I also learned that the best way to get your script produced is to get a star interested in the project. Once that happens, your movie's sure to be made. So what I do is paste a photograph on the cover of the script of whatever star I'm sending a copy to. I've sent it to the dudes who are the most obvious actors to play Abbé Faria—Salman Khan, Shahrukh Khan, and Hrithik Roshan—and I've bombarded them with e-mails, snail mails, faxes, telegrams, and tweets to inform them that my mesmerizing script has been sent to them. That's something else I learned at the seminar that you have to do. But, you know, if I don't hear from one of these guys soon, they'll be sorry because I'm going to translate it into English and send it to your own Mr. Brad Pitt of Hollywood, USA. And then you'll get to read it as well. Maybe, since you're a professor and you know a lot of things about Faria, you could help me polish the English a little bit for Brad. Of course you'll get screen credit for that. Don't worry about that. With the right makeup, Brad would be an excellent Faria. I recently read in an interview with him on ScreenIndia.com that he really wants to be in a Bollywood movie. Brad is completely fascinated by India. And so is Angelina. I might have to write in a part for her, you know, make her one of the French chicks that Faria hypnotizes. Brad is, by the way, really into hypnosis. Yeah, it's true. He used hypnotherapy to give up smoking and he's been hooked on hypnosis ever since. That's why if Salman, Shahrukh, or Hrithik don't get back to me soon, he'll get the part. The script is going to blow him away. I know it's great because last year when I was enrolled in the National Film Development Corporation India's Screenwriters' Workshop that was held during the Goa International Film Festival, the renowned screenwriter Viktor Acharya, who penned such smash hits as *Tashan* and *Dhoom 3*, told me he had never read anything quite like it. I learned a lot from Viktor, practical things like, for example, how to download software from hindi-script-software.fyxm.net, as well as more theoretical things, like you've got to give your audiences their paisa vasool, you know, their 'money's worth,' and that means plenty of songs and lots of dancing, exotic settings, a handsome hero and gorgeous heroine, malevolent villains, corrupt politicians, old-fashioned parents, a heartbroken mother, daredevil stunts, picturizations, dream sequences, and a bit of comedy to temper the melodrama. Let me buy you another Faria Trance and then I'll tell you all about my script. But you gotta be honest with me. As an expert on Abbé Faria, you must tell me if there is anything at all in it that is not great and advise me also if there is anything that I have left out.

"It begins in Goa, right here on this very beach two hundred and fifty years ago. Imagine it: a little boy named José Custodio de Faria watches horny Portuguese soldiers harassing Goan women. They beat up the poor fishermen who try to protect their daughters, sisters, wives, and mothers. That'll really get the audience's adrenaline pumping. Cut to a few years later. Using kalaripayat, Indian martial arts, José takes revenge in a thrill-packed fight scene with those colonialist Portuguese villains. And then the fishermen and their women do a folk dance and sing Konkani songs in celebration of Faria's victory.

"Where, you might be wondering, did he learn kalaripayat? From a yogi, a Tantric siddha with a long gray beard living the shrine of the goddess Mayavati in Dhargal. Because Faria's parents are Catholics, he must sneak out to meet with the yogi, who, having taken a liking to the boy, becomes his guru. First he teaches José yoga, then kalaripayat,which is based on yoga, and then sammohana—hypnotism, which is also based on yoga.

"Because the box-office success of a film depends on the dance numbers, there's another dance scene in which the rice farmers in Dhargal celebrate their harvest with Faria joining in. From working in the rice paddies, the women's saris are soaking wet. Who does not love beautiful women in wet saris? It's then and there, during that dance, that José first sees the gorgeous Aishwarya. I've named the heroine that in order to arouse Aishwarya Rai's interest in the script. With her on board the film is sure to be a smash. If not her, then I'll offer the part to Monica Bedi, who, ever since her appearance on the hypnosis reality show *Raaz Pichhle Janam*, has been promoting hypnotherapy and so will definitely be keen to be in my movie. And if not her, Julia Roberts would be okay with the right makeup. I know she'd be happy to play the part because she has become a devout Hindu and wants to spend a lot of time in India.

"Faria and Aishwarya, falling madly in love at first sight, sing to each other. They wish to marry but, because she is a Hindu and he's a Catholic, their parents adamantly oppose the marriage. Nevertheless they secretly vow to love one another for the rest of their lives. That's when we get the first dream sequence in which, while dancing in the French Alps, they sing a duet about the hypnotic power of love. It's great, isn't it?

"Then one day comes the terrible news," Mohan continued without pausing for my response. "Aishwarya's parents have arranged for her to marry the rich old zemindar. Aishwarya weeps as she sings a heartbreaking song about the agony of not being able to be with the man you love. She is consoled by her younger brother, a handsome boy named Mohan. Building on the tragic mood, I have written a scene in which Faria's mother dies of a heart attack."

It was only because the young man had asked for my feedback that I finally insisted on interrupting him: "Excuse me, Mohan, but I don't think that's quite right. I believe that she left her husband and son in order to become a nun in the Convent of Santa Monica. And then Faria's father became ordained as a Catholic priest here in Goa."

"That may or may not be true," the screenwriter informed me. "Who's to say what is true and what is not? In my version, his mother must die, because Indian audiences would never be able to forgive a woman for abandoning her husband and son. Also the death of his mother will increase audience sympathy for the boy. In my script, the Farias, both the father and the son, are so grief-stricken—the father over the death of his wife and the son over the marriage of Aishwarya—that they cannot endure remaining in Goa. In hopes of leaving their sorrows behind them, they decide to go to Portugal together, there to be ordained and take vows of celibacy for the sake of remaining true to the women they have so truly loved."

"But you do know," I had to ask, "that that isn't true?"

"Well, I suppose it may not be completely true historically, but it rings true dramatically. And that's what counts in a film. That's what Viktor Acharya says.

"Once the Farias are in Lisbon, it's a good thing that José has mastered *kalaripayat* because there is quite a lot of racism in Portugal and bullies there, calling him things like wog, Sambo, cow-kisser, and curry-muncher and teasing him for his Indian accent and dark skin, become so obnoxious that the audience will be sure to cheer when he beats them up. Of course that just makes them so angry that they plot to kill our hero. It becomes so dangerous for him in Lisbon that his father takes him to Rome where people to this day are better behaved and more cordial to Indian immigrants. The pope is so impressed with José that he invites him to give a sermon in the Sistine Chapel."

I was not surprised to hear the *kator re bhaji* story once again. But Mohan gave it a new twist in a scene taking place sometime later when the Farias have returned to Lisbon. The gang of Portuguese thugs that had previously been after José spot him and surround him with swords in their hands, ready to kill him. "You are all vegetables," Abbé Faria sneers, "Prepare to be chopped!"

"Because the chief of police in Lisbon is a racist, he arrests Faria for assaulting the gang and breaking their limbs. But our hero escapes from the jail before his trial and flees to France, and it's there that he runs into none other than Aishwarya's younger brother, Mohan, who reports to him that, because of her undying love for him, his sister has refused to consummate her marriage to the rich old geezer. This causes José to dream of his beloved, to imagine once again that they are dancing together and singing a duet in the Alps.

"Mohan, visiting Paris as member to the retinue of Tipu Sultan, who is in France to form an alliance with the King Louis, invites our hero

109

to attend a feast in Versailles where a troop of beautiful devadasis, who have been brought from India to show the French people Indian culture, put on a magnificent dance performance with lots of Indian music. Tipu Sultan should obviously be played by Amitabh Bachan. But if he is unavailable due to his busy shooting schedule, Ben Kingsley will do. If he can play Gandhi so well, then Tipu Sultan should be a piece of cake.

"The dance performance in Versailles is interrupted by the sound of canon fire. The French Revolution has just begun. And that's where the intermission comes. Let me get you another Faria Trance. But first be honest with me. What do you think?"

I told him that I heartily agreed with Viktor Acharya, attesting that I too had never heard anything quite like it.

The second half of the movie opened with lots of action-packed scenes of the Revolution scored with the roar of cannons, rockets exploding, a shouting mob, and the *Marseillaise*. After leading a battalion of revolutionaries to victory in a battle on the Champs-Élysées, Commander Faria celebrated the triumph of liberty, equality, and fraternity with rounds of champagne and the patriotic Hindi song *Ab ke Baras*. When one of the soldiers at this fête asked Faria why he would risk his life for France by fighting for the Revolution, the man from Goa gave a stirring speech about freedom in which he, as an Indian from the Portuguese East Indies, spoke so adamantly and eloquently about the colonial oppression of people in India that, several days later, he was arrested for conspiring for overthrow French colonial rule in Pondicherry and imprisoned without trial in the Chateau d'If where, just as in Dumas's *Le Comte de Monte-Cristo*, he met Edmond Dantès.

"In prison," the screenwriter explained, "by means of the self-hypnosis that he had learned from his guru as a boy in India, he is able to frolic with Aishwarya in the paddy fields of Goa. He also hypnotizes Dantès using sammohan to enable him to likewise be united with his fiancée, Mercédès, and the four of them dance together in the Alps.

"Having practiced on Dantès for many hours, he has refined his techniques for induction to the degree that he is able to hypnotize the prison guards merely by looking into their eyes, making a mesmeric pass with his hand, and commanding, 'Sleep.'

"With all the guards in deep hypnotic trance, Faria and Dantès leave the prison and joyfully bid each other adieu as Dantès heads out for the island of Montecristo and Faria returns to Paris. It would be great if we could get Jim Caviezel, who played Dantès so well in the Hollywood movie a few years ago, to repeat his performance in *Sammohan*. If not him, Prem Nazir, who played Prince Udayan, the character based on Dantès, in *Padayottam*, the Malayalam film version of *The Count of Monte Cristo*, would have been perfect for the part but unfortunately he is dead. Chiranjeevi, who played the part in *Veta*, the Telegu film based on the novel, is, however and fortunately, still alive.

"On returning to Paris, Abbé Faria gives demonstrations of the hypnotic practices he has perfected during his imprisonment in the Chateau d'If. In the scenes depicting those demonstrations I am, thanks to you, professor, for the inspiration, going to add a human plank scene. I think Gerard Depardieu would be perfect as Napoleon, who, after attending one of Faria's shows, hires him to hypnotize Josephine and use posthypnotic suggestion to keep her faithful and loyal to him.

"The soldier who arrested Faria years before, now a rotund civil judge, not realizing that the hypnotist is none other than the man he once incarcerated, attends one of the demonstrations. Recognizing him, Faria calls the man forward, hypnotizes him, and then, giving him a glass of water, tells him that it is cognac and, upon drinking it, the man becomes instantly drunk. Faria adds the posthypnotic suggestion that every time he drinks water he'll again become immediately soused. Drunkards are always a cinch for comic relief in Hindi films. Who does not find them amusing? Yes, Faria's revenge on that guy will tickle every funny bone in the theater.

"Now here's the exciting part, a scene that is sure to make my film a blockbuster. During this demonstration sequence, Faria turns to face the camera and we zoom in on his hypnotic eyes. 'Your eyelids are getting heavy,' he says, 'heavier and heavier, yes, you are getting very drowsy, very, very drowsy,' and so on until he commands, 'Sleep! Sleep!' And then many if not all of the people in the audience in the movie theaters, no less than those in the audience in his studio in Paris, will become hypnotized. And then he commands them to imagine they are in Goa, 'Imagine a beautiful woman there.' When the picture dissolves into a shot of Aishwarya in a wet sari the movie goers will not know whether they are looking at a film of her, imagining her in their minds' eyes, or actually seeing her in the flesh. Is that cool, or what?

"Aishwarya's husband has died and his family, blaming her for causing his death by refusing to consummate their marriage, is trying to force her to be a Sati, you know—to immolate herself on her husband's funeral pyre. Thankfully, the old yogi, the holy man who taught young Faria martial arts and hypnotism, uses mass hypnosis to put everyone asleep so that she can escape. Her younger brother, Mohan, takes her to Paris to be reunited with her long lost lover.

"Then we cut back to Faria in his studio, still facing the camera, and saying, 'when I count to three you will wake up feeling rested and happy. One . . . two . . . three.' If we don't do that some people in the movie audience might never wake up and we could be sued by their families. Just at that moment of awakening, Aishwarya dashes into Faria's studio, arms outstretched, crying, 'Oh, my beloved! Finally, finally we can be together.'

"Faria explains to her that he only became a priest and took a vow of celibacy in order to be faithful to her forever. He had never desired any woman but her. 'But now I will ask the archbishop to release me from my vows, which he will surely do once he hears the story of our love, true love. And then we can return to Goa to become man and wife.' They go back to India via the Alps where they sing a duet and dance again with the joy that, formerly just a dream, has finally become reality.

"The climax of my cinematic epic is a fabulously dazzling Hindu wedding right here on Anjuna Beach, where it all began. Everyone is dancing, dancing, dancing—the fishermen and their women, the rice farmers and theirs, the old yogi, Faria's father, even Tipu Sultan and his harem of devadasis, as well as a few Portuguese soliders and priests, Aishwarya's parents and her brother Mohan, who I plan to play. I've written a song for them to sing at the end of the film. It's called *Kator re Bhaji*. It's hard to capture the beauty of it in English but the gist of it is that all the obstacles standing in the way of people who are in love being together are just vegetables. '*Kator re bhaji*' is the refrain. 'Cut the vegetables! Cut the vegetables! Yes, cut the vegetables and be with the one you love.'

"My question to you, Professor Siegel, as an expert on Faria is this:

what do you think the abbé-hypnotist himself would think of my movie?"

"I can't imagine. But I met someone the other evening after my talk at the Casa de Moeda, a woman who came up to speak to me right after you, a person who might be able to answer that for you. She told me that under hypnosis she had discovered that in a previous lifetime she actually was Abbé Faria."

part two

Four Tales to be Read Aloud

During lucid sleep, there are adept
concentrators who are able to read from
a book even while their eyes are closed.

ABBÉ FARIA,
DE LA CAUSE DU SOMMEIL LUCIDE

THE TRANSLATOR'S TALE

Scared of flying? Maybe you once died in an aircrash. Unhappy in marriage? Maybe you mistreated your spouse in a former incarnation. Impotent or frigid and can't perform in bed? You might have suffered sexual abuse in a previous birth. Overly obese and can't lose weight? Maybe you starved to death in a former lifetime. In a country where the concept of reincarnation is as old as life itself, it isn't surprising that past life regression therapy (PLRT) has become the hottest treatment for upwardly mobile Indians demanding answers to all their life's problems.

ANUBHA SAWHNEY, "TODAY'S HOT FAD: REWIND TO YOUR PREVIOUS LIVES," *TIMES OF INDIA* (SEPTEMBER 9, 2007)

Following a public lecture based on his research on Abbé Faria and the history of hypnosis in India at the Casa de Moeda, a woman approached the writer to introduce herself as Mrs. De Souza, a language teacher recently retired from Our Lady of the Rosary High School for Girls in Dona Paula currently working on translating Abbé Faria's *De la cause du sommeil lucide* into English, Portuguese, and Konkani. She explained that she could contribute significantly to this book: "Much of what you said this evening about the abade was, I'm sorry to inform you, entirely wrong and gravely misleading. I do understand that this is because you have thus far had to rely on published accounts, fictions presented as factual biography, for your information and insights. But I am in the position to tell you the truth about Faria, things that no one else knows and have never been written. I am able to do this because, as I recently and much to my own astonishment discovered, I myself was José Custodio the Abbé de Faria in a former life. While I realize that this might be difficult for you to believe, I am hopeful that once you hear my story you will be convinced that it is true."

Startled, amused, and somewhat intrigued by the preposterousness of this announcement, the writer agreed to meet Mrs. De Souza for tea the next afternoon at the Vasco de Gama Club overlooking the Panjim Municipal Garden. After listening to her story, the writer wrote the tale and now, late at night, once again sitting in the chair by their bed in Goa, he reads it to his listener by candlelight.

SESSION ONE: *Trance-Fusions*

Imagine a rather demure South Asian woman, probably in her early sixties, with a wheatish complexion and shortly cropped, henna-black hair. The reserve with which her makeup has been applied enhances the impression that she is an essentially prim and conservative lady, in no way prone to frivolity or extravagance. The former schoolteacher wears a lavender polyester skirt with a matching jacket over a plain white blouse. On a chain around her neck, visible through the open collar of the blouse, is a silver, heart-shaped locket with a ruby center stone bordered with floral engraving.

As Mrs. De Souza begins to speak, imagine a voice that is pleasant, calm, and trustworthy. The accent and cadence are vaguely British:

"My voyage of discovery started in front of the television," she announces with a slight and possibly ironic smile. "I am, you see, rather a fan of reality TV shows, programs like *Kaun Banega Crorepati*, *Indian Idol*, and *Maa Exchange*. Reality is far more interesting to me, and ultimately more entertaining, than any story someone has fabricated. I prefer history books, biographies, and authobiographies to fiction. My favorite television show is *Raaz Pichhle Janam*, the series about past life regression. Do you watch it? No? Well, each week a celebrity guest is hypnotized by Dr. Trupti Jayin, a Mumbai-based hypnotherapist, and then transported back to a previous incarnation. The first time I saw the program the Bollywood actress Monica Bedi was able in hypnotic trance to remember that in a previous lifetime she had been a self-sacrificing American mother of three children whose husband died in a tragic automobile accident. That explained why Monica had always been afraid of driving. The following week, Dr. Jayin was pleased to announce that Monica, having relived the trauma and thereby overcoming it, had just purchased a new Bentley Continental and was taking driving lessons. The actor Aryan Vaid, the guest star on that week's show, was cured of chronic headaches when, after being regressed back to his former incarnation as a vegetable farmer in Gujarat, he remembered cracking his skull when he fell down his village well and drowned.

"That particular story especially intrigued me because I had, until my recent therapy, suffered with migraines for as long as I can remember. Since none of the medications prescribed by physicians had ever been significantly effective, I supposed that it might be worth a try to see what past life regression hypnotherapy might do for me. I found contact information on the Internet for a past life regression therapist here in Goa: Dr. Patanjali Mishra of the Faria Institute of Holistic Vedic Hypnosis and Trance-Personal Psychology.

"I must admit I was not entirely confident that Dr. Mishra would be able to help me. I had doubts as to whether or not I could even be hypnotized. And, to be perfectly honest, I wasn't sure whether or not the celebrities on *Raaz Pichhle Janam* had been merely imagining, fantasizing, or even just fabricating their past lives. They are, after all, actors.

"Despite these apprehensions, I telephoned Dr. Mishra for an appointment. The walls of his office are impressively adorned with degrees from prestigious Indian and U.S. institutes of psychology, parapsychology, and hypnosis. There is also a large and handsomely framed lithographic version of Ramachandra Pandurang Kamat's monumental statue of Abbé Faria. You've no doubt seen the statue in the square by the Old Secretariat. It was installed there in 1945, the year of my birth.

"Dr. Mishra invited me to be seated across from him at his desk. When he, wearing a spotless white khurta, explained his billing policies, I was disappointed to be informed that my Royal Sundaram medical insurance policy would not cover past life regression therapy. It was necessary for me to pay for each session in advance. Hypnosis is not cheap.

"Once I had written out a check for him, the therapist explained Vedic hypnosis to me: 'Thousands of years ago Patanjali, the venerable author of the *Yogasutras*, elucidated the psychological dynamics and therapeutic benefits of past life regression, what was known to the ancient sages of India in Sanskrit as pratiprasava, literally, "reverse birthing." We know from our hallowed wisdom literature that all enlightened beings—rishis, yogis, and mahatmas, holy men like Gautam Buddha, Shankaracharya, Ramakrishna, and Satya Sai Baba—were able to remember their past lives because they were adept at self-hypnosis. Hypnosis is a mode of yogic meditation by which the mental awareness that is described in our Upanishads as samadhi can be achieved. Hypnosis can provide us with a method of solving current problems through an evocation of memories of events in our previous incarnations. The hypnotic state is not, as many suppose, an unconscious one, a state of being asleep, but is rather an exaggerated state of wakefulness and highly focused concentration. Contrary to another of the many popular misconceptions about hypnosis, it is not in any way dangerous. You will do nothing under hypnosis that you do not want to do, and certainly nothing to violate your own moral standards. You will not divulge any information of a personal nature that you do not wish to reveal. You will be completely aware of all that is said and able to remember it. And you will discover that, as long as you really want it to, everything you experience under hypnosis will benefit you. You will be able to remember your former lives, but only if you really want to do so. By exploring your past lives, you will be able to discover in them the cause of your migraine headaches and thereby be cured. If you really wish to be cured, you will be. Let me assure you that you will wake up from the hypnotic state feeling refreshed and rejuvenated. I can assure you that it is a very pleasant experience.

'So, Mrs. De Souza, are you ready to be hypnotized? Yes? Very good. Why don't you lie down on the couch over there and make yourself comfortable. Yes, allow yourself to become as comfortable as you can be. Comfortable, calm, and relaxed.'

"His soft deep voice, the soft warm light in the room, and the soft plush couch all collaborated to help me become very, very comfortable indeed."

In preparation for Mrs. De Souza's tale, make yourself comfortable as well, taking a few breaths deeply in through your nostrils and letting them slowly out through your mouth. Allow yourself to do as Mrs. De Souza does, to fix your eyes, as she fixes hers, on a spot on the ceiling, any spot your choose. Allow yourself to play along with her.

"Notice," the hypnotist says to his subject, "that your eyelids are becoming heavy, heavy, so very, very heavy, and the heavier they become the more and more relaxed you feel . . . and the more relaxed you are, the heavier your eyelids will become. . . . And now, if you wish to go into a deep state of relaxation all you have to do is let those heavy eyelids close. Let them close. Yes, close your eyes. Yes, good, very good. . . .

"Now imagine that we are in the tower of an ancient castle, a palatial stronghold of memories, a safehold of the past. There is a door in this room, not the entrance through which you came, but another, an en-trance to the landing of a spiral staircase of twenty steps winding down into depths of your marvelous multistoried castle. Imagine yourself at the top of the staircase... visualize the softly illuminated hypnotic spiral of stairs beckoning... and take another deep breath in, yes, good, and now slowly let it out, and again ... again ... yes, good, very good, and again ... allowing each breath to put you more and more at ease, comfortable and ready for the descent. There's a handrail to hold if you wish, there to help you feel absolutely safe and secure as you go down, down, slowly, slowly, counting the stairs as you do, counting backward from twenty. With each step and number, breathe deeply in and slowly out, and as you do you will become more and more tran-quil, more calm and at ease. Nineteen, eighteen, going down... down, seventeen ... with each breath, step, and number, deeper and deeper, sixteen ... more and more relaxed ... fifteen, down into your castle of wonders... farther and farther back in time... fourteen, thirteen...."

As his voice becomes softer and softer, more and more hushed, slowly fading away, Mrs. De Souza hears her own voice slowly count-ing in whispers. "Twelve, eleven, ten, as with each step, breath, and number, I become more and more calm. Nine ... eight ... and I go deeper and deeper into my castle of soothing trance and serene dream ... seven, and with each step velvety shadows make the stairway darker and darker. Six... five... slowly, so slowly, and softly, so softly, around and around and down the spiral, my body becomes languorously light, lighter and lighter, lightly lilting with each step, sinking gently down at four, down, three, down, two down, one and then, by a line of light shining in through the bottom of a door on the landing of the staircase, I am surprised to see that I am wearing scuffed leather boots, not the comfy Bata pumps I had put on that morning."

I reach for the knob, turn it, and the door opens into a small but sunny garret furnished with an unmade bed, an old dresser with one drawer open, and a desk cluttered with pads of paper, pens, pencils, sticks of charcoal, and pieces of chalk pastels. I peruse the sketches pinned to a wall, portraits of people who, though unidentifiable, look vaguely familiar. There are several of a girl in various classical poses, naked except for an odalisque's turban. Imagine a washbasin on a wooden table near the window, and next to it a ceramic pitcher, razor, strop, soap dish, wet shaving brush, and a hand mirror.

I pick up the looking glass and see in it a clean-shaven young man with a tawny complexion, large brown eyes, and short black hair. Picture him. . . .

When I look out of the open window, I see the Panjim Municipal Garden and, beyond it, the Vasco de Gama Club, and I suddenly remember having danced with a beautiful girl one New Year's Eve long, long ago. It was the girl wearing the turban in the sketches on the wall.

Although I am alone in the room, I can still hear Dr. Mishra's voice: "Who are you? What is your name? And what are you doing here?"

"*Meu nome é Braulio, Braulio Pinto.* And this is my room. I'm an art student. These are my sketches."

Taking off my boots to lie down on the feather bed, soft, warm, and comfortable, I smell lilac cologne faintly infusing the pillow, a fragrance that brings back childhood memories of Lisbon. That's where I was born in the year, I remember my father telling me, that King Carlos was assassinated in the Praça do Comércio. I remember my mother's nectarous voice reminding me to stay close to her, not to wander off as she bought vegetables from the vendors in that very square. I remember that she died of cholera when I was a little boy, just seven or maybe eight years old. I remember seeing my father weep as he watched my mother's coffin lowered into the grave in the Cemitério dos Prazeres. And I remember looking up at the battlements of the tower on the banks of the Tagus where he was imprisoned on the day a military junta seized control of the government and installed Salazar as dictator. I remember having headaches as a child in Lisbon.

"Go to Goa," my father said to me as the soldiers were taking him again, "and stay with my parents there. They will take care of you." And so I made the voyage to the homeland my father had nostalgically evoked in the bedtime stories he had so often told me during my childhood.

I remember the journey to the east, a snake charmer entrancing a cobra with his flute in Port Said, the violent pitch and roll of the steamer in a storm on the Arabian Sea, and an English girl with auburn hair, faintly freckled skin, and a flirtatious smile who disembarked with her parents at Surat. I remember the flamboyantly grand mustache of the elfin clerk at the Secretariat who informed me that my grandparents, Verissimo and Benedita Pinto, had passed away. It seemed appropriate at the time to place myosotis flowers, so sentimentally called forget-me-nots in English, upon their graves in the cemetery of the Igreja de São Tomé in Aldona. I remember sketching the statues of the women installed in that church—Santas Isabel, Iria, and Beatriz. I remember allowing myself the fantasy that real women of flesh and blood were posing for me. I remember showing those drawings to Ramachandra Kamat in hopes that he would accept me as his student. I remember the aromas of turpentine, linseed oil, and damar in his studio as he added highlights and shadows to my portrait of the young girl posing in an odalisque's crimson silk turban. I remember the allure of her stillness, the sadness in her eyes, and the lushness of her nakedness. I remember the sweetness of the honeyed bebinca she, sitting next to me one afternoon on a bench in the municipal garden, shared with me. I remember asking her to teach me Konkani. I wanted to learn that language so that in her tongue I could tell her how much I loved her. I remember her fingers on my temples as she massaged my head in hopes that it would relieve me of the pain of the migraine. I remember the pungent taste of the cashew feni I drank with Kamat in his studio on the night he asked me to be the model for his proposed sculpture of Abbé Faria. The girl who was accustomed to being naked in the studio put on a French frock with billowing sleeves to pose as Faria's somnambule. I remember the uncomfortably heavy woolen black clerical robes I had to wear while trying to stand still with my arms dramatically extended and fingers spread above her. "Perfect," the artist exclaimed, "Yes, Braulio, you *are* Faria!" While making the preliminary studies for the monumental statue, Kamat told me fanciful stories about Faria. "That he was an abbot," the artist proposed, "did not prevent him from enjoying voluptuous adventures with countless beautiful women in Paris. In fact, it served him well. Making love with clerics thrills women, particularly Catholic women, even more than making love with artists." I remember the melody of a plaintive fado sung by an old, blind woman dressed in black mourning clothes in the municipal garden at dusk. And I remember the hungry howl of feral dogs prowling around the Casa de Moeda. The sound of it aggravated a headache. I remember so many things, and I remember remembering them so keenly that it seemed more like reliving than remembering.

The last thing I can recall about being Braulio Pinto is how I trembled, so terribly frightened, as he walked to the Goa Medical College Hospital, which was in Panjim then, near the market, not in Bambolim as it is now. I was going there for surgery for chronic migraine headaches, enxaquecas, as we called them in those days. None of the treatments—not the morphine, lumbar punctures, mustard baths, nor any of the Ayur Vedic potions—had provided any lasting relief. But Dr. Vas, the professor of neurological surgery at the college, had diagnosed increased intracranial pressure as the cause of my migraines, and he was confident that the pain would be relieved once and for all by trepanation, "an operation," he claimed, "that will be as effective today on you as it was thousands of years ago when it was first performed on Raja Bhoja. The physician made the procedure painless by hypnotizing the king. Likewise, there was a surgeon in Bengal some years ago, a Dr. Esdaile from Scotland, who successfully trepanned a farmer with headaches using mesmerism as the anesthetic for the operation, thereby sparing the patient the danger of ether. With ether, there is always the risk that the patient may go under too deeply, so deeply that he cannot be wakened. There is no such risk with mesmerism. I'm eager to try it, but I'll let you choose—ether or mesmerism?"

I remember the penetrating petroleum smell of the ether I had chosen in fear that I might not be as susceptible to hypnotic suggestion as either the king of Malwa or the farmer of Bengal had been.

As I breathed the ether in, deeply in and slowly out, my body became light, lighter and lighter, my eyelids heavy, heavier and heavier with each breath. They closed as I drifted into a silken sleep in which I was no longer afraid, in which thought and feeling faded, floating in the silent darkness of anesthetic somnolence.

The next thing I remember was slowly ascending a staircase out of that darkness and counting the stairs as I did. One, two, three, four, and higher, five, six, seven, higher and higher, and as I approached the top I hear a voice I recognize as Dr. Mishra's: "At twenty your eyes will open and you will be wide awake, feeling rested and refreshed. And you will remember everything about your previous life.

"Eighteen . . . nineteen . . . twenty . . . wake up, Mrs. Souza, and open your eyes."

Yes, open your eyes.

"It was the first time in my life that I had been hypnotized and, although I did indeed feel pleasantly refreshed, I was, I must confess, still a bit unsure what to make of it, still somewhat skeptical about past life hypnotic regression. Despite the acuteness of my memories of Braulio Pinto's memories, I wondered if perhaps I might have been merely imagining the whole thing, dreaming it, making up a story that Dr. Mishra, with hypnotic suggestion, had encouraged me to compose.

"The therapist confidently assured me that we had been successful, that I had indeed been regressed to a previous incarnation. Recalling that Aryan Vaid had been cured of his headaches by remembering that he had cracked his skull when falling down a well in his previous life, I asked Dr. Mishra if I might likewise be cured of mine by remembering that I had died during brain surgery for migraines in my former incarnation.

"'No,' he said, 'no, I don't think we have discovered the actual origin of your migraines, but merely witnessed their presence in your last life. Why did Braulio suffer with headaches? My experience with past life regression tells me that we must go deeper in the castle to find out when they began, farther back into your past during our next session.'

"It occurred to me that the therapist might be merely pretending to believe I had been Braulio Pinto in a previous lifetime in order to encourage me to believe it so that I would keep my appointment with him the following week. I was, after all, paying rather dearly for his services. One thousand and one rupees per session!

"Dr. Mishra's office is on Mahatma Gandhi Road, just around the corner from the Broadway Book Centre. After that first hypnotic session I went to that shop to find books on hypnosis and past life regression, as it seemed prudent to do some research before committing myself to a continuation of the rather costly therapy. While browsing the self-help books, I was drawn to a large picture book on the adjacent shelf of travel books with the title *Portugal Past and Present* on its spine.

"I have, you must understand, never been to Portugal, not in this life anyway, and thus you can surely imagine my astonishment when, thumbing through the volume, I came upon a photograph of the Torre de São Vicente on the banks of the Tagus River in Lisbon, the prison in which Braulio's father had been confined. The battlements of the tower were identical to those I had envisioned under hypnosis. And, other than the fact that there were no vegetable stalls in the photograph of the Praça do Comércio, it looked exactly as I had remembered it.

"How could this be explained? I wondered and considered the possibility that I had actually once seen photographs or drawings of that tower and square somewhere and just did not remember having done so. But how and where did I come up with the name Braulio Pinto?

"Curiosity took me to the Directorate of Archives & Archaeology on rua Orem here in Panjim the next day in order to see if, by any chance, I might be able to find any records documenting the prior existence of a man with that name in Goa. I was surprised—and yet, at the same time, paradoxically strangely not surprised—to discover an obituary in the June 1945 issue of a Konkani weekly, *Sanjechem Noketr*, reporting that an art student, "Shri B. S. Pinto of Panaji," had died from complications during surgery at the Goa Medical College Hospital on June 4, 1945, not very long before I was born on July 22 of that year. The newspaper announced that he would be buried in the cemetery of the St. Thomas Church in Aldona.

"Mr. Dicholkar, the director of the archives who had dutifully helped me locate the obituary, telephoned several days later to report that he had unearthed a colonial immigration permit for Braulio Pinto. It was dated May 31, 1926, and there was a photograph attached to it. Mr. Dicholkar showed it to me. It was unmistakably the same face I saw in the hand mirror on the table in the garret overlooking the municipal garden.

"While still searching for surviving examples of Braulio's artwork, I have so far only been able to discover one painting, a portrait in oils of a nun, signed 'B. S. Pinto '39.' It's in the visitor's gallery of the Church and Convent of Santa Monica in Old Goa, the convent where Rosa de Sousa-Faria, the mother of José Custodio de Faria, was cloistered after her separation from her husband and child.

"It seemed appropriate for me to place a garland of blue myosotis flowers on the unkempt grave of Braulio Pinto in Aldona. Gazing at his moldering tombstone, I began to sense that everything I had remembered about him in hypnotherapeutic transport was true. I felt assured that all of us have been here before and that what we have experienced in our past lives influences us, whether we remember it or not, no less than what we have experienced earlier in our current lives.

"Having attended a Roman Catholic school for girls here in Goa, I had been taught by the nuns that the Hindu doctrine of reincarnation is heretical, that we live but once and that our behavior during this singular lifetime is judged by God to determine whether we are resurrected in Heaven or condemned to Hell. Contrary to that teaching, one of the books on past life regression that I purchased at the Broadway Book Centre proposes and convincingly argues that Christ himself believed in reincarnation. Yes, it's true. Jesus explicitly declared in the Gospels that his cousin John the Baptist was none other than the prophet Elijah reincarnated. There is, furthermore, evidence in that book that Peter the Apostle had once been Aaron the Israelite, and that the Pharaoh Ramses eventually became reincarnated as Herod Antipas."

Mrs. De Souza suggested to the writer that, for the continuation of her story, they might meet at the same time on the next day across the street in the municipal garden. He agreed to it more out of politeness than out of the kind of interest that would have been aroused by credulity.

SESSION TWO: *Trance-Mutations*

As the writer joined Mrs. De Souza, again dressed in polyester, on a bench in the municipal garden, she pointed out the Hindu pharmacy building: "See that open window on the fourth floor, the one with the empty flower box beneath it? It's from that very window that Braulio Pinto looked out from his garret and down at this park. He would have been able to see us here on this bench."

Mrs. De Souza began by assuring the writer that she had arrived for her next appointment with the therapist fully convinced that it was indeed possible to accurately remember past lives under hypnosis. Given that conviction, she had been eager to descend deeper into the castle of memory.

"Fix your eyes on a spot on the ceiling again, the same spot, and again take a few breaths deeply in, slowly out, allowing each breath to relax you more and more . . . again . . . let your eyes close and again imagine the spiral staircase leading down into the castle, forty steps down, twenty to Braulio's garret and then another twenty steps down into the past.

"Counting thirty-nine, thirty-eight . . ." I settle into the comfort of trance more rapidly than before and feel the balmy pleasure of tranquility as I float down, down, soon down into Braulio's garret. Resting on the bed there for a few moments, I become even more relaxed, comfortable and calm. Dr. Mishra's disembodied voice brings to my attention a door by the dresser that I hadn't noticed before. It opens to another spiral staircase, leading deeper down into a lower story of the citadel.

Beginning the descent and slowly counting, *trinta e sete, trinta e seis,* Braulio takes a deep breath in on each odd number, *trinta e cinco,* and slowly breathes out on the even ones, *trinta e quarto,* in as the left foot comes to rest on a step, out with the right foot, in and out . . . down, down . . . and with each number, step, and breath, the staircase becomes darker and darker with a soothing, dreamy darkness, and Braulio becomes more and more sedate . . . seeing nothing and hearing only faintly murmured numbers.

Três, dois, um, zero, and, reaching out, I touch a door, feel for the knob, turn it, and step into an alcova redolent of decaying roses.

"*Menina mal, Raisa-Maria, estão atrasados,*" a woman shouts: "You're late again, Raisa-Maria. You've kept Senhora Chochota waiting. Come here. Sit on the bed."

I remember the harsh voice of a heartless mother—Aranha Boceta of Ponta Delgado in the Azores, a *fofista,* which is to say a *cortesã,* a euphemism for *puta.* Pardon the vulgarity, but that is what she was. And if Aranha Boceta had had her shameless way, I would have followed in her footsteps for the sake of the money that was, with the progressive graying of her hair, wrinkling of her skin, and drooping of her breasts, becoming more and more difficult for her to come by.

It would make sense enough that the daughter of a wanton prostitute who brought home and into bed all sorts of lustful reprobates would be disgusted by the idea of intimacy with a man. As a young child I had smelled the unctuous liquor lacing the rancid breath of my mother's panting customers, seen their filthy hands lasciviously reaching up under her skirts, and heard their repulsive grunts and gruesome groans as Aranha Boceta lewdly serviced them. But now, because of what I have discovered about myself in past life regression therapy, I understand that Raisa-Maria was afraid of men because an unconscious aspect of a soul imprinted with the scars of an excruciating sorrow that love had caused long, so long, ago. Who and why and how we love or hate is determined no less by the experiences we have in this life as it is by our experiences in former lives.

The only man young Raisa-Maria would ever love, she promised herself and Him, was our mighty Lord and gentle Shepherd. Although she vowed to die a virgin, an inviolably chaste lover of the Redeemer, she had no inclination to take the veil as a Bride of Christ because she did not want to share His love with sisters in a convent. Raisa-Maria naively yearned to be His one and only clandestine lover, an illicit acolyte communing with Him in secret reveries. Imagining Him on the cross was a consolation during migraine attacks, assuring the child that our salvation is not from suffering but through it.

Senhora Chochota called herself an *enfermeira*, a nurse, but she was really a *mulher encantadora*, a *bruxam sacana*—a witch. Picture fierce fires in her eyes and amulets around her neck and wrists, and imagine the rank smell of camphor on the blotched and cockled skin of the hands she waved rhythmically in front of Raisa-Maria's eyes.

"A tormented spirit, the soul of someone who died a violent death," the crone informed Aranha Boceta, "has taken refuge in your daughter's skull. She feels his anguish as her own. I must contact this malevolent specter to lure him out and banish him from the child."

Within the hypnotic trance induced by Dr. Mishra, the old woman induced a deeper trance, a trance within a trance, a dream within a dream. "*Calma, calma, afrouxa*," the *exorcista* muttered again and again, lulling eyelids closed, sedating with monotonous murmurs, deeper and deeper, more and more susceptible to every utterance: "*Sim, sim, bom, bom, vá dormer, Raisa-Maria, vá dormer.*"

"*Fala, fala, espectro, fala!*" the witch commanded and a man's voice, grave and hoarse with despair, issued from my trembling lips.

"*Há dezessete anos, que aqui estou morto*," the revenant moaned. "I have been dead for seventeen years. *Só o espírito vive: vela absorto num fixo, inexorável pensamento.* Only my spirit lives, absorbed by a single, inexorable thought. *Morto, enterrado em esta rapariga virgem!* Dead and buried in this virgin girl! *O meu tormento é isto só.* That is my torment."

"*Qual é o teu nome?*" The *exorcista* demanded. "What is your name?"

"Antero," the revenant soughed. "*Antero desanimado, alma lastimosa de Antero.*

"*Sai, Antero, sai!*" Senhora Chochota commanded. "Come out, come out!"

"*Não posso,*" the spirit whimpered and then fell dead silent.

The witch called out his name again and again, but Antero refused to answer.

While hypnotists unequivocally insist that people cannot be made to do what they do not wish to do under hypnosis, I can attest to the fact, based on my own experience as Raisa-Maria Boceta, that it is not so. Acting on my mother's behalf, and amply imbursed for her thaumaturgical services, Senhora Chochota used her hypnotic prowess to coerce me to later do something that was absolutely repugnant and utterly horrifying to me in the waking state, an act that was in flagrant violation of human decency.

While Raisa-Maria had no memory of what the *encantadora* had said to her in trance and of what those words had impelled her to do, once I was back in Dr. Mishra's office with my eyes wide open I was able to recall the true and terrible story of what happened to Raisa-Maria so many years ago. Although the story is very sad, there was a feeling of relief in being able to recall it, and some solace in that relief, some freedom from the past.

It was rumored among the *cortesãs* of Lisbon that King Carlos had an obsession with nubile virgins, that he would pay as much as one thousand *milréis* to deflower a maiden. Well aware that her innocent little Raisa-Maria would never willingly consent to sexual relations with any man, not even His Majesty the King, Aranha Boceta paid Senhora Chochota to once more entrance her daughter and cast a spell that would cause the girl to do what would allow the greedy mother to collect those one thousand *milréis*.

Hypnotized under the pretext that the sorceress was again attempting to exorcise the tormented ghost who caused her headaches, Raisa-Maria, in a deep cataleptic state, was introduced to Luis Filipe, the Duke of Braganza, and Dr. Mizrahi, the royal physician.

"Lie down on the bed, Raisa-Maria," Senhora Chochota commanded, "so that the doctor can examine you."

The entranced Raisa-Maria obeyed and, once the physician had determined and announced that her virginity was intact, the Duke smiled: "This pretty vestal child will certainly please His Highness."

"You are very fortunate, *minha pequena querida*," the witch announced. "You have been chosen to serve our king. He will honor you in the chambers of his palace with regal embraces. In gratitude for this you will surrender yourself entirely to him, doing for him whatever he asks of you. You will awaken from this dream only when you return home tonight, only when you hear my voice again, only when I tell you to wake up. And when you wake up, you will remember nothing of what I have told you and nothing of what you have done. Nothing. As far as you will know, nothing will have happened."

Taking me by the hand, Braganza led me into the courtyard where King Carlos was waiting in the royal carriage. Nodding to the duke with approval, the king then gestured for me to climb in and be seated next to Prince Manuel. I complied willingly, without either desire or fear—without, as I remember it now, any feeling whatsoever.

Now I remember the military police on horseback, armed with swords and rifles, accompanying us through the streets of Lisbon. I remember watching King Carlos ceremoniously wave to the cheering crowds.

The carriage was crossing through the Praça do Comércio when suddenly there was the sound of gunfire. Raisa-Maria saw the explosive gush of crimson and splinters of bone from the king's obliterated face. Screams. More gunshots. More screams. Then silence. Darkness. Nothing.

In keeping with her childhood vow, Raisa-Maria died a virgin.

A voice was beckoning me out of the darkness, urging me to find the door to the spiral staircase and climb up, up from Lisbon to Goa, up past Braulio's garret and back into Dr. Mishra's office.

"When I count to three, you will open your eyes. You will wake up, wide awake, feeling rested and refreshed."

One . . . two . . . three . . . and open your eyes.

It was only when she was back in her therapist's office, Mrs. De Souza told the writer, that she had been able to remember what the witch had forced Raisa-Maria to do under hypnosis. And then, as she discussed the memory with Dr. Mishra, she realized something utterly marvelous and amazing to her: "The spirit who spoke from Raisa-Maria's mouth—I know who it was! Because they were illiterate, neither Raisa-Maria nor her mother nor the witch knew. But as a teacher of the Portuguese language and its literature, I am very familiar with his poetry. I recognized the words he uttered in Raisa-Maria's trance: *Só o espírito vive: vela absorto num fixo, inexorável pensamento.* It's a line from a sonnet by the illustrious Portuguese poet Antero Tarquínio de Quental. I must have been him in a previous lifetime. That's another story and, if you wish to hear it, I'll tell it to you the next time we meet."

"Of course I want to hear it," the writer claimed. "But what about Abbé Faria? When are you going to tell me about him?"

"You mustn't be impatient," Mrs. De Souza responded. "It's important for me to tell you about you the succession of lives I have lived since being Abbé Faria. Because his spirit was incarnated in each of those figures, I believe knowing something about them will enable you to better understand Faria. So let's meet at the statue of him in the small square by the Old Secretariat building. There's a bench in the shade there where we can sit comfortably. Yes, let's meet again in a few days in the presence of Abbé Faria."

SESSION THREE: *Trance-Figurations*

Entering the square by the Old Secretariat, the writer saw that Mrs. De Souza, wearing a wide brimmed straw sunhat and casual floral print cotton dress, was holding a book in one hand and her purse in the other. She was staring at the dramatic life-size bronze statue of Abbé Faria, gazing at it so intently that the writer felt as if he were awakening her from a trance by saying hello.

"It's unbelievable," she exclaimed without greeting him in turn. "But it's true. Yes, that's actually what Abbé Faria looked like. Artistically embellished of course, and appropriately stylized, but quite accurate. It used to seem plausible to me to trust that the anonymous portrait of him, posted on the Internet, published in various biographies, and shown in your lecture, having supposedly been sketched by a contemporary of Faria, was a truer likeness to the actual man. So you can imagine my surprise when remembering in a hypnotic trance to come that when I was Faria, the face I saw when I looked at myself in a mirror was almost exactly the face of this statue.

"How is it that Kamat could have known what I had looked like? The only reasonable explanation is that, whether he was conscious of it or not, Kamat knew Faria in one of his own past lives. Thinking about that, several days after my last session with Dr. Mishra, I suddenly remembered that Faria remembered that his friend General Nosier had brought a guest to one of his lecture-demonstrations, a gentleman who was introduced as Monsieur François Rude, a sculptor who had recently been awarded the Prix de Rome. After complimenting Faria on the brilliance of his theory and the mystifying dramatic appeal of his demonstration, he confessed to having made a few sketches of the hypnotist and his subject during that demonstration. 'I would be honored,' the sculptor explained, 'if, Monsieur Faria, you would be so generous as to grant me permission to do a sculpture in bronze of you inducing the girl into trance.'

"'And I, in turn, Monsieur Rude, would be honored,' Faria responded, 'to pose for you and I furthermore can assure you that my nubile somnambule will likewise be willing to pose as herself in *un sommeil lucide*.'

"The sculptor explained that he was going to Brussels for a commission but would begin work on the statue as soon as he returned to Paris. Unfortunately Faria had died by the time of that return.

"It seems obvious to me that after several lifetimes, Rude must have been reborn as Kamat to finally, after some hundred and thirty years, fulfill his wish. And that would explain why he was drawn to Braulio Pinto as a model for Faria. It seems likely, furthermore, that a young lady named Seraphine Goéland, about whom you will soon hear, was reborn as the girl with the odalisque's turban who posed as the reclining woman being hypnotized by Faria in this marvelous statue.

"So do please look carefully at the statue so that you can remember it when you listen to the story of Abbé Faria."

"Are you going to tell it to me today?" the writer asked hopefully.

"No. No, today I want you to hear the story of Antero Quental. I brought this book to show you. It's his *Primaveras Românticas*.

"I could hardly wait for my next appointment with Dr. Mishra, eager as I was to remember my life as Antero Tarquínio de Quental," Mrs. De Souza began. "I imagined that the memories of that avatar of my peregrine soul would reveal the origin of my migraines. And that, according to my understanding of the principles of past life regression therapy, would be my cure. Of course, at that time, I did not yet know that several lifetimes previously I had been Abbé Faria and that it was with him that my headaches began.

"Having read Victor de Sá's biography of the poet when I was a postgraduate student in the Comparative Literature Faculty of Goa University, I had long been aware that he also suffered from migraines. That we shared a common pain had allowed me a sense of an affinity with the poet that informed my understanding and enhanced my appreciation of his poetry. That affinity frightened me as well, since I accepted Sá's thesis that his headaches had caused bouts of depression and so exacerbated them that, sitting on a bench in the municipal Jardim dos Amores one afternoon, he put a pistol to his temple and pulled the trigger. I supposed that Antero had imagined that death would be deliverance from suffering. Little did he know that the pain and sadness would follow and afflict him in the body of the young girl, Raisa-Maria Boceto.

"When I informed Dr. Mishra of my intimations of a cure during our previous session, he smiled, urged me to be patient and to lie back down on the couch, make myself comfortable again and relax. And then he began the induction."

While listening to Mrs. De Souza's account of the induction, the writer looked at the statue of Faria hypnotizing the reclining bronze woman.

With eyes fixed upon the spot on the ceiling, I listen again to the hypnotic suggestions: "Take a deep breath in . . . and slowly let it out . . . and again . . . and as you do so notice once again how heavy your eyelids are becoming, heavier and heavier until you no longer wish to keep them open . . . and, as they close, yes, let them close, once again you drift into a deep state of contemplative relaxation. . . . A few more deep breaths and you are on the spiral staircase, descending again, down another twenty steps, deeper . . . and deeper into your castle, counting again, sixty-nine, sixty-eight, six-ty-seven . . . down, down, more and more calm and relaxed with each number, breath, and step . . . "

Having become familiar with the sound of induction, the vision of the tenebrous stairwell, and the calm engendered by hypnotic trans-port, I am able to descend into the castle more easily and rapidly than during my first two sessions, gliding down, down, barely aware of the stairs beneath my feet, deeper, down past Braulio's garret, deeper, down past Raisa-Maria's mother's alcove, deeper and deeper into the hypnotic darkness of the castle keep, feeling that it is not I who was descending, nor is it Braulio or Raisa-Maria. It is a disembodied spirit who had fleetingly been both the art student in Goa and the abject girl in Lisbon, and who had been, and would again become, me, but is in that moment and place outside of time and space, seeking a body in which to reexperience the world.

"*Quarto,*" the spirit whispered, "*três, dois, um,*" and a door swung open to the brightly illuminated and bustling Café d'Esculape on the rue de Clichy in Paris.

As I seated myself at the only vacant table there, a waiter greeted me: "*Bonjour Monsieur Quental. Le pichet habituel du Vin Mariani?*"

While waiting for my drink, I happened to notice that the woman drinking tea at the table to the left of mine was reading a book and was startled indeed to see that it was a collection of my poetry, yes, my own *Primaveras Românticas.*

"*Desculpe, Senhora,*" I said, unable to restrain myself: "Excuse me, Madame, but I must tell you what unexpected joy it gives me to en-counter a perfect stranger here in Paris reading verses composed by me. Please permit me to introduce myself, and do forgive me if I am intruding in any way, but I am Antero Tarquínio de Quental."

"Then I must tell you, Mestre," she responded in our common lan-guage as she turned to face me with a generously delighted smile of surprise, "of the enormous complementary pleasure that is mine in having the equally unexpected pleasure and honor of meeting the poet whose compositions have so enriched my life. Please join me, Senhor Quental. Please."

As I shifted my chair to her table in acceptance of her gracious invi-tation, she laughed. "Perhaps you should pinch me so that I can be sure this is not a dream. There are so many things I'd like to ask you, Senhor Quental, so much I'd like to know about you, major things like 'Are you really as darkly pessimistic and despairing as your poetry insinuates?' and little things like 'What has brought you to the City of Light?'"

There was something familiar about the woman, some quality that appealed to me, not in an amorous way, no, not at all. No, it seemed rather the sort of attraction that is rooted in the kind of affection one feels for a sister or perhaps a best friend from childhood. It was a safe and calm attraction allowing me to imagine that she cared about me and was genuinely interested in my story. Because I trusted that from reading my poetry she understood my torments, I felt free to divulge some of the intimate things that have been the source and substance of my literary endeavors.

I explained to her that after the death of my wife Ana the previous year, Lisbon had become utterly unbearable. I could not remain in our house and sleep in the bed in which we had slept next to each other for so many years, the bed in which, on so many nights, I read my poetry to her, lulling her into dream with the images that particular words, combined in certain ways, can so magically generate. She died in that bed.

No longer could I enter the church where we celebrated the Mass together each Sunday, nor walk through the Jardim dos Amores where we had strolled hand in hand on so many afternoons. I could not go anywhere near the Praço do Commércia where some twenty-five years before I first saw her. It was *o amor à primeira vista*, as we say, but with the conviction that it's not really first sight but rather the recognition of someone that you have loved and always will, someone from a dream, another lifetime, or different world, when and where you vowed to make love eternal.

Needing to escape the Portugal that had been so darkened by shadows of death, I chose to come to Paris for various reasons, literary and political ones, but a medical reason as well. I'm here because I suffer from severe migraine headaches. Frustrated by his failure to cure me with hydroelectric baths and strong galvanic currents applied to my temples, my doctor in Lisbon referred me to a physician at the Salpêtrière hospital here in Paris, a certain Dr. Charcot, who has lately become rather celebrated in medical circles for his successful treatment of neurological disorders with mesmerism, what he calls *l'hypnotisation*. Unfortunately it's impossible to determine the degree to which Charcot's *hypnotisations* would have helped me in the long run because, after only two sessions with him, he abruptly refused to continue treatment. I'll get to that in a bit.

The woman was entirely sympathetic for she too, so she confided, suffered from migraine headaches. She was familiar with hypnosis as well: "I am from the Portuguese Indies, you know, from Goa, the birthplace of José Custodio de Faria, an abade who gave weekly demonstrations of hypnotism here in Paris some years ago and wrote a pioneering treatise on the subject that, once I've sufficiently mastered French, I hope to translate into Konkani, his and my own native language. Translation is such a difficult task."

"Yes, but such a metaphysical one," I added. "Translation is reincarnation."

Intrigued to learn that she was from the Malabar coast, I explained that I had dreamed of someday visiting the Indies. "As a young man at university in Coimbra, while reading Camões' marvelous *Os Lusíadas*, I became so utterly enchanted as to yearn to retrace the poet's voyage from Lisbon, down around the Cape and on up to Calicut, Cochin, Diu, and Goa. Imagining your lush land in enchanted reveries, I fashioned my fecund fantasies into odes:

> *Onde a noite é balsâmica e fulgente*
> *E a lua cheia sobre as águas brilha*
> *O aroma da magnólia e da baunilha*
> *Paira no ar diáfano e dormente . . .*

"While I'd like to make the journey, I am at the same time afraid that, if I do, reality, vicious as it tends to be, will dispel the dream. If our Oriental colony is as idyllic as I have imagined, you would not have left home. You would not be here with me right now."

"Familiar as I am with both that ode, '*Sonho Oriental*,' and with the real Goa, I can assure you that, as in your dream, the moon really does shine on the water on balmy nights there and that the fragrances of magnolia and vanilla do truly lace the air. Don't be afraid to come to Goa. I'm going back soon and I would be pleased to receive you there. I imagine you'd feel quite at home. I'm only here in Paris to take an advanced French course. I am, you see, a Portuguese language and literature teacher at Our Lady of the Rosary Academy, a convent school in Goa, and French is the language all the young girls want to learn these days. French is fashionable. Konkani is my mother tongue, but Portuguese is the language that transports me most profoundly. Konkani is earthy, Portuguese ethereal. With a conviction that it will inspire my students to appreciate the sublime softness and elegant sweetness of Portuguese, I require them to read your poetry. And because it is more meaningfully heard than read, I insist on reading it aloud to them so that they might be enchanted by the sound of your words. Yes, the sound is the sense. And so I'm sure you can understand what it would mean to me, Senhor Quental, if you would be so gracious as to read to me one of the poems I read to my students. Here, I've marked the place of one of my favorites in your book. This one. Please read to me."

> *Almas no limbo ainda da existência,*
> *Acordareis um dia na consciência,*
> *E pairando, já puro pensamento,*
> *Vereis as Formas, filhas da Ilusão,*
> *Cair desfeitas, como um sonho vão . . .*
> *E acabará por fim vosso tormento.*

"I explain to the students," the woman from Goa told me, "that the gist of the poem is that our spirits, passing from body to body in the limbo of existence, will awaken someday to hover as pure thought in a transcendent consciousness. And then we'll witness the bodily forms we have assumed in our many lives disintegrating like illusory daughters of a dream. We shall be free then, our torments finally ended. Of course, the girls understand that the poem is sad. But I try to show them that, because of the language you have used to evoke your sadness, an ineffable beauty begins to shimmer mysteriously in that sorrow. And beauty, I would like them to imagine, can be a redemption from all our sorrows."

I felt constrained to confess that I should not be given so much credit for the poem. I divulged my suspicion that the spirit of a grieving woman is lodged within me. "My acceptance of Charcot's diagnosis of migraines as a symptom of hysteria, a woman's affliction, had led me to believe that my migraines are really hers. But so too, I imagine, is much of the poetry for which I have been but the medium. Yes, it was, I believe, a heartbroken, lovesick, disconsolate woman who composed that verse. The hand that held the pen to write it down is mine, but the torment is hers. While I had hoped that Charcot would be able to cure my headaches, I also feared that, once healed, I would no longer be able to write poetry. I would be abandoned by the tormented woman. So perhaps it is for the better that Charcot terminated my treatment."

"Why," the woman from Goa asked, "would he do such a thing?"

"It's a long story and not a felicitous one," I told her, "a story I'm rather ashamed to tell." That, of course, made her all the more eager to hear it.

"Please, Senhor Quental, please tell me," she pleaded. "I really do want to hear the story."

On the condition that she promised never to repeat it, I allowed myself to divulge my sins, to confess to her as one does to a priest in hopes of forgiveness. Not God's forgiveness in my case, but rather my own.

"Some months ago, arriving at the Salpêtrière for my second session with Charcot, I was introduced to an old man, a Monsieur le Baron Jules Dupotet de Sennevoy, whom Charcot had commissioned as a consultant on magnetic procedures for which the Baron, as an apostle of Mesmer and member of the Société théosophique, had some knowledge and much experience. At the Hôtel Dieu he had experimented with the use of animal magnetism as a surgical anesthetic and therapeutic aid in the treatment of vaginal pain, frigidity, nymphomania, migraine, and other female disorders. There was something familiar about the aged theosophical magnetizer, something I did not trust. It was a sort of *antipatia à primeira vista*.

"When Charcot presented me to him as 'a poet of some accomplishment and renown in Portugal,' the doddering mesmerist excitedly informed me that his daughter aspired to become a poet herself. 'She is a gifted young lady,' he boasted, 'so much so that it would be a shameful waste if her innate talent were to go uncultivated. A mastery of the formal technicalities of poetic composition would certainly serve that cultivation.'

"The baron offered to pay me whatever salary I considered appropriate for a professional poet to receive for teaching a literary debutante those technicalities. In need as I was at the time of an income to support myself here in Paris, I agreed to tutor the girl and was then invited to meet his daughter and dine with them that same evening at his home on the rue de l'Abbaye.

"Pythie Dupotet was some twenty years my junior and not at all beautiful, but substantially more pretty than she was talented, as I was to discover after dinner when her father requested that she read aloud for us his favorite of her compositions. Her lips quivered and the hands that held the poem trembled with a domestic display of stage fright:

> *L'amour est un fluide coulant magique,*
> *Un pouvoir mystérieux et magnétique,*
> *Subtil, divin, ancien, qui remplit tout,*
> *Cet intermédiaire entre les célestes et nous.*

"After suffering through the lumpen sound of her reading of that inane doggerel, I, both out of politeness to my host and for the sake of the salary he had offered to pay me, congratulated the girl on the rhymed invocation of magnetism as a metaphor for love. In order to reassure the baron that I was capable of teaching his daughter what he considered poetic technicalities, I suggested that the substitution of an a-b-a-b rhyme scheme for her a-a-b-b, as well as a metrical adjustment into the classical French Alexandrine line of two hemistiches of six syllables each, might enhance the feeling of sophistication that was latent in the poem but yet to be fully realized.

"The suggestion so stimulated the baron's enthusiasm that he insisted I begin my instruction the very next afternoon. 'I'll be at the Salpêtrière,' he announced, 'and so there will be no one here to disturb you. And please, Monsieur Quental, do bring along a book of your poetry. Even though I do not, I'm sorry to say, read Portuguese, I do collect books composed and autographed for me by authors whose acquaintance I have made, some of them quite illustrious. I don't mean to boast, but, to name a few, I have Mesmer's revolutionary *Catéchisme du magnétisme animal*, Puységur's marvelous *Du magnétisme animal*, and Deleuze's *Histoire critique du magnétisme animal*, as well as the great Balzac's *Ursala*, which contains a charming chapter on mesmerism, and a copy of both Dumas's *Joseph Balsamo* and his *Le Collier de la reine*, signed to me "*avec mon admiration et ma gratitude*" for my diligence in teaching him mesmeric theory and the technicalities of its applications that figure so significantly in those novels. Monsieur Dumas also gave me a fine edition of his *Le Comte de Monte-Cristo*, signed "*avec reconnaissance*" for my suggestion that he name the mad monk in that novel Abbé Faria. I'd be honored to add your volume to my collection, to purchase it from you or, if you prefer, to receive it in exchange for my own text, *Manuel de l'étudiant magnétiseur*. Although it was written a long time ago, it might interest you to read in it the case report of my use of mesmerism to treat a young lady who, like yourself, suffered from migraine headaches.'

"Greeting me at the door the next day as '*cher Maître*,' a seemingly nervous Pythie Dupotet escorted me into the library, where her father's book collection was on display. She invited me to make myself comfortable on the plush sofa there, a Louis XVI recamier with a high headrest and low footrest, upholstered with beige chenille embroidered with dainty pink roses.

"The aspiring poetess had chosen to wear a white linen high-waisted day gown, the cut, pleating, and folds of which were, I supposed, meant to suggest classical antiquity and thereby set the mood for her reading of a limp versification she had titled 'Erato' and dedicated to that muse of lyric love poetry.

> *O Erato, Erato! Ma Muse et mon âme sœur,*
> *Princesse d'amour qui serre mon cœur,*
> *Erato, c'est vous qui m'envahit de bonheur. . . .*

"'Please be honest with me,' Mademoiselle Duport declared upon finishing her reading of the puerile verse. 'Do I really have as much talent as my father says I do? Tell me the truth.'

"Certain that she, like most of us, did not really want to know any truth that was not flattering, I said that if I hadn't known she had composed the poem I would supposed that it was the work of Sappho, the immortal poetess of Lesbos. I asked if I might read it to myself and, in order to spare myself the embarrassment of having to hear her read again, I added that I would be honored if she would permit me to translate the stanza into Portuguese in order to see whether or not I could capture its nuances and lyrical beauty in my native tongue.

"Delighted by the proposal, she listened in rapt attention as I, pretending to be reading and simultaneously translating her banal couplets, recited an emended version of one of my own poems:

> *O Erato, Erato! Almas no limbo ainda da existência,*
> *Acordareis um dia na consciência,*
> *Erato, epairando, já puro pensamento. . . .*

"Although having to insert 'Erato' into my stanza the same number of times it had appeared in hers compromised the rhythm of the verse, she was enthralled.

"'*Vraiment sublime en portugais aussi!*' she moaned with delight as she sat down next to me on the recamier. 'I can hardly believe I wrote that. It's even more enchanting in Portuguese than it is in French. And now, *mon Maître*, perhaps you would be so kind as to read one of your Portuguese poems to me?'

"'*Amortalhei na fé o pensamento,*' I read. '*E achei a paz na inércia e esquecimento,*' and, apparently captivated by my words, she leaned close to me to exclaim: 'Portuguese is so beautiful. I must learn it. Would you teach me? Teach me so that I can read everything you've written and also so that I can translate my own oeuvre into your language. Read another. Please, *cher Maître*, read to me in your mesmeric Portuguese.'

"'*Verbo crepuscular e íntimo alento,*' I began and felt her head come to rest upon my shoulder. '*Das cousas mudas,*' I continued as her left arm reached around my back and her fingers began to rhythmically stroke my side.

"'Because I don't know what the words mean I can listen purely to the sound of them,' Mademoiselle Dupotet noted. 'The music enraptures me. Please read another,' she begged as her right hand settled upon my knee. '*S'il vous plait, mon cher, mon cher Maître, lisez.*'

"Although I had certainly not intended to seduce Pythie Dupotet, for some reason that still baffles and troubles me, I did not resist as she pushed me back on the recamier and feverishly kissed my forehead, cheeks, neck, and again and again my mouth with savagely ravenous kisses.

"'*Je vous aime, mon Maître. Je vous adore,*' she moaned again and again as, lifting her skirts to straddle me, she pulled open my shirt. Given the intensity of the girl's lust and the impetuous indecency of her behavior, I was shocked to see the stain of hymenal blood on the recamier.

"As I struggled to unshackle myself from her fervent clutch so that I might dress and escape the premises, the unabashedly grinning and immodestly sprawling girl declared that she had never in her life been as happy as at that moment. She was certain, she proclaimed, that the joy she was feeling would forever be the inspiration for the composition of immortal poetic masterpieces: '*Oui, des chansons d'amour sans fin. Dans vos bras, mon Maître, je me sens la plus douée des poétesses et la plus aimante des femmes. Dans votre amour, je me perds et je me découvre. Je vous aime mon Maître.*'

"The aura of a shimmering patch of light and spinning spirals, the tingling of my lips and tongue, the vertigo and nausea, augured the onset of a migraine.

"Appalled by what I had just done, ashamed of my weakness and, at the same time, annoyed by her pathetic professions of love, I spoke out: 'You said that you wanted me to be honest with you. And so I will. I do not love you, Mademoiselle Dupotet. And, I'm truly sorry, but I do not wish to see you again.'

"'*Non,*' she shrieked, '*c'est pas vrai. Impossible!*' In a fit of despair, she was babbling some histrionic nonsense about destiny having united us as '*deux poètes inspirés par l'amour.*' The aura gave way to a migraine that was exacerbated by the noise of her clamorous caterwaul. I suppose that I deserved the pain of it as a punishment for my transgression.

"Putting on my overcoat, hat, and gloves, I interrupted the frenzied lovelorn rant: 'Mademoiselle Dupotet, your father tells you that you have talent because he loves you. Love makes liars of us all. But because I do not love you, I can tell you the truth. You are not a poet. *Adieu Mademoiselle.*' I left my unsigned copy of *Primaveras Românticas* behind.

"It's hard for me to imagine how I could have allowed myself any physical intimacy with the innocent girl only to reject her so heartlessly. It felt as though the tormented spirit of that migrainous woman in me had angrily incited me to do something I did not want to do. Perhaps she was impelled to hurt that girl as she had herself once been hurt, to transfer her anguish to another. I don't know.

"When several days later I arrived at the Salpêtrière for my therapy, Charcot curtly informed me that it was impossible for him to continue to treat me in that his venerable advisor, Monsieur le Baron Dupotet de Sennevoy, was refusing to work with him as long as I was his patient.

'The baron insists that in breaking his daughter's heart, you have irreparably shattered his own as well,' Charcot reported. 'Mademoiselle Dupotet has been admitted to the hospital. Because of you, I am now treating her for acute hysteria.'

"I've given up hope and resigned myself to suffer for the remainder of my life, not only with migraines, but with countless other torments as well, to suffer until all the forms I have assumed disintegrate as in a dream. All the pleasures of this world have an illusory aspect and dimension to them, but pain is always real. Thus, just a little while ago, you said, 'Perhaps you should pinch me so that I can be sure this is not a dream.' The migraine is but a reminder that reality itself is, by its very nature, essentially painful. And the most any medication or procedure can do is provide a transient distraction from that pain."

"Poor girl," the listener to my story remarked. "But poor man as well. Yes, poor you. I suspect, as you do, that you could not help doing what you did. In the Indies, you know, the Hindus believe that all of us have lived before and that we carry with us the transmigrating soul of our previous incarnations. We can't help being who we are in this life and being who we are determines what we do. Try to forgive yourself. I'm sorry, but I really must go now. I have an appointment."

That said, the woman from Goa signaled the waiter for her bill, paid it, rose from the table, bid me *adeus*, hesitated, and then added, "I imagine that someday you will finally make the journey to Goa. I hope to see you there. In any case I will remember you always."

No sooner had she disappeared through the doorway from which I had entered the Café de Esculape than I noticed she had forgotten her copy of *Primaveras Românticas*. Picking it up from the table, I rushed after her, hoping to catch up with her on the spiral staircase. Hearing footsteps above me, I called out: "Wait, wait for me, Senhora! You've forgotten something. Wait for me."

In pursuit of the woman from Goa I climbed the stairs as quickly as I could, twenty stairs up to Raisa-Maria's mother's boudoir, racing up from there up another twenty steps, past Braulio's garret, then rushing from there up and into the office where I saw her lying on the couch with closed eyes.

"One ... two ... three. . . . Wake up, Mrs. De Souza. Open your eyes," Dr. Mishra said and I opened my eyes.

One . . . two . . . three. . . . Open your eyes.

Sitting up on the couch and turning to place her feet on the floor, Mrs. De Souza wanted to talk with Dr. Mishra about the woman from Goa whom she had met in a past life in Paris. "She wore her hair cropped short like mine. And her voice sounded very much like mine. And this antique silver heart-shaped locket on this chain around my neck—she was wearing this very piece with its ruby center stone and identical engraved floral border. And when I was in Paris some years ago, on leave from my teaching post to study French there, I would often take afternoon tea at a café on the rue de Clichy. I can't explain it. I don't know what it means. It seems that woman was me even though I know that I could not have been her. No, I could not have been her because I was the poet Antero Tarquínio de Quental."

"I was stunned," Mrs. De Souza told the writer, "to encounter in my next trance someone that I knew, a magnetizer with whom you are now familiar—yes, Monsieur le Baron Jules-Denis Dupotet de Sennevoy, the father of the broken-hearted girl, Pythie Dupotet. He was, of course, a much younger man at that time than the elderly consultant to Charcot whose daughter was seduced and abandoned by Antero Quental. I'll tell you the story when we next meet.

The writer suggested that Mrs. De Souza might, for that occasion, come to the house he was renting.

"No," she exclaimed as if his invitation suggested something improper. "No, let's meet near the Panjim market in the garden of what was the site of the Goa Medical College Hospital before it was moved to Bambolim.

SESSION FOUR: *Trance-Actions*

On his way to the meeting, the writer had stopped at the Broadway Book Centre, where he purchased Luis Vas's just-published *Abbé Faria: The Life of a Pioneer Indian Hypnotist.* While there, he thumbed through *Portugal Past and Present*, curious to see the photographs of the Torre de São Vicente and the Praça do Comércio.

He was reading the Vas biography when Mrs. Souza arrived a half-hour late for their appointment. She responded to his question about her opinion of the book with, "I haven't read it yet, but I'm sure that Mr. Vas means well and that he has done the best he can with the limited and unreliable information available to him. I have, as a matter of fact, written to him to inform him that I would be willing to assist him in revising his book in accordance with my firsthand experience in my incarnation as Abbé Faria. I have not yet heard back from him. But let's not waste time talking about misinformed biographies of Faria. Let's get to the truth. As I mentioned at our last meeting, I once again met Monsieur le Baron Jules-Denis Dupotet de Sennevoy during my next past life regression session with Dr. Mishra. Let me tell you the story.

"Make yourself comfortable again, taking in and out a few deep and relaxing breaths as you rest your head comfortably back. Just as you did before the last story, direct your eyes upward to focus on a spot on the ceiling as you listen to my voice. Notice your eyelids becoming heavy, so very heavy, and the heavier they become the more and more relaxed you feel. . . . If you wish to go into an even deeper state of relaxation all you have to do is let your eyelids close . . . . Yes, let them close . . . yes, close your eyes and remember the spiral staircase and how very calm and deeply relaxed you become, more and more relaxed with the descent, story after story down, down, deeper and deeper into the mansions of memory."

Mrs. De Souza told the writer that she had not taken more than a dozen steps, hadn't counted back beyond sixty-eight or so, when she lost track of numbers and stairs, of time and space, and of who she was as she entered a room lambent with flickering candles. Imagining that the couch in the hypnotist's office in Goa was a plush recamier in a private library in Paris with a high headrest and low footrest, elegantly upholstered with a beige chenille richly embroidered with dainty pink roses, she reclined, took a few deep breaths and rested her back.

Comfortable there and calm, she imagined that the hypnotist was speaking French: *"Je vous ai attendu pendant si longtemps,"* he told her in a seductively soft whisper. "Yes, Renée, I've been waiting for you for such a long time, waiting for you to remember."

Imagine hands gracefully moving in rhythmic circular passes, slowly around and around your face, to and fro, up and down, hands at once delicate and virile with fingers slightly spread, patiently making the soporific gestures that lull the mind into restful trance as a vertiginous voice flows softly from flush lips: "*Regardez-moi fixement, Renée, fixez-moi. . . . Fixez-moi intensément. Concentrez-vous. Fixez-moi . . . vous ne voyez plus que moi. . . .*"

The hands lower as he leans in close, closer and closer, staring with the hauntingly blue-gray eyes that arouse fear and at the same time an uncanny illusion that fear will vanish as soon as one surrenders. Surrender bestows serenity.

As heavy eyelids close, there's an anodyne warmth of fingers gently and rhythmically massaging the temples, the mere touch of fingertips transforming the intensely sharp pain of *les crises migraineuses* into dreamy clouds of billowing pleasure. Nausea disappears as soon as a palm comes to rest on the stomach. The penetrating warmth of a strong hand radiates into every fiber of the nubile body, pulsating in every organ, vibrant in every cell.

In hypnotic trance I remember remembering my father, Monsieur Gabriel Reverdy, a prosperous importer of Oriental fabrics, gems, perfumes, and spices, my sweetly doting Papa who, after Maman abandoned us, contracted agents to conduct his business in Mahé des Indes so that he could stay home and care for his daughter. I remember his face illuminated by candlelight as he sat on the edge of my bed at night telling stories and reading tales about the French East Indies.

As he stroked my cheeks, my eyes would close and out of my darkness there would appear a resplendent procession of lavishly caparisoned, slowly swaying, elephants with turbaned maharajas in ornate howdahs on their backs followed by lithe dancing girls and servants bearing trays of ambrosial sweets.

Sometimes he'd read fables translated from an ancient Indian language into French. I remember the tale "*Le marchand enchanté.*" "*Dans la ville de Mohapur sur les rives de la rivière Svapna,*" it began and, with closing eyes, I was transported to that town on the banks of the River Svapna.

Whenever I had a headache Papa would tuck me into his bed, cool my forehead with compresses, gently massage my temples, and whisper, "*Dors, ma fifille, dors bien.*" He'd refuse to leave the bedside until I had fallen asleep. And in that sleep I'd often dream of his idyllic Malabar, a dream in which I was cleansed by a warm nocturnal downpour of monsoon rain.

None of the physicians to whom my father had taken me had, been able to provide, with their blisters, cups, and leeches, their allopathic tisanes and doses of laudanum, any relief from my pain. An article he read in *Le Siècle*, "*Application du magnétisme au traitement des céphalées*," so aroused his hopes for me that he contacted the author, Monsieur le Baron Jules-Denis Dupotet de Sennevoy and arranged for the magnetizer to treat me.

Reclining on the recamier in the library of Baron Dupotet's home, I listened to the somniferous voice: "*Fixez-moi. Vous êtes bien tranquille, Renée, et vous respirez profondément . . . profondément . . . tranquillement, et vos paupières sont lourdes, si lourdes. . . . Vous les fermez et vous sentez une agréable sensation de lourdeur vous envahir. Vous glissez lentement . . . irrésistiblement dans un sommeil réparateur. . . .*"

Pleasure gently pulsating in my entrails, warmly radiating into my buttocks, loins, thighs, warmer and warmer, seeping down my legs, tingling into my toes, and up, up into my stomach, filling and warming my chest, flowing into my arms, and down, down into my fingertips, up, up into my neck, glowing on my face, as deeply I breathed, deeper and deeper, languid with bliss, heart enraptured, flesh quivering with exhilaration, a soul transported to ethereal realms of exquisitely strange pleasures.

In the trance induced by Dr. Mishra, I remembered trances induced by the baron, recalling transports that Renée herself could not recollect. I remembered words, actions, and feelings that Dupotet had told Renée she, upon being wakened, would not be able to recall. He told her that she would not remember that he had ever undressed her, cradled her head in his lap, and delicately stroked her cheek with fingers, the tips of which then meandered down her neck, down, down and around her breasts, around and around, and down to her belly, down, down, as he guided her with suggestive whispers into "*un jardin secret.*"

As the creator of that garden, fashioned with expressions of desire and suggestions of bliss, the Baron Dupotet was god. And into the garden he brought a girl and caused a deep sleep to fall upon her, a sleep in which she inhaled deeply the breath and words of her creator as slowly she exhaled her own spirit and will. With each breath the garden became more vividly lush and fragrant with blossoming flowers of every color. The baron-god was at once around and within the spellbound girl. She was naked and not ashamed. He gave her a commandment: "In the middle of our garden there are two trees, the Tree of Dreams and the Tree of Memory. You may eat from the Tree of Dreams, for its fruit is lusciously sweet, but the fruit from the Tree of Memory must never be tasted. The day you eat of that bitter fruit, you will become ashamed of your nakedness and you will be expelled from the garden of delight, never to return again. Open your mouth," the baron-god ordered as he took the naked girl into his arms, "and taste the intoxicating fruit of the Tree of Dreams."

Although Renée, upon being wakened from the somnambulistic trances induced by the baron during each of their weekly meetings, had no conscious memory of the garden into which he transported her during those hypnotic sessions, no recollection whatsoever of any physical intimacy with the magnetist, she soon began to dream about the garden, and in that garden to imagine that he embraced her.

In bed in the morning she'd resist awakening, keeping her eyes closed to concentrate on her memories of the somnolent dalliances for fear that those sweet dreams might fade away. In hypnopompic reverie she'd cling to her pillow, pretending it was the baron. "*Je vous aime*," she'd whisper. "*Je vous adore, mon rédempteur.*"

In my incarnation as Renée Reverdy, I was vulnerable, susceptible, and naive. I could not help falling as passionately in love as only inexperienced young girls can do. It was an impetuous love that disregarded all obstacles and rules and imagined itself to be the only thing that mattered in the world. That my beloved was more than twenty years my senior, that he was married and had recently fathered a baby girl, intensified rather than discouraged or hindered love. The novels of Charles Paul de Kock that I had so avidly read during the period of my transformation from a little girl into a young woman had given me the impression that all married men of means kept mistresses and that they loved their mistresses more intensely than their wives. While devotion to the latter was a matter of duty, attention to the former was a matter of passion. And duty was as dull as passion was glorious.

In bed at night I'd rehearse declarations of love. "*Je vous aime, mon rédempteur, pour toujours et à jamais*" would preface oaths that I would keep our love affair secret and never expect him to compromise his conjugal obligations. I memorized a line spoken by the beautiful courtesan in De Kock's *Le mari, la femme, et l'amante*." Passing it off as my own, I planned to recite at just the right moment: "*L'étincelle magnétique qui brille dans vos yeux a réveillé un amour qui dormait tapi comme dans une transe au plus profond de moi.*"

No sooner had I arrived for my next appointment with the mesmerist and taken my customary place on the recamier in his library than I began the declaration: "*Je vous aime, je vous aime, mon rédempteur, pour toujours et à jamais.*"

Putting a finger to my lips, my beloved stopped me. "Do not say anything. Not yet. No, just allow yourself to relax. Rest your head back. And let's begin."

I surrendered. I obeyed.

"*Vos paupières sont lourdes, si lourdes. Vous les fermez et vous sentez une sensation de lourdeur vous envahir. Vous glissez lentement . . .*"

Only in the trance induced by Dr. Mishra almost a century later did I remember the baron's posthypnotic suggestions and commandments: "Listen to me, Mademoiselle Reverdy. Listen and concentrate on what I am saying. You will not remember any physical intimacy between us. You will never be able to recall what we have done. If you ever have any intimations of such memories, you will imagine that you are merely imagining them, that it happened only in your dreams. I am going to wake you now. And when I do, you will not remember any of this. And you will not be in love with me. You will wake up on the count of three. And when you do, you will not love me. You do not love me. You do not love me. And we shall not see each other again. It is over."

"*Un, deux, trois*," the magnetist said firmly. But Renée's eyes did not open. And they remained closed while he repeated it more sternly. "*Un, deux, trois*." It had to be reiterated three more times before the girl emerged from hypnotic trance.

"I have done all I can do for your migraines, Mademoiselle Reverdy. There is no need for further treatment," I remember the baron announcing frostily. "So, you will not come here again. It's over. Do you understand?"

"You can't do this to me," I desperately protested. "The migraines are fewer and less intense since I began therapy with you. If you discontinue treatment, they'll become more frequent and severe. I'm certain of it."

"I am convinced by what you have revealed in the somnambulistic state that your headaches are imaginary, Mademoiselle Reverdy. You will continue to have them only if you want to have them. Our work together is over. You must leave now. Yes, go. *Adieu Mademoiselle.* Please, go."

I nodded, obediently rose, and started for the door, but then suddenly stopped, turned back to face the Baron, lost control of myself, and cried out, "*Non, ce n'est pas possible. Je vous aime pour toujours et à jamais.*"

"No," the baron responded in a clinical tone of voice. "You do not love me. Your love is imaginary. It is a magnetic illusion. A dream. It's not real."

"*Il n'est rien de réel,*" I protested, "*que les rêves de l'amour. Tout le reste est imaginé et sans importance.*"

The magnetist repeated it forcefully: "You do not love me, Mademoiselle Reverdy. And I do not love you. Wake up from the dream. Yes, wake up," he said as he opened the door, expelled me from the garden, and condemned me to a lifetime of pain.

As I stepped through the threshold, I heard the door close behind me and the sliding of the bolt that locked it. Standing on the landing, I noticed that in addition to the staircase heading upward, there was another leading down and, curious as to where it might take me, I started to descend. I hadn't taken but a few steps down when I heard a voice from above beckoning me back up. I tried to resist its control over me, but could not. Obediently I climbed back up, past the baron's door, past the café in Paris, past the bedroom in Lisbon and the garret in Goa, higher and higher until I heard the voice counting:

"One . . . two . . . three. . . . Wake up, Mrs. Souza, and open your eyes. Yes, open your eyes.

"After that particular session with Dr. Mishra," Mrs. De Souza told the writer, "fraught as it was with troubling—and yet in some way liberating—memories of the Baron Dupotet, I was anxious to go home to search the Internet for information about the mesmerist. Given the faith I had developed in the reality of past lives and the efficacy of hypnosis as a method of remembering them, I was not surprised to discover that Monsieur le Baron Dupotet de Sennevoy was a very real person. A portrait of him was posted on a site dedicated to the history of hypnosis. The digital biography validated various facts that I had discovered under hypnosis—he really was a disciple of Mesmer, a friend of Dumas, and a consultant to Charcot. How could I have known those things if I had not once truly been Renée Reverdy and Antero Quental after her?

"The biography included a bibliography of Dupotet's writings, two of which were, I discovered, for sale on eBay.fr. I purchased both: *Le magnétisme animal opposé à la médecine, mémoire pour servir a l'histoire du magnetism* and *Manuel de l'étudiant magnétiseur, ou nouvelle instruction pratique sur le magnetism.*

"The former, an impressionistic history of magnetism, includes, incidentally, the author's recollection of being taken, when he was an impressionable young man, by his father to a demonstration in Paris of Oriental hypnotism given by '*Monsieur l'abbé de Faria, un brahmine des Indes, sa couleur malabare et son régard séduisant, qui attribue les phénomènes du somnambulisme à l'impressionnabilité psychique du sujet.*'

"The second text, *Manuel de l'étudiant magnétiseur*, sent to me by an antiquarian bookseller in Marseille, didn't arrive here until a few days ago. It's ponderous reading, so pompous and tediously repetitious, in fact, that while trying to work my way through it, my eyelids would frequently become heavy and I'd almost drift off into asleep. But then, in an appendix consisting of case reports, I read something that has kept me awake, tossing with anger and turning with sadness, for the past few nights. It's an account of the author's use of *le magnétisme* to treat twenty-year-old Mademoiselle R—— for '*une céphalée grave, chronique, invalidante et caractérisée par des maux de tête et des nausées.*'

"Despite a distance of seven thousand kilometers and four lifetimes from the residence on the rue de l'Abbaye, I could not help being at once distraught and infuriated to read Dupotet's claim that he had terminated treatment because Mademoiselle R—— had become dangerously dependent upon him. I've brought the book along. It's here in my purse. Here it is. Let me read it to you. I'll translate it for you as I do. Listen to this: 'The novice magnetizer should be cognizant of the potential dangers of mesmerizing young women. The story of Mademoiselle R—— provides a typical example. She had come to me complaining of migraine headaches, a condition that can normally be cured in one or two magnetic sessions. But Mademoiselle R——, reporting no improvement, insisted on returning week after week for additional treatment. Since many young women experience physical pleasure in the somnambulistic state, this did not surprise me, but it did suggest the possibility that she could have been coming to see me under the mere pretext of persistent migraines. I began to suspect that she might be either fabricating her headaches or imagining them so vividly as to believe they were real. That Mademoiselle R—— seemed to be a perfectly demure, modest, and reserved young lady made it quite shocking when, during her fourth magnetization, she was suddenly transformed into a brazen *cocotte* who shamelessly attempted to lure me into indulging in the wildest of carnal debaucheries with her. She said and did things that propriety forbids me from reporting here. Upon being wakened from magnetic trance, however, she regained her respectable, decorous manner and seemed to have no recollection of her wanton entreaties and lewd performances. "Seemed," I say, because it is possible that she was merely feigning innocence and only pretending to be unaware of her licentious somnambulistic displays. Whatever the case, I am certain that it was in both her best interest and my own that I terminated her therapy. She begged me not to do so, sobbing and weeping, and, preposterous as it may seem, declared that she loved me and wished to be my mistress. The student magnetizer should be aware of the fact that incidents of female subjects falling in love with their magnetizers or imagining that their magnetizers have seduced and taken advantage of them are not uncommon and have been reported by Mesmer, Puységur, Faria, Deleuze, Liébeault, and others.'"

Closing the book and then her eyes, Mrs. De Souza shook her head with disapproval, muttered, "calumny," and then fell gravely silent.

"What happened to Renée?" the writer asked.

"I don't now remember very much at all of what I must have remembered under hypnosis about the sad remainder of her life. Just as we forget so many things about the life we are currently living, so we repress, even under hypnosis, even more about our past lives.

"But I do remember that after being rejected by the man she had loved as her lord and master, with all her heart, soul, and might, Renée suffered from bouts of depression, deep and dismal, overwhelmed by unbearable feelings of helplessness and hopelessness. The migraines, as I remember, occurred with greater and greater frequency and intensity, so exacerbated the depression as to cause her to contemplate suicide. Although she did not act on that impulse in that life in Paris, she did, I believe, do so in her next life in Lisbon. Yes, it was, I imagine, Renée Reverdy who put the pistol to Antero Quental's temple in the Jardim dos Amores and pulled the trigger.

"I do remember that during her depressions Renée was too wearied by sorrow to get out of bed and yet too agitated by that same sorrow to sleep. She struggled with all her might to rid herself of the painful recollections of the pleasure the Baron Dupotet had given her. But the more rigorously she struggled, the more vivid the memories became. She could not forget the penetrating hypnotic gaze of the blue-gray eyes, at once ice and ashes, the spellbinding hands, at once delicate and virile, circling her body in rhythmic passes, at once relaxing and arousing, and the flush lips flowing with suggestive whispers: *'Regardez-moi fixement, Renée, fixez-moi . . . concentrez-vous . . . vos paupières sont lourdes . . . vous les fermez et vous sentez une sensation de lourdeur vous envahir.'*

"Memories of the inductions were so vivid that, just by remembering them, they would inevitably lull Renée into a deep self-hypnotic state, into trances in which she was a child again. She imagined that her parents were happily married in that childhood and that her father took his wife and daughter with him to Mahé des Indes. The moon was shining on the waters of the Arabian Sea and the air was laced with fragrances of magnolia, vanilla, and burning sandalwood and coir. She watched a resplendent procession of lavishly caparisoned elephants with turbaned maharajas in ornate howdahs on their backs followed by lithe dancing girls and servants bearing trays of ambrosial sweets. The child heard rolling thunder and then listened to the sound of nocturnal monsoon rain on palm, mango, and plantain leaves. Naked she stepped out from under a thatched roof to bathe herself in its warm soothing downpour.

"Renée's spirit had to wait until 1945 for her actual passage through four deaths and births to India. She was not aware that it was a return, a journey home. No, not until undergoing past life regression hypnotherapy did I remember my childhood here in Goa some two hundred and fifty years ago."

"So, Renée was Faria in her previous life?" the writer asked.

"Yes. But, I'm sorry, I really must go now. I have an appointment. I'll tell you the true story of Abbé Faria next time so that you can retell it in your book. For that occasion I propose that we meet for lunch in Candolim at the Taj Fort Aguada Resort Hotel, and then, after lunch, we can visit the house in which José Custudio the Abbé de Faria was born. That, it seems to me, would be an appropriate place to hear the end of my story."

SESSION FIVE: *Trance-Formations*

When the writer joined Mrs. De Souza several days later at the resort hotel for lunch on a sunny terrace overlooking the majestic inlet where the River Mandovi flows into the Arabian Sea, she was wearing a light blue floral-print cotton salwar kameez. The woman from Goa seemed more relaxed and comfortable in Condolim than she had been in Panjim.

"Imagine this place," she said with an air of nostalgia, "as it was more than two hundred years ago when José Custodio de Faria was a child. He played down there on Sinquerim Beach just as those boys are doing now. I remember looking up from there to where you and I are now and seeing the battery of scores of huge-caliber cast-iron canons that were exultantly aimed out to sea.

"I was so eager to venture further down into the depths of my castle that I was, as I am sure you can imagine, grievously disappointed when I had to cancel my next appointment with Dr. Mishra on account of a migraine and wait another week to discover who Renée had been in her previous life. I had no idea who I would find one hundred steps down into my castle."

With each repeated experience of hypnosis, Mrs. De Souza explained to the writer, she had become more and more readily susceptible to induction, finding it easier and easier with each successive session to relax more and more completely, to surrender more entirely to suggestion, and to go more and more quickly and deeply into lucid sleep.

"I had no idea what to expect as, with my eyes focused on a spot on the ceiling, I began, without even waiting for Dr. Mishra to tell me to do so, to breathe deeply in and slowly out. Almost immediately my eyelids became heavy, heavy . . ."

"*. . . So very heavy and, as before, the heavier they become, the* more relaxed you feel. Remember how relaxed you became during the last story? If you wish to go into an even deeper state of relaxation and greater concentration all you have to do is let your eyelids close . . . yes, close your eyes to see the spiral staircase again and imagine the descent past Braulio's garret . . . again past the door to Aranha Boceto's alcove . . . deeper down past the Café d'Esculape . . . past the library of the mesmerist on the rue de l'Abbaye . . . again breathing deeply in and slowly out . . . more and more relaxed with each breath and step . . . counting, ten, nine, eight, more calm and relaxed, seven, six, five, another story of the castle down . . . down into a state of deeper relaxation . . . counting to yourself, four, three, two, one . . . and now imagine an opening door. . . ."

Pushed though the entrance, I tumbled into pitch-darkness.

Crawling slowly forward I came to a wall, turned to lean against it, and sat waiting, waiting until slowly, slowly my pupils began to dilate so that I could see where I was, and slowly, slowly I began to remember stories of my life as José Custodia de Faria.

I remembered being unjustly imprisoned in the cramped and gloomy cell that the French call an *oubliette*, a chamber of forgetting and being forgotten, in the dungeon of the prison on the small Isle of If in the bay of Marseille. I imagine that just as there is bondage in memory, so too there is freedom.

It is ironic that I ended up in a prison in France by attempting to avoid imprisonment in Portugal when, because of the rebellion against Portuguese rule in India, Goans in Lisbon were being rounded up for questioning as to their knowledge of and possible involvement in the plot to overthrow the colonial government. Many were arrested on suspicion of treason.

My father urged me to flee to France where there was sympathetic support for our revolution. An apoplectic stroke had left my father hemiplegic. Supposing that his paralysis would be burdensome to me, he did not accompany me. He imagined that, in any case, the paralysis would render him immune to arrest.

Alone in Marseille with nothing to do there, I yearned to return home, to once again be lulled into sleep by the sound of nocturnal monsoon rains on palm, mango, and plantain leaves, to smell the smoke of burning coir and sandalwood, to taste dodol and bebinca, to bathe in the warm currents of the Mandovi, and to hold Kamala in my arms again.

I booked passage on a ship that was sailing in several weeks time for Mahé des Indes, the French colony on the Arabian Sea, a short journey south of Goa. While wiling away those lonely weeks of waiting, waywardly I went one night to a rowdy tavern on the docks, into which, just before midnight, an old drunkard bounded, exultantly shouting, "*Me voici! C'est moi!*" He laughed, "I'm back, I'm home, and I've been cured." Dancing about in drunken delight, wildly waving his arms in the air, rushing up to this and that old comrade, he hugged and kissed each of them in turn. "It's me! Look, look at me! It's a miracle," he bellowed, belched, and begged us one and all to join him in hearty celebratory toasts to his regained fitness and to the man who cured him of his affliction—"the honorable Marquis de Puységur. *Hourra pour le Marquis et hourra pour le magnétisme animal! Hourra, houra!*"

A loquacious lascar at my table bought me an absinthe and let me in on the story. The jubilant rascal was a fisherman who hadn't been able to work ever since a blow to the head by the swinging boom of his boat had rendered the right side of his body paralyzed.

"*Mais régardez-moi maintenant!*" the soused gaffer exuberantly exclaimed with tears of joy forming in his eyes and rolling down into his beard as he climbed up onto one of the tables to tell his tale.

"The quacks here who said nothing could be done for me should see me now. Haha! I've been in Soissons, up in the north, on the estate of an aristocrat, a real marquis, a Mason, and a mesmeric magnetizer, as he styles himself. The Marquis de Puységuy, a liberal gentleman, uncommonly both rich and generous and so much so that he didn't charge even a sou for my treatment, undertaking my case, he said, because my condition intrigued him. He wondered if his magnetic cure would work on me. I had my doubts but, as you can see, my friends, it did! Haha! It worked! *Hourra!*"

Downing two more drams, he danced a capricious solo tarantella, guffawing as he did, then belched a few more times and stopped to momentarily catch his breath for the continuation of his happy tale. "I heard about him from my brother-in-law who attended one of his demonstrations in Paris last year. He swore that with his own eyes he had seen the marquis restore a blind woman's sight and put an end to an epileptic's fits, and swore furthermore that he had with his own ears heard testimonials of patients who swore that they had been cured of syphilis, tuberculosis, fistulas, goiters, gout, flatulence, worms, and what have you. Since I couldn't travel on my own, my wife and her brother took me to his estate. Supposing as I did that there wasn't any hope for me, I didn't want to undertake the journey. But my wife insisted, complaining that there wasn't much pleasure in being married to a cripple. So let's drink to my wife and brother-in-law! *Hourra, hourra!* Haha, Haha! And now I'm back and fit to fish and please my wife to boot. *Hourra! Hourra!* How did he do it? All that I remember is drinking some water that he said was magnetized, and holding two sticks, magnetized as well, and then he was moving his hands, likewise magnetized, around and around in front of my face. Then he placed those hands of his upon my head and told me that his magnetic fluid and mine were mixing. '*En mélangeant . . . en mélangeant,*' he kept repeating, and that's the last thing I remember until I woke up and much to my amazement realized I could move my arm and leg again.

"My wife, bearing witness to the treatment, informed me that I had been in some kind of deep sleep in which the marquis, mumbling things into my ear she couldn't hear, seemed to have complete control over me. The marquis raised his right arm, she remembered, and when he did, I, although my eyes were closed, did the same. Yes I raised the arm I hadn't been able to move for eighteen months. When he lowered his arm, I did the same. When he raised his right leg and bent his knee, I did just that. He stood up and I stood up. He walked about the room and I walked with him. Faster and faster we trotted and then jumped up and down, yes, up and down we jumped for joy."

To demonstrate the miraculous recovery and bring the story to life, the intoxicated fisherman jumped up and down on the table, leaping about with such frenetic delight that he slipped, fell, and rolled about on the floor moaning in pain. His right arm was broken.

I resolved at that very moment to postpone my journey home and travel to Soissons in hopes that the Marquis de Puységur might consent to teach me the magnetic procedures that could enable me to return to Lisbon and cure my father's paralysis.

Upon introducing myself to him as an Abbé Brahmine des Indes, the marquis, apparently intrigued by my Oriental origins, asked if the tales he had heard about the East were true, if it was so that methods for manipulations of a magnetic fluid had been used for thousands of years in the East Indies, if there really were charmers in Hindustan who magnetized deadly serpents, rendering them docile as they danced in Mesmeric trance. Was it true that there were fakirs and yogis who could put themselves into somnambulistic states in which they could walk through fire and over water, lie down naked on broken glass, touch their breasts with white-hot pokers, and painlessly run needles through their flesh? Was it true that in those self-induced trances there were adepts who recalled former lives and divined future ones?

"Yes," I told him, "all of that is true. What you refer to as *un fluide magnétique* they call *prana*. But because those men are Hindus I was never privy to the secrets of their magic practices, for I am a Christian, baptized in the Roman Catholic Church."

Astonished, if not amused, when, elaborating on my religious upbringing, I informed him that both my mother and father had taken Holy Orders, the marquis asked, "So nuns and priests in the Indies are permitted to have conjugal relations?"

"No, no, not at all," I answered and explained that at the time of my conception my mother was not a nun and not particularly devout. "And although he was a pious layman, my abstentious father never intended to be ordained. Although his piety included a conviction that chastity, as mastery over the most potent of passions, was an essential aspect of Christian spiritual practice, he consented, following Saint Paul's dictum that it is better to marry than to burn, to the marriage his parents had arranged for him with the parents of Rosa-Maria de Sousa. I imagine that it was his essentially ascetic proclivities that eventually caused my mother to seek satisfaction of a natural desire outside that marriage."

The marquis wanted to hear about my mother's extramarital adventures.

"Several months before gossip about her adulterous affair with Sebastião José de Cacete, the Portuguese Capitão de Corveta in charge the artillery at Fort Aguada, reached my father's ears, I was playing with some friends on Sinquerim Beach when I happened to look up at the battlements of that fort, and notice there, amidst the scores of canons, a man in a Portuguese officer's uniform with a woman who I was startled and confused to recognize as my mother. What were they doing together? Whatever it was, I sensed that it would culminate in sadness for us all.

"Capitão Cacete had been called back to Lisbon by the time my father was told, by whom I do not know, about the clandestine love affair. When, in the presence of her parents, myself, our servants, and several of our neighbors, he questioned his wife about the rumor, she confessed, fell repentantly to her knees, wept, swore to God that the liaison was long over, avowed regret, proclaimed remorse, and begged for forgiveness. Without uttering a word, my father took me by the hand, pulled me from the room, and took me from the home where I had been born to live in his parents' house in the village of Colvale.

"I imagine that it was my father's firm refusal to pardon his wife that caused my mother to turn in supplication to the only one whose love is so abundant and generous as to forgive her, He who would understand that what she had done was done for love. The love that had made her weak, she imagined, could give her, with His guidance, the strength to transform despair into joy. The love that had impelled her to sin would become, by His grace, the source of her salvation. And so she turned to Him and, in love, took the veil and lived the remainder of her life in the Convento de Santa Monica, enclosed in Christ's presence there, consecrated to Him as his penitent and obedient bride by solemn vows of silence, solitude, poverty, chastity, and perpetual prayers of adoration."

"Did you visit her there?" the marquis asked.

"I never saw my mother again in what we imagine to be real life. But, alone in bed at night, I'd pretend she was at my side and reading to me as she used to do: '*Transforma-se o amador na cousa amada,*' my mother enunciated the majestic Portuguese words arranged in richly resonant and rhythmic phrases, *'por virtude do muito imaginar.'* Such soothing sounds lulled the senses and rendered eyelids heavy. I'd blink, yawn, and yawn again as, with closing eyes I saw my bedroom slowly trance-formed into a cabin in a caravel. The bedposts were the spars and my sheet the sail of a vessel rocking out of the Mandovi's mouth into vast ocean, rocking on soporific slopes and swells of salty sea, rocking in the cadences of my mother's voice, tempered by tremolos of splashing rain, gently swaying me into reverie.

"I remember languid lullabies sung in the mother tongue: *Tori tuji prapti tunttoli na, na unni zali na, na, na, sorolina.* Konkani is a dulcet, seminal, spontaneous parlance, not learned like grandiloquent Portu-guese, but congenital, embryonic, brewed in blood. The breezes from the Western Ghats are Konkani whispers, Malabari monsoon thunder Konkani shouts. Each word of the native language was to my ear what each morsel of dodol, lusciously sticky and sumptuously sweet with coconut, jaggery, and ghee, was to my tongue: *Tuje bogor hanga konnach na mhonn. . . ."*

"And your father," the marquis asked, "What happened to your father?"

"After taking me from Candolim, my father began to read to me from the Vulgate he was diligently studying at the Seminário de Rachol in preparation for the sacrament of Holy Orders. *'Implete hydrias aqua,'* I heard Jesus say and imagined a wedding guest drinking water that had been turned into sweet wine. *'Tu autem servasti bonum vinum usque adhuc.'* My father read not to calm me, but to teach me, not to put me to sleep, but to wake me.

"After the completion of his theological studies and ordination as a deacon, my father was dispatched by the bishop of Goa to Lisbon for full ordination into the priesthood. I was fifteen years old at the time and did not want to leave Colvale. It was for no other reason than that I had fallen in love as recklessly and passionately as my mother had. It would have infuriated my father to know about it since, given his in-tention that I follow his footsteps into the Church and become a priest as well, he considered women stumbling blocks to any state of grace. *'Hi sogli baji,'* he'd say of women in Konkani. 'They are all vegetables. *Kator re baji!* Cut the vegetables!'

"If women are vegetables, I mused, I was hungry for the most luscious of all, the delectable one called Kamala, a ripe delicacy served secretly warm with the sweet creaminess of coconut milk, her words, and the tangy spiciness of chilies and ginger, her kisses."

"Tell me about her," the marquis said. "I'm very fond of love stories."

"Kamala was a servant in our home, a few years older than I and a devotee of the Hindu goddess Shanta Durga, the beautiful slayer of demons, who, as far as I was concerned, was wildly alive in her. She was a doe-eyed beauty with a plump berry of a lower lip, teeth as white as jasmine flowers blossoming in her smile, rounded pumpkin hips, and swollen breasts as firm and fragrant as any Goa summer mango.

"I followed her as she ambled with a languid swaying gait into a grove of coconut palms where she made a bed of leaves, covered it with a patch-work quilt she herself had sewn, decorated it with holy tulsi leaves, richly perfumed mogari buds and sunlight yellow shevati blossoms, and then beckoned me with a playful smile and winking eye to lie down with her.

"Enflaming me with sparkling glances, heated kisses, and feverish breath, Kamala made me understand what Saint Paul had meant by 'burn.' I was enthralled by her honeyed voice, entranced by her tender touch, and enchanted by the voluptuous perfumes of her ruddy skin and sumptuous shining hair.

"Other than such second-person singular imperatives as 'fetch, pick up, sweep, and wash,' Kamala knew hardly a word of Portuguese until I taught her phrases I ached to hear repeated: '*Eu quero você por toda a minha vida. Eu não posso viver sem você. Eu quero te tocar, abraçar você.*'

"When in our palm grove bower I kissed her with the last of countless desperate goodbye kisses, I could restrain neither tears nor vows to always love her. When I promised to return to her someday, she smiled with the delight and pride of being able to respond with a Portuguese phrase that I had taught her: '*Eu sonho com você.*'

"I wrote to her from Lisbon in Konkani. '*Dispedir korchea velar kosolo akant amcher ailo, kuddinto atmo asleari muzo, kedinch mogu visrum nuzo, te tuj' inocente kallzacho.*' In translation it loses the amorous anxiousness insinuated by those repeated, embedded *k*'s—*ko, ko, ka, ku, ke, ka*: 'At the time we said goodbye we were engulfed by fear, but in whatever body my soul resides I will never forget your innocent heart.'

"There was no point in actually sending the letter, since Kamala was illiterate. But when so often she appeared to me in dreams, I'd whisper those words to her and in embrace we'd fall asleep and in that sleep we'd dream we were embracing in Colvale, and in a dream within that dream within a dream we embraced in Lisbon."

"And what brought you from Lisbon here to Paris, Monsieur Faria? Why did you not return to the Indies?"

"After my father's ordination, he was assigned to an ecclesiastical post in Rome," I explained, "and despite my entreaties that he let me return to Goa, he insisted that I accompany him and that I study theology at the Propaganda Fide College there. I planned to return to Goa as soon as I completed my degree.

"When my father had a stroke that paralyzed him, the bishop who supervised his work in Rome sent us back to Lisbon so that he might be cared for by the nuns of the Catholic Hospital Real de Todos os Santos. That's where we were when news came of the rebellion in Goa against Portuguese rule. Because Goans in Lisbon were being arrested on suspicion of aiding and abetting the plot to overthrow the colonial government, I came here to France, initially to Marseille where, while waiting for a ship to take me home to the Indies, I heard about you, Monsieur le Marquis, and about the extraordinary therapeutic powers of animal magnetism. I want to learn from you so that I can return to Lisbon and cure my father."

The marquis prefaced a cordial agreement to tutor me in the mesmeric arts and sciences with the caveat that not all people have the ability to control the flow of magnetic fluid. "But we shall see, Monsieur l'Abbé de Faria, if you have that power."

The marquis taught me the theory and practices he had learned from his master, Anton Mesmer of Austria. "Your father's paralysis results from an imbalance, maladjustment, or interruption of an invisible magnetic fluid that pervades all living beings and nonliving things, all things including the earth, planets, and stars. It is the force that holds the moon in its orbit around the earth, and the earth in its orbit around the sun. Since your own body contains this ethereal magnetic substance, passing your hands over a patient can rebalance or correct the flow of the body's magnetic fluid. It is crucial that there be a close harmonious connection between you and your subject, so that the patient, once magnetized and somnambulistic, is entirely subject to your will. I have discovered that it is very often the case that the somnambule can diagnose and prescribe treatment for his or her own malady."

I had been studying with the marquis for some months, observing his methods, asking him both practical and theoretical questions, and practicing magnetic passes over beakers of water, iron rods, and branches of laurel, when finally he announced that he believed I was ready to work with a patient.

A groom employed by the marquis, the father of a little girl named Seraphine, brought the child to the marquis in hopes that he might cure the seizures which were so violent as to threaten her life. The marquis asked me to be seated and then directed the father to place the convulsing girl on my lap.

"Put your arms around her," my teacher instructed, "and hold her tightly so as to suppress her thrashing about. Cradle her firmly and yet gently, and concentrate entirely on holding her in such a way as to calm and relax her. Feel what she is feeling. Concentrate on that feeling and nothing else."

Closing my eyes as I had watched the marquis do on so many occasions, and holding the girl securely in my arms, squeezing her legs between my legs to arrest their relentlessly restless kicking, I, conscious of the heat of her body, gradually began to feel it merging with the heat of my own flesh, and then that heat seemed to become a fluid seeping from me into her, mixing with her fluid, and then flowing back into me as our fluid, back and forth in a rhythmic, magnetic ebb and flow. She was held close to me by the same force that holds the moon in its orbit around the earth. Her muscles began to relax as her breath became progressively more steady and regular as she went deeper and deeper, more and more relaxed, into a somnambulistic trance. And in that sleeplike state her body was so magnetically balanced that upon being awakened she was calm, perfectly at ease, and never again had another convulsion.

It seemed obvious to me that the *spiritus sancti* of the theologians in Rome is nothing but the magnetic fluid that I had myself just felt flowing from within me into the child, and from her back into me again. And what we imagine to be God, I reasoned, is the absolute manifestation of that universal fluid that once upon a time was made flesh in Christ.

I remained in Soissons for several months, assisting the marquis in the treatment of the many patients who came to the estate with hopes of being redeemed from their sundry illnesses. Once I was assured that I had acquired a mastery over the flow of magnetic fluid, I prepared for my return to Portugal to deliver my father from paralysis. And then I would go home to Goa. It was on the eve of my departure from France that the self-inducted soldiers of the Revolution raided the estate of the marquis and arrested both of us in accordance with the *Loi des suspects* that sanctioned the arrest of anyone who, in the opinion of the empowered rabble, had not consistently demonstrated sufficient allegiance to the Revolution. This included many aristocrats like the marquis and, like myself, many foreigners without citizenship certificates. The marquis was imprisoned in the Bastille, and I was held in the Chateau d'If.

Because it was impossible to distinguish between night and day in the cramped and windowless oubliette, I lost all sense of time. And with that loss the demarcations between reality and illusion were blurred. And in that blur, I began to imagine that I was imagining the oubliette. I was imprisoned in a trance. In that case, I realized, there was no need to try, like some character in a novel, to dig my way out, scratching away night after night at mortar and stone with a stolen spoon. Rather than that, it occured to me, I might use the mesmeric skills I had acquired to self-induce a lucid trance within my trance, and in that trance to stand up, to envision a rope, and use that rope to scale the wall up to the door of my cell. The power of concentration unlocks and opens doors. I saw myself crawling onto the landing of a staircase that winds upward and out of the castle.

I began to climb, higher and higher, counting as I ascended: One . . . two . . . three. . . .

Yes, count: one . . . two . . . three . . . and open your eyes.

SESSION SIX: *Trance-Substantiations*

At the end of her tale, Mrs. De Souza insisted that the writer try the sweet bebinca for dessert, noting that Abbé Faria's mother was credited for the original recipe for that pastry. "You are tasting the taste that young José Custodio so often tasted. Imagine that!"

After the lunch at Fort Aguada, Mrs. De Souza took the writer to a house in a clearing at the end of a rubbled and puddled path, a dilapidated single-story Indo-Portuguese *bangalô* with rain-stained, whitewashed walls and crackled, reddish laterite steps leading up to a dusty pillared *balcõe*, its ornamental window shutters closed, its warped and rotting sheesham double doors bolted shut, and its painted blue concrete benches water-stained and fading into dappled gray.

On an eave beneath the drab, red Mangalore tile roof there was a weather-worn memorial plaque: LOCAL ONDE NASCEU AOS 31 DE MAIO DE 1756 O GENIAL CRIADOR DO HYPNOTISMO CIENTIFICO, PE JOSE CUSTODIO DE FARIA CONHECIDO NO MUNDO CULTO POR ABADE FARIA. There were no signs of life in this scene other than the woman from Goa, the writer from abroad, a flock of scavenging crows, a pack of ravening dogs, and a lone sow with muddied, bloated teats hungrily rooting in a pile of refuse.

"Once upon a time," began the preface to Mrs. De Souza's story as, followed by the writer up the stairs onto the unswept veranda, she made herself comfortable in the shade there, "this was the home of one of my ancestor, Senhor Alexandre de Sousa. He lived here with his wife, Dores-Renata, his daughter, Rosa-Maria, her husband, Caetano Vitorino de Faria, and their only child, José Custodio. Both the De Sousas and the Farias were descendants of orthodox Saraswat Brahmins who, despite their conversion to Catholicism, retained many of the customs and manners of their Hindu forebears. See that ornamental planter there in front of the house? It's an altar for Tulsi, deified basil, a bush that is venerated and cared for as a manifestation of the goddess.

"It is probable that, just as they maintained their caste status and respect for that Hindu deity, the Goan Catholics of the time would not have relinquished a native worldview in which it is generally assumed that souls transmigrate from one lifetime to another.

"The Government Department of North Goa Planning and Development donated this house to Provedoria, the Institute for Public Assistance to the Destitute, to be used as a home for orphan boys. But because of the government corruption that plagues India, Provedoria lacks sufficient funds to manage the home. I have a plan to solve this situation. My idea is to turn this house into a museum and school of hypnosis dedicated to the memory of Abbé Faria. In order to institute this, I have written letters of proposal to the Minister of Culture, the Minister of Tourism, and the Minister of Planning and Development, with copies of each sent to the Director of Provedoria. In these I have disclosed that, in my past life regression hypnotherapy with the internationally eminent Dr. Patanjali Mishra of the Faria Institute of Holistic Vedic Hypnosis and Trace-Personal Psychology, I discovered that I myself was once, in a previous lifetime, José Custodio de Faria, and that as such I have vivid memories of my childhood here in Candolim. Included with those letters were copies of an affidavit, personally signed by Dr. Mishra, attesting to the fact I truly once was Abbé Faria. I have informed the government ministers that, having retired from my job at the Our Lady of the Rosary High School for Girls, I would have the time, for which I would ask no remuneration, to supervise a restoration of this house, to refurbish and furnish it exactly as it was in the eighteenth century when I lived here in the body of Abbé Faria. Once restored, I have explained to them, it would be the ideal place for an institution dedicated to preserving and perpetuating the legacy of Goa's most illustrious son, the father of scientific hypnotism. Tourists, history buffs, scholars like yourself, and all people interested in hypnosis would flock here from all around the globe. And the revenue, raised by the sale of tickets of admission as well as by charitable donations, could be given to Provedoria. Additional funds for the maintenance of the museum could be provided by the sale of souvenirs—Abbé Faria coffee mugs, T-shirts, and postcards; miniature reproductions of Kamat's statue of him; portraits of him by local artists; and books about him, including, of course, the one you are currently writing. I have not as yet, I am disappointed to report, received any response to my letters. I realize that this might be because these government bureaucrats do not believe, despite Dr. Mishra's affidavit and endorsement as a medical scientist, that I really once was the abbé. That is why it is so important for me to tell you my story. I do so with the hope that once your book is published I will have the credibility necessary to put my plan into action.

"Your book should correct many of the things that have been written about the abade, things that are drastically misleading, such significantly false assertions, for example, that he was a teacher of philosophy at a lycée in Marseille, that he frequented the gaming halls of the Palais Royale, and that he made a fool of himself in a botched attempt to use magnetism to kill a canary at a dinner party in Paris. People believe that because of Chateaubriand's memoirs. But Chateaubriand was, among other things, both a diplomat and a novelist, and we know that neither diplomats nor novelists can be trusted to tell the truth. In actual fact, not only did the canary, as I remember the evening at chez la Marquise de Custine, become cataleptic under Faria's influence, but Madame Custine's lap dog was also entranced. After making a series of rhythmic circular passes with my hands in front the animal's face, I pointed to a silk pillow, uttered 'meow, meow, meow,' and all at once, the pup, obviously imagining that pillow was a cat, barked, leapt from Madame Custine's lap to attack the pillow and rip it into shreds.

"Perhaps the most misleading of all the misconceptions about Faria is the assumption, based on the fact that he was called abade, that he was a Roman Catholic priest. As you no doubt surmised from the story I told you over lunch, he resisted his father's attempts to convince him to take Holy Orders. During the eighteenth century in Goa, the title 'abade' was a hereditary honorific bestowed by an archbishop on laymen who were descendants, like both the De Sousas and the Farias, of particularly distinguished orthodox Brahmin families. As such, high-caste Saraswat Brahmins, in their conversion to Christianity, did not lose the titular prestige they had enjoyed in the community as Vedic priests and scholars. The pews in the front of the churches were reserved for those commendatory abades and their families. I would imagine that maintaining the title in Paris enhanced the mystique of the Catholic Brahmin hypnotist from India. People were intrigued by him, eager to see his demonstrations and hear his story. And now, let's get back to that story."

Once Mrs. De Souza had made herself comfortable on the therapist's couch, Dr. Mishra asked if during their last session there had been any indication that Faria suffered from the migraine headaches that had transmigrated through Renée, Antero, Raisa-Maria, and Braulio to her. That there had not been, he pointed out, suggested that Faria only began to have the headaches late in life. "So," the hypnotherapist promised, "by recalling the later years of Faria's life in today's session, we should be able to discover the cause and origin of your migraines. And doing so will free you from them. After today's session you will be cured."

So eager was she for that cure, and so accustomed to induction, that the mere closing of her eyes allowed Mrs. De Souza a vivid sensation of descent into the hypnotic castle wherein her previous lifetimes were so clearly remembered. And there, in the depths of that castle, she became José Custudio the Abbé de Faria once more.

*Having become accustomed to listening to these tales, your imagination should, if you'd like it to, become more and more readily stimulated by what the tales suggest, and con*centration on what is imagined should then become more acute. The mere closing of eyelids and a few deep breaths should allow you to follow the woman from Goa down, counting backward, ninety-nine, ninety-eight, ninety-seven, down . . . down . . . soon losing count and floating six stories down into a room where Abbé Faria is waiting to tell you a story. . . .

It's a candlelit salon with a large black marble-topped table at one end and a painting on the wall behind the table, an ornately gold-framed depiction of an Oriental landscape with a procession of lavishly caparisoned elephants with turbaned maharajas in the howdahs on their back. On the wall at the other end of the room is a crucifix, a wooden body of an emaciated Christ painted ash-white, splashed with blood red, and nailed to an ebonized cross with three rusted spikes. Imagine the gaping, empty eye sockets of the skull beneath his feet.

Looking at you from across the table, the abbé is wearing a black academic robe under a darker black clerical cape. His once raven-black hair is now streaked with gray, and his face is deeply wrinkled above the brow and around the eyes. Although his thin lips suggest an ascetic constitution, the dark eyes are sensual and the sonorous voice is seductive: "I'm dying," he says.

Yes, dying. It's true. My physician prescribed *sel de Drosne*, what he poetically calls *le morphium* after the god of dreams, to relieve me of my agony. He imagines, however, that the excruciating headaches are benign somatic expressions of painful emotions aroused by the public mockery of me and the denunciations of my endeavors by both the Church and the Conseil de l'Ordre des Médecins. But I know he is wrong. I know it is symptomatic of the tumor that is rapaciously feeding upon my brain. I am certain of it and I'll tell you why.

Years ago, during my apprenticeship with the Marquis de Puységur in Soissons, it became evident to us that a few of our patients had an innate and uncanny ability when in the somnambulistic state not only to correctly diagnose their own illnesses but also to clairvoyantly diagnose the illnesses of others and to determine with extraordinary precision the outcome of those illnesses. We had several opportunities to verify this with autopsy.

One particularly psychically gifted somnambule was a mere child, a little girl named Seraphine Goéland, the daughter of a stable hand on the marquis's estate. She was the first patient I ever treated with what I, as a disciple of a disciple of Mesmer, quite mistakenly imagined to be a manipulation of magnetic fluid.

I saw her again several years later when, after being released from the Chateau d'If, I returned to Soissons to continue my work with the marquis. During my incarceration, I had imagined that if I were ever to be freed, I would return to Lisbon to treat my father for his paralysis. Upon being released from my oubliette, however, I was given a letter from Lisbon that had been delivered to the prison months before but withheld from me until my discharge. In it, Capitão General José de Cacete, Portugal's Minister of Military Justice, duly informed me that my father had been arrested on suspicion of treason shortly after my departure from Portugal and imprisoned in the Torre de São Vicente, where he died after suffering several severe strokes.

I would have returned to Goa if I could have allowed myself to imagine that Kamala, after such an extended separation with no communication between us, might still be waiting for me. I realized that even if she still loved me, her parents would surely have arranged a marriage for her long ago. And so I returned to Soissons to resume work with the Marquis de Puységur.

Both the marquis and Seraphine's father consented to allow me to experiment on the girl. Although her convulsions had been stopped, I wanted to work with her on account of her ample susceptibility, using her to formulate new methods for inducing somnambulism and to test those inductions for both rapidity and depth. Just as I had done years before, I seated the girl on my lap and held her tightly in my arms, allowing the heat of her body to merge with mine and regulating my breathing to coincide with hers, deeply in and slowly out, in and out, until I imagined my magnetic fluid beginning to flow into her, and then I'd concentrate on that fluid mingling with hers and flowing back into me, ebbing and flowing until she became cataleptic. With repeated inductions, she became more and more accustomed to the procedure and so increasingly relished the pleasure of the bodily relaxation it provided that I was able with each successive induction to entrance her more and more quickly and deeply. Soon, while just holding in her arms, I could entrance her merely with the command, "*Dormez.*" And not long after that, I was able to effect somnambulistic trance without even touching her, just by waving my hand in front of her eyes and saying, "*Dormez!*"

Seraphine was in that state, the depth of which I had just tested by piercing her palm with a needle, when a gardener from the estate arrived in what Puységur referred to as our *salle magnétique* complaining of a progressive deafness that had culminated that morning in a severe earache.

Hearing this, Seraphine suddenly sat up, opened her eyes, gazed at the man's face for a moment, and then, though still deeply entranced, spoke: "I see an abscess. If it is punctured through the nose so as to allow the pus to be discharged from the nostrils, his pain will disappear, his hearing will return, and he will live. If it is not surgically lanced, it will burst in three days and its contents will flow into his throat, causing him to choke to death." Her eyes then closed and her body slumped back into catalepsy.

Upon being wakened, the girl had no recollection of the prognostications she had made in trance.

A physician summoned by Puységur from nearby Buzancy to perform the operation prescribed by the groom's young daughter scoffed at the diagnosis, assuring us that the earache was merely the symptom of a harmless inflammation that would go away on its own with a few days of rest. The marquis trusted the doctor more than the girl, and three days later the gardener choked to death in his bed.

Three nights ago in a deep and lucid sleep, Seraphine Goéland diagnosed my brain tumor, indicated that it is inoperable, and foretold that I will die in four days.

Seraphine's visitation was as unexpected as a second coming of Christ. Other than in my tormenting dreams and irrepressibly amorous reveries, I hadn't seen her for several sorrowful years. She looked ghostly pale, but the pallor in contrast to the ripe red of her flush lips and the lush golden ginger of her hair, a loose curl of which dangled carelessly over her temple, made her all the more hauntingly beautiful.

Upon opening my door to the discovery that Seraphine was within my reach, I realized that the strenuous struggle not to love her had been in vain, that I had lost the battle with myself in the long war against love. But, despite the overwhelming tidal force of her presence, I was somehow able to restrain myself from the humiliation of bursting into tears and falling to my knees to clutch her ankles, kiss her feet, and profess my love. As much as love had promised to ennoble my heart, sanctify my soul, and bestow its abundant joy, it had more readily rendered my heart pathetic, damned my soul, and doled out its intractable misery. Despite the perverse treacheries of love, I was somehow able to control my impulses and summon the strength to pretend to be so calm as to cordially say, *"Il est agréable de vous revoir, Mademoiselle Goéland. Voulez-vous entrer?"*

It was the same thing I had said to her ten years ago when she came to my studio for the first time. The then fifteen-year-old girl had just arrived in Paris with a letter from the Marquis de Puységur in which he expressed his wish that I might be so kind as to help Seraphine settle in the city. As a favor to my mentor, I offered the pretty girl a room in my apartments on the rue de Clichy.

Seraphine had come to the capital, she explained with naive ebullience, to become an actress. While playing Joan of Arc in a pageant performed for the annual spring festival in Buzancy, she had received enough accolades from her parents as well as an impressive number of the folks of rural Soissons to allow her to imagine, like thousands of other young girls from the provinces, most of them destined to become prostitutes, that she might have sufficient talent to successfully audition for the Comédie Française.

I used my influence with both Madame Marie-Rose Sainte-Clarie la Marquise de Somme and Madame Louise-Eléonore de Sabran la Marquise de Custine to arrange an appointment for Seraphine with the scandalously illustrious Mademoiselle Raucourt, who was amusing herself at the time by auditioning debutante actresses at the venerable Parisian temple of Thespis.

At the conclusion of Seraphine's recitation of a tragic monologue from Racine's *Phèdre*, Mademoiselle Racourt wrapped her arm warmly around the girl's shoulders and coldly said, "No. It's impossible. Go back to the country, marry a farmer, and use the bit of talent you have to entertain him in his bed."

"And then, after shockingly forcibly kissing me on the lips, she heartily laughed and left me alone on the empty stage," Seraphine reported, burst into tears, and slumped into my arms for refuge from the despair of rejection. She wanted to flee Paris but could not bring herself to face the dreadful humiliation of returning home in failure.

So disturbing were her subsequent persistent fits of sobbing, self-deprecatory tirades, and even suicidal threats that I invited her to sit on my lap so that I might try to relieve her from her misery in the same manner that I had once cured her childhood seizures.

Cradling Seraphine in my arms and breathing in harmony with her, I whispered, "*Dormez*," to ease her into somnambulistic trance, calm, relaxed, and entirely under my control. I had the power to please her. It was in that moment that I was certain of something I had suspected, absolutely certain that Mesmer and his disciples, including my own mentor, Puységur, were completely mistaken, that what I had been instructed to recognize as a magnetic fluid, hers and mine mingling and flowing back and forth between us, was not some ethereal magnetic substance. No, it was quite simply love. And as such, I imagined, love was the *spiritus sancti*. I was in love with Seraphine Goéland. And I had the power to make her love me.

Based on this revelation I formulated a revisionary theory of somnambulism, a rejection of magnetic theory, a vocabulary with which to articulate it, and a plan to disseminate it to the public. I was confident that French intellectuals, philosophers, and physicians, poets and pedants, dilettantes and dabblers in the occult sciences, aristocratic and bourgeois alike, would be happy to hear denunciations of the Austrian Mesmer that did not dismiss, but rather illuminated, the intriguing phenomenon he had so flamboyantly brought to their attention. I believed that I could make somnambulism fashionable in Paris once more.

I realized that the popular success of my lectures would depend upon dramatic demonstrations of what I would call *le sommeil lucide*. I would play myself in the spectacles, *l'abbé brahmine des Indes Françaises*, adept in Oriental mystical rites and practices. And, deeply absorbed in a *sommeil lucide*, Seraphine was easily convinced to remain with me in Paris to play the *épopte*, my nubile initiate into the Greater Mysteries of antiquity. She would appear in the fluttering diaphanous Doric chiton that her mother in Soissons had sewn for her to wear at her audition as Phédre at the Comédie Française.

Seraphine was a remarkable subject, so profoundly susceptible to suggestion and so prodigiously accomplished at imagination and concentration that, when in lucid sleep, she did not flinch or even blister when I touched her breast with a white-hot poker; she did not wince or even bleed when I ran a needle through her hand; she maintained the faculty she had demonstrated years before of correctly diagnosing illnesses and predicting their outcome; with closed or blindfolded eyes she could read from a book or describe in detail a painting held up behind her. She'd become comically drunk when she drank water that I said was wine, or woefully ill if I told her it was ipecac.

Furthermore, and much to my own amazement, she seemed to understand and speak languages with which she was unfamiliar in the waking state. I discovered this quite accidentally when I absentmindedly happened to ask her in my native tongue, *"Tudo Bem?"* Seraphine spontaneously responded, *"Estou bem, obrigada."*

Supposing that perhaps she had some exposure to Portuguese pleasantries, I tested her by asking the same question in Konkani, a language I was certain no one in France could understand: *"Ko-shem-asa?"* *"Aoo tsaud kooshi,"* she answered with a perfect Malabari accent. When I asked her name, *"Tuchem naum kitay?"* I was dumbfounded by the response, *"Mojem naum Kamala."* She then recounted in Konkani that she had died of a brain hemorrhage a few months after I left Goa. Her spirit, Seraphine reported, released from the confines of Kamala's flesh, had followed me and, in the convulsing body of a child in Soissons, had finally found me. *"Dispedir korchea velar kosolo akant amcher ailo,"* she recited with tears seeping out from in between closed eyelids, *"kuddinto atmo asleari muzo, kedinch mogu visrum nuzo, te tuj' inocente kallzacho."* In Konkani, the spirit told me that she loved me.

Moved by those words, I held her close to me, kissed her neck, closed my tearing eyes and was transported back to the palm bower in Colvale where we had clung to each other in love.

Dazed upon being wakened from her lucid trance, Seraphine did not seem to be aware of what had transpired. She knew not a word of Portuguese and had never heard of the language called Konkani. Although she had no conscious memory of a rapturous union in a lush bower that had been conjured up by suggestion in my studio on the rue de Clichy, the spirit of the Goan servant girl must have been awakened in her. It was, I suspect, that spirit who prompted her to kiss me on the lips, to ask if she could move from her room into mine, and to tell me for the first time that she loved me.

Spreading word of Seraphine's amazing abilities to endure pain, see with closed eyes, diagnose diseases, and speak foreign languages in lucid sleep drew more and more curious witnesses to my demonstrations each week and made celebrities of us in Paris.

We were drinking champagne at La Procope one night in celebration of our success when she posed an intriguing question. "If in lucid sleep you told me this champagne was water, would I be able to drink the whole bottle without getting drunk?" An experiment at home that night proved that by the power of suggestion, just as Seraphine could become drunk on water she was told to be wine, so too suggestions given in lucid sleep could keep Seraphine sober no matter how much effervescent wine she consumed.

Several weeks later, Seraphine informed me she would be leaving the following day to spend the month of August with a new friend on his father's estate in Sennevoy-le-Haut in Burgundy. His name, she said, was Jules-Denis and his father, Charles Dupotet, had brought him to several of my lectures. Unbeknownst to me he had introduced himself to her after one of my demonstrations and invited her to join him on an afternoon walk in the Bois de Boulogne.

"He's absolutely mystified by our demonstrations of *le sommeil lucide*," Seraphine announced with a cheerful enthusiasm that belied any suspicion on her part that I might be jealous of the boy.

I interrupted, "You cannot go, Seraphine. No, you must not leave me. Do you understand? You will not go."

"No, I am going," she adamantly insisted. "Yes, I'm going. You cannot stop me."

"Come, Seraphine," I beckoned, preparing myself to render her compliant to my will. "Come and sit here on my lap so that we can talk about this more calmly."

"No," she snapped with uncharacteristic defiance, "No, I won't let you do it."

Raising my hand in front of her face, I commanded, "*Dormez!*"

She looked away. "No, I don't want to be controlled by you any longer. I want to be free, wide awake, and in control of myself."

"You must not leave me because I love you," I said in hopes that sentiment might be more effective than demand. "And you cannot leave me because you love me. Remember? You're in love with me. You told me you love me."

"I have been in love with you in the same way that I have been drunk on the water you gave me to drink telling me it was wine. Yes, my love for you was a drunkenness on water. It felt real but it was only imagined."

With that shattering pronouncement Seraphine made a dramatic exit, slamming the door to my studio behind her.

That was several years ago, a difficult, bitter, remorseful period during which I was defamed and denigrated, accused by the scientific community of quackery, censured by the Church for heresy, mocked as a charlatan and buffoon in both satirical theatrical farces and vulgar journalist caricatures. And, most painful of all, I did not hear from Seraphine or see her again. Not until three nights ago when, standing in the doorway by which she had left, she appeared more stunningly beautiful than I had ever imagined her to be.

"*Il est agréable de vous revoir, Mademoiselle Goéland,*" I politely said, "*Voulez-vous entrer?*"

Walking in and past me, she carelessly let her black cape slip to the floor just as a courtesan might do upon arriving in the apartment of an aristocratic client, and then turned to face me and speak with trembling lips.

"I'm sorry to visit you like this, so unexpectedly and suddenly after such a long time. Yes, very sorry, but I'm desperate. I need your help. You must help me. You're the only one who can. My head began to ache several weeks ago, and the pain has become more and more intense each day. It is now quite unbearable. And the large doses of laudanum

I've been given do nothing to alleviate the pain. I imagine you can cure me just as you did when I was a child suffering with seizures. I want to believe what I imagine. I want it to be so. Please forgive me for any sadness I might have caused you. Forgive me, and try to help me. Please, please help me."

"Sit here, Seraphine, sit on my lap," I instructed and, holding her in my arms, I felt a pleasure I had imagined would never again be felt. Asking her to close her eyes, I closed mine and, as I became conscious of the warmth of her body, it began to mingle with my own warmth. I felt the relaxation of her musculature as her breath became progressively more steady and regular. I coordinated my breath with hers to slowly and deeply breathe in and out together.

"*Dormez*," I commanded and instantly she went to a profound *sommeil lucide*. And then I asked her to reveal the cause of her headache.

"I see a malignant tumor devouring my brain. It's inoperable. I'm dying. Yes, I shall die in four days."

Placing my palm across her forehead where she had indicated the pain was most severe, I guided my *épopte*: "Concentrate on the tumor and on my open hand. Imagine that the tumor is being drawn out of you by my hand as a magnet draws on iron. Concentrate on the sensation as it emerges from your skull directly into my hand, drawn out of you and into me."

As I said this, I could not help imagining the tumor beginning to penetrate my palm. I felt it slowly moving into my wrist, gradually crawling up my arm, foraging further into my shoulder, and from there up my neck, and finally burrowing deep inside my brain. Seraphine's pain was mine.

Suddenly straightening up and opening her eyes, she stared intently at my face. "I see it," she said without a trace of emotion. "I see a malignant brain tumor. It's inoperable. You will die in four days." Her eyes closed and her head dropped forward.

Upon being wakened, dazed from lucid sleep, she had no recollection of what had transpired. She knew only that her pain was gone and I assured her that it would be gone forever.

She smiled with enormous joy, thanked me again and again, and noted that she had not doubted that I could cure her.

"*Prenez bien soin de vous, mon cher ange-guardien*," she said as she picked her cape up from the floor to wrap it snugly around her shoulders. She thanked me yet again, rose up on her toes to kiss me on each cheek, added, "*Adieu,*" and vanished.

Alone in my studio, gazing at the crucifix on the wall, wracked with pain, I regretted that I had not stopped her to disclose that I loved her enough to gladly suffer for the sake of her salvation, that indeed I did love her enough to die for her as Christ died for those would love him. Unlike Christ, I wanted her to believe, I loved her whether she loved me or not.

Opium has done nothing to alleviate my pain. The agony has been so excruciating that my impending death should rightfully be welcomed as deliverance. And yet I dread it and am horribly afraid of dying in this place so far from where I was born. I ache to return to Goa, to die only there and be buried in Candolim so that my body might be absorbed into its fertile soil.

Imagining that it might be somehow possible, I open the door to my studio eager to try to make my way home. I begin to climb the spiral staircase in hopes of making it up the one hundred and twenty steps to Goa in time, breathlessly climbing as fast as I can, desperately climbing out of Paris and past the Isle of If, hurriedly climbing from there up to Lisbon. I suddenly realize that with each step my pain diminishes and it continues to fade as I climb still higher . . . higher . . . and it has disappeared entirely by the time I hear the familiar voice: "When I count to three you will wake up feeling refreshed and rejuvenated and, having discovered the origin of your migraines, you will be free from them forever. Never again will you have another headache. Never. One . . . two . . . three . . . you can wake up now."

Yes, one . . . two . . . three. . . . and open your eyes.

"And since that moment, I've not had a single migraine," Mrs. De Souza announced with a satisfied smile. "Past life regression therapy cured me as effectively as it did Monica Bedi and Aryan Vaid on *Raaz Pichhle Janam.*"

As the writer walked with her to her car, the storyteller reflected: "You know, I can't help but wonder whether or not Seraphine Goéland became reincarnated as Ana Guilhermina da Maia, Antero Quental's wife. That would account for the poet's disclosure that his attraction to Ana was a matter of 'love at first sight.' Perhaps she was also the girl who posed for Braulio Pinto in the odalisque's turban. I can't imagine there's any way to find out if that's true, but I'd like to imagine that it is. Well, in any case, now that you've heard the real story of Abbé Faria, you can write about it in your book. Readers will appreciate it all the more for knowing it is the truth."

Although the writer doesn't believe in reincarnation and thus cannot imagine that it is possible to remember a past life, he does believe in the capacity and tendency of imagination to construct out of disparate shards of memory fantasies that are as believable as any empirical reality. And he also believes that Mrs. De Souza believes that the tale she told is true and that her account of Faria's life is, in its own way, as valid as the more authoritative biographies by Delgado, Moniz, and Vas. And so when, just before they parted company, she asked him to be completely honest with her and tell her whether or not he believed the story she had told him, he felt justified in saying "yes," he did.

To what extent and in what way, the writer had wondered throughout his sessions with Mrs. Souza, were the stories of her imagined previous lives actually a story about her real present life? Who, he was curious to know, was Mr. De Souza? Did they have a happy marriage like the one she had imagined for Antero and Ana Quental? Or had she been in some way as tormented by love as all of her female incarnations had been? But the writer did not ask. He had realized that such questions would be considered impertinent ever since the day when, sitting together near the statue of Abbé Faria, he asked Mrs. De Souza if she had children.

"Other than the fact that I have been cured of migraines by past life regression hypnotherapy," she answered, "and that in the course of that therapy I discovered that I was Abbé Faria in a previous lifetime, the personal particulars of my current life are unimportant and quite irrelevant. You are writing about Abbé Faria, not about me."

Several weeks later, the writer sits on the edge of the bed on which his listener has reclined to listen to this story. When he finishes the reading, she sits up, shakes her head and says, "I don't believe it. You made it up, didn't you? Tell me the truth."

"It is the truth," he claims. "If I were making it up, if this were a novel, Mrs. De Souza would have been beautiful and we would have had a love affair. In my fictional telling of the tales you've heard, there would have been explicit sex scenes: descriptions of Braulio making love to the girl in the odalisque's turban and Raisa-Maria watching her mother crudely and lewdly fellating a drunken client, perhaps a dwarf or a hunchback just to spice it up. My Antero Quental, after arousing the woman from Goa by reading his poetry to her, would have had sex with her on the landing of the spiral staircase outside the Café d'Esculape, and my lusty Baron Dupotet, tightly binding his hypnotized Renée with silk ropes, leather straps, and silver chains would have spanked her with a riding crop and then sodomized her. The hallowed conventions of erotica do demand some S&M. And, as the hero of my tale, Abbé Faria would have had lots of affairs, making love in Goa not just to Kamala but to many other women as well, a nun, maybe the abbess of the Convent of Santa Monica, or perhaps both of them in a ménage à trois beneath a crucifix in the convent chapel. In Lisbon, Rome, and Paris there of course would be a slew of voluptuous demimondaines, both raunchy whores and elegant courtesans, and he would use his hypnotic powers to turn countless wives, including Puysegur's and the mother of young Jules-Denis Dupotet, into adulteresses. In my version of the Faria story you would listen to rapturous descriptions of a naked Seraphine's pale breasts, the nipples hard and glowing ruby red, and her luscious loins, the pubic hair a fluffy ginger. All of this would have led up to the denouement of the frame story, a vivid description of Mrs. De Souza and me so aroused by the erotic stories of her past lives and so unable to harness desire and impulse that we could not stop ourselves from making impassioned love on the bare floor of the abandoned house in Candolim in which Abbé Faria was born. In my tale Mrs. De Souza would not have gone for past life regression therapy because of headaches but rather on account of frigidity. And the climax in Candolim would dramatize her cure. The fiction would be a lot more entertaining, more amusing and arousing, than the truth."

After pausing for a moment to consider what the writer was saying, the listener speaks seriously to him. "Actually it does seem a little strange to me that although you've met with your Mrs. De Souza at least six times, I've never been introduced to her. Why is that? You do know, don't you, that if I were to discover that you are actually having or have had an affair with her, I'd leave you? Our story would end right here. You'd have to find another listener."

"I'd stop you!" the writer protests. "I'd swear to you that there really is no Mrs. De Souza, that she's just a character I've imagined. I'd try to use hypnotism to convince you that the story of my affair with her was fiction."

After another moment of reflection, the listener allows herself to smile and then concedes, "Okay, I'll stay with you here in real life and listen to your stories on the condition that if you compose a story in which you are unfaithful to me, you will write that I leave you. In that story you are alone and have no one to read it to but yourself.

THE WRITER'S TALE

Perhaps we first met a long time ago, many years ago in a previous lifetime. Yes, I suspect that it is likely that we knew each other in Paris, or possibly Lisbon, or even here in Goa when I was Abbé Faria. That would explain your interest in him as well as my readiness to talk to you about him. And it would explain why I've trusted you, believed that you'd believe me, and thus feel comfortable telling you so many intimate things about him. I wonder who you might have been at that time.

MRS. DE SOUZA, THE LAST CONVERSATION IN GOA (2011)

Intrigued by the psychological implications and compelled by the literary potential of Mrs. De Souza's seemingly genuine conviction that under hypnosis she had been able to actually be Abbé Faria, to remember the life of another, experiencing what he had experienced, feeling what he had felt, knowing him as herself and herself as him, the writer experiments by attempting to self-induce hypnosis and, in whatever depth of trance he is able to achieve, to allow imagination to construe, out of suggestive fragments of biographical information, some of which he believes to be true and others not, a story to be written posthypnotically about an Abbé Faria who is as real, although differently so, as the abbés of Mrs. De Souza, Dr. Hedge, Johnson Eyeroor,

Alexander Dumas, D. G. Delgado, Etienne de Jouy, Egaz Moniz, Luis Vas, and others. In so doing, he encourages listeners to the tale of his Faria to imagine, in a state of concentrated relaxation, their own abbé, to trance-form the writer's Faria with sensations, images, sounds, smells, and feelings from their own banks of memory.

In preparation for going along with the writer, doing what he does, imagining what he imagines, make yourself comfortable. . . . Just as you've done for the previous tales, take a few breaths deeply in through your nostrils and let them slowly out through your mouth, letting each breath allow you to feel more and more calm and relaxed, and picture the writer. Lying in bed next to his sleeping listener, he adjusts the pillows and shifts about to find the position in which he is most comfortable. His hands rest at his sides. Candlelight, the tropical warmth of the Goan night, the sound of rain on palm and plantain leaves outside the open windows, and several glasses of cashew feni have put him at ease. Fixing his gaze upward at the spinning blades of the rhythmically wobbling ceiling fan, the writer begins to recite the lines of a conventional hypnotic induction script.

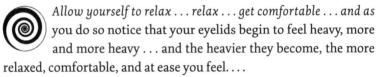 *Allow yourself to relax . . . relax . . . get comfortable . . . and as you do so notice that your eyelids begin to feel heavy, more and more heavy . . . and the heavier they become, the more* relaxed, comfortable, and at ease you feel. . . .

The writer breathes deeply in through his nostrils, and slowly out through his mouth, and again . . . deeply in and slowly out, and again . . . and with each breath his eyelids do become heavier and heavier and the voice seems disembodied, no longer his own. . . . It guides him. . . .

And now if you want to go into an even deeper state of relaxation and concentration, let your eyes close . . . yes close your eyes and feel the relaxation spreading throughout your body . . . feel it moving down into the muscles of your legs . . . feel it warming you . . . flowing down your arms into your hands . . . up your back, radiating into your shoulders . . . your neck . . . up into your face . . . every muscle of the body relaxed . . . deeply relaxed . . . warm, calm . . . relaxed. . . .

Now imagine a large salon in an apartment in Paris some two hundred years ago, its walls paneled with madder mahogany, windows draped with burgundy velvet, heavy and thick. There are thirty or forty empty café chairs facing a large table, on the black marble top of which is a black leather-bound Bible, a wine goblet, a crystal carafe of water, a long silver hat pin, a votive candle burning, and an Oriental incense burner with wisps of sandal-scented smoke curlicuing from it. Imagine it. . . .

As if in a flagrant sneer at the snowdrifts outside, the grate of a black iron stove is open, a fervid mouth, yellow flames its teeth, red coals its glowing tongue, breathing heat into the room. Feel the warmth, comfortable and calming, as you imagine the light of the stove, the candle, the brass lamps around the room, and a chandelier up above you.

Imagine a painting in an ornate gilded frame on the wall behind the table. Its details are difficult to discern at this distance and in this light, but you can just make out what appears to be an Oriental landscape with a procession of lavishly caparisoned elephants and turbaned maharajas in ornate howdahs on their back. Nubile nautch girls dancing in deshabille and servants bearing trays of fruit and flagons of wine follow. Onlookers wave peacock feathers in the air. There are palm trees in the background, beyond them gold-encrusted towers of pagan pagodas and icy Himalayan peaks in the distance.

Now look at the crucifix mounted on the wall at the other end of the room, the life-size wooden body of an emaciated Christ painted ash-white, splattered with blood-crimson on its brow, side, hands, and feet, and nailed to an ebonized cross with three large, rusted spikes. There is what appears to be a real skull beneath his feet. . . .

Turning toward the entrance to the room, picture ladies and gentlemen arriving for the evening's *divertissement. C'est le beau monde*: aristocrats and wealthy bourgeoisie, military officers, several renowned courtesans, a few painters, a couple of playwrights, and some poets of course, a physician, a priest, a judge, a diplomat perhaps, and a professor or two. . . . Watch them entrusting hats, gloves, overcoats, and capes to a black African boy in Oriental livery and hear murmured French cordialities as the spectators are ushered to their seats. There's a scuffle of chairs and boots. In the muffled muttering hear here and there a *oui*, a few *mais nons*, some *bien surs* for sure, a laugh or two, a cough, a "*shhh.*" Shhh. . . .

Imagine some of them in particular, determining for yourself what each of them is wearing, deciding whether they are tall or short, gaunt or stocky, young or old, rendering their complexions, the colors of their hair or styles of their wigs, construing their postures and demeanors, and lending expressions to their faces. They are yours to conjure up one by one:

Imagine Faria's patron, Madame la Marquise de Custine, who witnessed the guillotining of her husband some years ago . . . picture her eyes. . . .

Imagine a battle-weary General François-Joseph Noizet just back from Hungary and here to learn techniques of somnambulistic induction . . . picture his uniform, his medals, his boots. . . .

Imagine the sculptor François Rude, whose liberal passions have been so blatantly articulated in his monumental bronze portraits of Napoleon, unabashedly here with his mistress. . . . Picture his hands. . . .

Imagine the librettist, journalist, and social satirist Etienne de Jouy, who, convinced as he is that le magnétisme is quackery, is here to write a lampoon of tonight's demonstration for the Gazette de France. . . . Picture the flamboyant gestures with which he greets La Marquise de Custine. . . .

Imagine the champion of Bourbon restoration and friend of Louis XVIII, Monsieur Charles Dupotet, Seigneur de La Chapelle et de Sennevoy, here with his young son Jules-Denis. . . . Does the boy resemble his father? . . . Why are they here tonight? . . .

Imagine the venerable physician Horace Bianchon of the Académie Royale de Médecine, here with his wife. . . . Is she young . . . pretty? . . . Does she love her elderly husband? . . .

Imagine the aged actress Mademoiselle Raucourt, whose beauty, talent, and scandalous love affairs with women have made her so notorious in Paris, here because of an obsession with all things occult. . . . Picture lips that have kissed so many mouths. . . . Picture hands that have caressed so many limbs. . . .

Imagine them and others too, whoever you would like be here, friends or acquaintances, historical or fictional characters . . . it's up to you . . . and imagine yourself among them . . . yes, picture yourself here. . . .

Scanning the people gathered in this room, the writer imagines a woman from Goa in the back, her henna-black hair cropped short,

wearing a light-blue floral print salwar kameez. And over there he no-
tices his listener and her eyes are closed. . . .

He imagines taking a seat next to a woman whose neck, shoulders,
and bosom are modestly concealed by layers of organdy and lace.
Picture dark, wide-open eyes, dark with desperation and wide-open
with yearning. He gives her both a grand name—Madame Marie-Rose
Sainte-Claire la Marquise de Somme—and a sad story: she's here hoping to be assured that *le somnambulisme* can cure what medicines have
not, and that by initiating her into its mysteries, Abbé Faria might
help her. Madame la Marquise de Somme would be rather beautiful if
only it could be imagined that she is smiling.

While waiting for Faria's entrance, take another breath deeply in
and slowly out, and again . . . again . . . with each breath allowing yourself to see the room more and more vividly, to feel the warmth of the
stove and of the bodies gathered here, to hear the whispers and smell
the scent of sandalwood incense burning. . . .

Just now, if you look toward the doorway again you can, if you wish,
see the Abbé enter with his head lowered, slowly walking toward the
table at the front of the room, followed by a girl with ribboned ring-
lets of ginger hair, wearing a short-waisted diaphanous Doric chiton,
fluttering loose, white and light, exposing her pale neck, supple shoulders, lithe arms, and, to the degree that decency barely allows, her
powdered soft bosom. Remember her? She takes a seat next to the
hypnotist.

He wears the black robe of a doctor of philosophy under an open,
black-collared clerical cape. There are black streaks in the long flow of
his gray hair. His face, glowing darkly in this light, is deeply wrinkled
above the brow and around the eyes. Although his thin lips suggest
an ascetic constitution, the large eyes, surveying the room, are those
of a sensualist. They stop to stare at you. Look into those eyes to get a
feeling of who he is. . . .

His voice is seductively sonorous, but he speaks so softly that it's
hard to make out what he's saying. It seems to be French, but the
strong foreign accent makes it all the more difficult to understand.
It's something about the soul being bonded with the body through
the blood, and something about the thinness of that blood facilitating
somnambulistic transport. The words *sommeil, lucidité, esprit, intuition,*

conviction, and *imagination* are repeated again and again. In lucid sleep, he proposes, the soul, freed from the body, experiences transcendental realities and gains insights into eternal truths.

The monotony of the lecture, warmth of the room, the hour of the night and dimness of the light, cause eyelids to droop, mouths to yawn, heads to nod, shoulders to slump.

There's a protracted silence. . . .

And now, finally, the demonstration.

Placing a hand gently on his assistant's shoulder, the abbé encourages the girl to make herself comfortable, to be at ease, calm, relaxed, and to breathe slowly and deeply in and out. Her hands rest lightly on the arms of the chair.

"Fix your eyes on the flame of the candle," *le concentrateur* says. "*Concentrez-vous, Seraphine*," he urges and repeats it: "*Concentrez-vous*." Picture the flicker of the flame and concentrate on it . . . listen to the sound of my voice, only my voice . . . and concentrate.

The eyelids of the abbé's subject flutter. When she yawns it prompts several spectators to yawn as well, and that, in turn, causes still others to do so. It's difficult to suppress a yawn . . . if you yawn you will notice that you become even more deeply relaxed and as you relax you may yawn again. . . .

"Heavy, deep, asleep," the abbé whispers, pauses, and then commands, "*Dormez, Seraphine. . . . Dormez. . . . Dormez.*"

The girl's head drops forward, shoulders slump, and breathing is visibly more deep and rhythmic.

"Her body is asleep," the abbé informs us, "but the soul of the *épopte* is awake, wide awake, and the mind is concentrated on whatever is suggested. *C'est le sommeil lucide.*"

When the abbé suggests that the room is cold and getting colder and colder, so cold that icicles hang from the chandelier, the girl begins to shiver. Her teeth chatter. And you too may begin to feel a chill in the room. . . .

Now the abbé suggests that the stove has been rekindled and the room is warming up, getting warmer, warmer . . . now hot . . . soon so hot that the somnambule pants and wipes the perspiration from her face with the hem of her dress. And you too may feel the room becoming warmer. . . .

The abbé opens the Bible on the table and points to a passage which his somnambule reads with closed eyes: *"Tu autem servasti bonum vinum usque adhuc."* She translates the Latin of the Vulgate back into the Gospel Greek: *"Sy teterekas ton kalon oinon heos arti."* And that into French: *"Vous avez gardé le bon vin jusqu'à present,"* and then, as commanded, into languages that in the waking state, it is claimed, she does not know: Italian (*"Hai conservato il buon vino fino ad ora"*), Portuguese (*"Mas vocês guardaram o melhor para o fim"*), English ("You have kept the good wine until now"), and an Indian language (*"Tukare asa dovola boro soro jevalya upran"*). "Konkani," Faria explains, "my mother tongue."

Pouring water from the crystal carafe on the table into a wine goblet and offering it to the girl, the abbé demonstrates how Jesus performed the miracle at Cana: "I have saved the good wine for you to drink. See in the cup a ruby redness rich with reflections of violet. . . . And now, breathe in, deeply in, the fragrance of ripe black currants. . . . And now, take a small sip and imagine the soft, supple sweetness on your tongue. Taste a delicate spiciness . . . another sip, and another. . . . Drink, Seraphine, and with each sip you become more and more lightheaded . . . lighthearted . . . another sip and you are feeling a bit drunk, pleasantly drunk, happily drunk, yes, very happy. . . ."

The somnambule smiles.

"So happy, so tipsy that it makes you laugh."

The girl's giggle causes the spectators laugh as well.

"Silence," the hypnotist orders and both the girl and the audience obey.

The subject is told to extend her right arm and open her hand. Picture her, expressionless, passive, lips parted, breathing deeply, eyes closed, arm outstretched, hand open. Taking the long silver hatpin from the table, and holding it up so that it glistens ominously, the concentrator tells the girl that her hand is completely numb, entirely insensitive to all sensation. "You feel nothing. Nothing at all," he suggests as slowly he pushes the pin into her palm, turning it slowly, forcing it deeper and deeper until you see it emerge from the back of her hand. She does not flinch. And there is no blood.

The abbé removes the pin from the girl's hand, sets it back on the table and looks directly at you. Imagining that you are not deeply enough absorbed in lucid sleep to truly believe in what you are seeing, he approaches you to help you realize a deeper hypnotic state.

As he speaks to you, concentrate on his words. Hear nothing else . . . only his voice . . . my voice . . . listen: "Imagine the candle on the table burning . . . imagine its flickering flame . . . and imagine its white wax melting, dripping down the candle . . . melting . . . melting . . . as you watch candle becoming smaller and smaller drifting deeper and deeper into a state of tranquility . . . deeper into a peaceful sleep . . . deeper. . . . Sleep. . . . Sleep. . . . In the depths of this deeper and more lucid sleeplike trance you can, if you wish, feel that you really are in this room. You can feel its warmth and vividly see the dark wood paneled walls. . . .

Notice now that the spectators are leaving, slowly, silently, as if entranced, walking toward the doorway, out of the room, into dreams of their own. . . .

Only the Marquise de Somme and Abbé Faria remain. They are seated across from each other at the black marble–topped table. The marquise, unable to imagine that you, the omniscient listener, can hear the urgency and despair so resonant in her voice, is speaking. Listen to her:

"I appeal to you both as a magnetizer and a member of Société médicale de Marseille, an abbot of the Church and also, I am told, one familiar with Oriental healing procedures. I hope that you might be able to help me. I'm desperate. The most esteemed physicians of Paris— Rousset, Récamier, and Bianchon—have failed me. The Duchesse de Langeais assures me that she was effectively treated with magnetic therapy by the Marquis de Chastenet de Puységur for a condition similar to my own. But the marquis has retired from Paris to his estates in Soissons and, according to the Duchesse, is no longer administering magnetic therapy. You were, I understand, his assistant. Is that not so? Will you help me? Can you? I want to become as insensible to pain as was the young lady into whose hand you inserted a pin this evening. Please listen to me, please.

"Each month with the onset of what my mother called *les fleurs*, but what are more like flames than flowers to me, I experience the excruciating pain of Eve's curse, a persistent agony that begins even before the first discharge of blood. It is as if a barbed spear, its tip white-hot, is being rammed violently into my womb, brutally twisted around inside of me, ferociously thrust in and out, churning, scouring, shredding, and blistering my entrails, scorching my uterus with a blaze that burns down from my pelvis into my cramping legs, and swelters up my spine into my head. The torture continues as long as I am unclean. I am confined to a bed that might as well, for all I suffer, be the rack. Copious doses of laudanum only make me vomit. I scream and moan, writhe, convulse, and want to die.

"Please, Monsieur l'Abbé, please try, if you can, to deliver me from this misery. I menstruated for the first time on the night my father was executed at the guillotine by Robespierre. It came later for me than for most girls. I was fifteen years old. It was terribly painful from the beginning and became all the more so with each subsequent period. I live each month in dread of the next sign of blood.

"My mother assured me that this would pass once I was married and in a position to fully enjoy the pleasures of womanhood. But that was not so for me. When, on my wedding night, the marquis embraced me for the first time, the pain was even more intense than my monthly anguish. While warning me that the first experience of carnal intimacy might be unpleasant, my mother had promised that, with each repetition of it, the discomfort would diminish, soon disappear, and that I would eventually come to enjoy intercourse and, on account of the pleasure it would afford me, would even some day desire it. But that was not the case. No. The pain of copulation became worse and worse each time, so terribly unendurable that, after no more than a month or so of marriage, I insisted on ending our physical relationship. The marquis consented to honor my abstinence on the condition that, while maintaining manners and behavior in public that would create the impression that our marriage was in all ways felicitous, I would allow him whatever amorous adventures he might arrange. I was relieved to agree to that and so thankful to terminate physical intimacy with him that I often hosted his sundry mistresses in our home. But while spared the pain of intercourse, I still suffer each month to such a degree that I recently tried to convince Dr. Bianchon to consent to performing a surgical removal of my uterus. But, informing me of the high mortality rate in such operations, he refused and has offered me no more consolation than a reminder that at some point as I get older I will naturally cease to menstruate. But I am not yet thirty years old. It could be many years until I am spared this suffering. And so I am turning to you. Will you try to help me? Do you think you can?"

"Come to me," the abbé says, "at the onset of your next menstruation. Come to me in pain, and you will be cured. Believe in that. You must believe in me."

Imagine that all the wax has melted, the candle gone out, and it is dark in the room. Take another breath, a deep breath slowly in . . . slowly out . . . and again . . . and again, deeper and deeper with each breath.

Understand that some time has passed, a few days, a week or so, whatever you suppose. And imagine the room again softly illuminated by brass lamps and warmed by the stove. Perhaps you smell the faint scent of kerosene, coal, and a lingering trace of sandalwood.

Imagine the marquise again, this time lying on her back on a down mattress that has been placed on the marble-topped table and draped with a soft cover of black wool. Following Faria's instructions she has removed her gloves, shoes, bonnet, shawl, and the quilted russet pelisse in which she arrived. She's wearing a cloud-white muslin day chemise. She winces, grimaces, and moans. Her fists are clenched.

The hypnotist begins the induction by asking the marquise to look directly into his eyes, to fix her eyes there and to try, despite the pain, to concentrate on his gaze and voice.

"*Concentrez-vous,*" he commands, and repeats it. "*Concentrez-vous.*" Concentrate. Imagine it: bringing his lips close to her face, he blows gently on her cheek. . . .

"*Dormez,*" he orders and repeats it. "*Dormez! Dormez dans un sommeil lucide.*"

Eyelids close as hands open . . . breathing becomes deeper and more regular. Listen to the moans becoming softer and softer and longer and longer apart. Watch as limbs become more and more relaxed. . . .

"While the anguished body sleeps," the concentrator suggests, "the soul, wide awake, lucid, and unburdened, is released."

The marquise feels disembodied. She sees herself on the table, sees that her eyes are closed, sees that her body is naked and her menstrual belt has been removed.

Imagine the ruddy hand, long fingers extended, coming to rest on the pale flesh of the lower belly, just above the patch of auburn hair, and listen to the ethereal voice: "The pain that had radiated out from the pelvis is drawn back to its source by this hand as iron filings are drawn to a magnet. The filings are pulled from the head down the spine, pulled up the legs, pulled from all parts of the body back into the womb. The uterus is hot, so hot that the filings melt into a molten ball. And now the body is ready to expel it. Legs open, spreading wider apart, wider . . . wider . . . as the body pushes, pushes . . . harder . . . harder. . . . And there, there, it comes out of you. There!"

The marquise hears a scream as the body releases the tar-black egg of anguish into the hands of the healer. As he disposes it into the open stove, she sees an explosive flash of flames, hears a thunderous roar . . . and now you may hear soft sighs.

The hand returns to slowly, rhythmically, gently rotate over the wan belly, down, moving down and up each leg in turn, around and around, and then across the stomach to one breast, there around and around, then back down the torso, around, around, and up again to the other breast, around and around, up and down, and up again to lightly caress the neck, to tenderly touch each cheek and then the lips. As dark fingers come to rest on the pale belly, the marquise concentrates on words slowly, softly spoken:

"Where there was pain, pleasure germinates. The pleasure swells gently, warm and soothing, to fill the womb. The body feels the pleasure following the hand, feels it seeping down the thighs, into the knees, down the calves, into each foot, each toe, now flowing back up the legs, feels it pulsating in the pelvis, seeping from there into the stomach, up into the breasts, the neck, the cheeks. And now the soul, for the sake of pleasure, returns to the body. Come back into the sleeping body. Come back."

The marquise feels a rhythmic throbbing of warm pleasure that begins gently, becoming more rapid, gently becoming stronger, more undulant . . . more . . . and more . . . a wild quake and ecstatic pounding of pleasure, more . . . still more, and more . . . and then the sudden eruption. . . . Body and soul moan with bliss and then sigh with joy as the marquise falls into deep and peaceful slumber. . . .

"When you awaken," the abbé suggests, "you will not feel any pain at all. You will understand and be confident and pleased that you have been cured. Never again will you dread menstruation. You will believe that the blood signals a release of tension around the uterus, and you will be eager for the pleasure that such release affords you. No longer will you dread your husband's embrace. No, you will yearn for the delight that you will derive from it. Where there has been pain, there will only be pleasure. When you awaken you will feel rested, refreshed, and well. You will wake up on the count of three. One . . . two . . . three . . . wake up. Yes, wake up and open your eyes."

Yes, open your eyes.

Upon hearing the abbé's command the writer's eyes automatically open. And a few nights later when he reads the end of the tale he has written to his listener, she opens her eyes at the same moment in this story that the writer and the marquise open theirs, at the same moment, the writer imagines, that you have opened yours.

THE READER'S TALE

Faria noticed that both the hypnotizer and the hypnotized play up to each other as if putting on a show.
MIKHAIL BUYANOV, *CHILD PSYCHIATRY AND YOU* (1989)

In finishing the composition of a story and allowing someone to read or hear it, the writer abdicates all rights to an exclusive understanding or evaluation of that tale. Authorial ideas, intentions, and notions of accomplishment are beside the point. It is the prerogative of each reader or listener to establish a meaning of the story.

"A week or so later," the writer tells the listener a week or so later, "the marquise returns to the abbé's salon. I've written the story but instead of reading it to you, I'd like you to read it to me so that you, the listener, become the reader so that I, the writer, can be the listener.

"In so doing I'm disowning the tale, giving it to you in order to hear it trance-formed by your voice, to be lulled by the voice of another deeply enough into a hypnotic state so as to imagine that you are its source."

The active reader and passive listener, hypnotist and hypnotized, agent and subject, are trance-posed.

Reclining on the bed, the writer, handing this story over to the new reader in preparation for becoming the listener, raises an arm so that his fingers are pointing toward the ceiling to ready himself for the conventional arm-drop hypnotic induction.

Do the same, dear reader. Yes, pass this book to your listener to turn that listener into our reader and you into the listener.

Change places.

And now lift your hand up, above your head, toward the ceiling as the new reader begins.

Look at your raised hand and concentrate on it. You may wish to continue looking at it with your eyes open or, if you prefer you may close your eyes and visualize it. In either case as you fix your gaze upon it you'll soon notice that your arm begins to feel heavy.... The longer you concentrate on your raised hand, the heavier your arm becomes ... feel it becoming heavier ... and heavier.... You will not go into a deep state of relaxation until your arm has come all the way down to rest at your side. Continue to concentrate on that hand ... concentrate ... and notice that your arm is becoming heavier and heavier ... so heavy that it begins to come down ... heavier ... slowly coming down ... down ... slowly ... and as it comes down it feels even more heavy, heavier and heavier with each breath you take. ... Take a deep breath and feel how heavy your arm is becoming ... it's coming down ... down ... and when it comes all the way down to finally rest at your side, it will allow you to go into a deeper state of relaxation ... becoming even heavier ... heavier ... and coming down ... down ... deeper and deeper down ... deeper into a lucid sleep in which, when your arm rests comfortably at your side, you will be able, if you wish to play along, to imagine you are the Abbé Faria of this tale. Imagine me, here with you, recognizing me and remembering my voice . . . the voice of the Marquise de Somme. Remember? Dress me tonight as you'd like to imagine I'm dressed. What is the color of my gown? What jewelry am I wearing, and how is my hair arranged? It's up to you. . . . Can you smell my perfume? Imagine a fragrance that's pleasing to you. . . . Look into my eyes and listen to me . . . please. . . .

"Yes, please listen to me. And help me . . . you must help me. You must because of the part you've played in what has happened to me. . . . It's not your fault of course, but I do hope you will feel some responsibility or at least some compassion and help me. Let me confess my sins to you . . . sins . . . yes, terrible mortal sins for which, if you do not help me, I shall certainly and quite justly suffer for all eternity in Hell. Innocent though your intentions may have been, you were instrumental in my . . . fall, yes, fall . . . I would not have the courage or immodesty to speak of what I have done, or to divulge what I have become, to anyone but you . . . you as the man who has done this to me. Don't misunderstand me, no . . . I do not blame you, no, it is I who have sinned. It was not your fault . . . no . . . I accuse not you but only myself of the mortal sin of lust, the sins of fornication and adultery . . . sins I have committed in both thought and action every day and night since I was last here. In both my waking life and in my dreams I have sinned again and again without hesitation or regret. . . . I have sinned eagerly, ecstatically . . . yes . . . thrilled and transported by sin, oh God . . . my God, oh the rapturous sins for which I'll suffer in Hell if you do not help me. I've come to you with the hope that by once again magnetizing me you might instill in me the resolve in a lucid sleep to sin no more . . . just as you delivered me from pain, so now you must redeem me from iniquity . . . cure me of wantonness. . . . I pray that, after listening to my confession, you will grant me penance and absolution . . . and that you will use your magnetic powers to undo what has been done. . . . I must tell you everything . . . please, listen to me. . . . Ever since being treated by you, I have been a stranger to the pain that had since adolescence caused me to abhor my womanhood . . . the pain that had so demonically haunted me, the agony that had caused me to refuse my husband's embraces . . . the pain that had made me chaste. I turned to you . . . and you cured me. It seemed miraculous. . . . The pain was gone. But then, on my return home from here, that night the rhythmic bounce of my carriage on the cobble stones, aroused a pleasant feeling in my loins and a curiosity as to the possibilities of intensifying it. Although I was still bleeding, I was in no way tormented . . . no, on the contrary, I felt the pleasure of it, pleasure in the warm pulsation and moist swelling and . . . I could not resist the temptation . . . I lifted my coat, dress, and underskirts and began to massage myself, at first very gently, tenderly caressing that part of myself that had formerly been the focus of anguish . . . slowly at first, rhythmically, then more vigorously . . . ardently and faster . . . harder and faster . . . faster . . . faster . . . and then, all of sudden, there was a tumultuous explosion of exquisite bliss, followed by a soothing warmth radiating throughout my entire body, a calm pleasure to which you had introduced me in lucid trance. . . . And as the anguish of conjugal intercourse had been far more excruciating than my monthly pain, so I was about to discover, the pleasure of sexual union was even more intensely glorious than my private pleasure. I can think of nothing but that feeling. It is never ever enough. The fading of the pleasure made me crave its repetition. In defiance of the transience of the glorious sensation, I could not restrain my fingers from frantically rubbing, desperately pressing and pushing to invoke another moment of the convulsive pleasure when suddenly the carriage stopped and, opening the door for me, Valentin, a sturdy young coachman from Picardy recently hired by my husband, gasped at the sight of his ladyship reclining on the seat of the carriage with her private parts exposed. 'Come in,' I heard myself command. 'Come into the cab. Valentin, come into me. Hurry, hurry, come in!' . . . Oh God, I committed the mortal sin of adultery, and have committed it again and again . . . can I ever be forgiven? . . . The penetration which had previously, every time since an excruciating nuptial deflowering, made me suffer, enthralled me with delirious delight. I was transported by the feeling of undulant hips pounding between my gaping thighs, the swelling, burrowing, fervent thrusts and heated throb, smelling the simmering ooze, bubble and drip of sex, the ardent palpations of engorged flesh, hearing the passionate pant, moan, grunt, the climactic screech of pleasure, a sigh, and then the beatific silence . . . oh . . . oh my God, I have sinned and relished sin's sweetness. . . . I dismissed Valentin, straightened my clothes, and hurried into the house and up to my husband's bedroom, aching for more. The marquis was asleep and snoring. After hastily undressing, I awakened him with my fingers and my tongue ... and my husband entered me for the first time in nine years. Afterward he yawned, mumbled, 'What a pleasant surprise,' and fell back asleep. Hardly ready for sleep myself, aching for more and more, I reached down to feel the luscious liquid, my menses, exudations, and sweat, laced with the semen of two men. I massaged it into my thighs and belly, touched it to my breasts, sniffed it on my fingertips, and then, licking those fingers, I savored the pungent taste of love. . . . The following morning I ordered Valentin to drive me to the Bois de Boulogne so that he might repeat his service to me there. This he has done every day since you last saw me. . . . In addition to my husband and our driver, I have, during the past week, had the occasion, a shameful compulsion contrary to my moral standards, to seduce two muscular carpenters doing repairs on the staircase of our home, as well as the fishmonger who a few days ago delivered the oysters my husband had ordered in hopes that they might enable him to better satisfy my carnal demands. The bloated face, hairy body, boozy breath, and piscatorial odor aroused rather than repulsed me. . . . And yesterday afternoon a gentleman with whom you are, I believe, acquainted, the writer of lampoons, Monsieur Etienne de Jouy, called upon my husband who was, both fortunately and not, away from home. Despite his friendship with the marquis, he consented to gratify my craving in retaliation, I suspect, for his suspicion that my husband has been clandestinely intimate with his wife. I am not the only adulteress in Paris. . . . Oh, but of course, that does not absolve me of my sins, sins for which I should be punished . . . yes, punish me. Strip me as the Roman lictors stripped our Lord and flog me as He was beaten, scourging me until I bleed as He bled. . . . Because of you, however, that punishment would only delight me. By transforming what caused pain into a source of pleasure, your treatment transformed a chaste woman into an insatiable whore, a faithful wife into a wanton adulteress. . . . Just now, even as I speak with pure intentions, demanding redemptive punishment, expressing repentance and hopes for absolution and cure, the words I hear coming from my lips arouse my desire all the more for the pleasures of sin. . . . I feared this, feared coming here this evening, feared that in making sacramental confession I would not be able to restrain myself from throwing my arms around you, kissing your neck, your cheeks, your lips. . . . Help me . . . beat me or embrace me, there would be no difference . . . you must entrance me once more, guide me into a lucid sleep and deliver me from desire there . . . and please forgive me . . . please. . . ."

The marquise becomes silent. She turns away from you to look at the crucifix illuminated by votive candles on the wall at the back of the room. Her gaze moves up from blanched skull upon which the overlapping, impaled, wounded feet of Christ rest, up the deathly white legs, across the dirty gray cloth wrapped around his loins, up the lean torso, over the stretched stomach muscles and protruding ribs, over the crimson gash beneath his breast, up and across to one of the pierced hands. His fingers are curled around a rusted iron stake, up now to the crown of thorns and droplets of blood on his forehead and in his hair. Her eyes are fixed on His face. . . .

What is the abbé thinking, feeling, desiring? How does he respond? With condemnation or sympathy? With abhorrence or arousal? Imagine it. . . . Whatever you suppose is true. . . .

"Sleep," he commands. "Sleep, sleep in a deep and lucid sleep."

And the marquise obeys. Her eyes close, her head falls forward, and her arms fall loose and limp at her sides. She will imagine whatever you imagine she imagines.

Imagine what she sees: the crucified Christ's chest expands, very slightly at first, but then His breathing becomes fuller, deeper, more apparent. Glistening scarlet droplets begin to trickle from the wound in His side as slowly He raises his head to look at her. A splendid golden aureole emanating from Him spreads radiantly out to illuminate the room. He descends from the cross and approaches.

Imagine what she feels: His wounded hand reaching for her so that His fingertips may tenderly touch her neck, her cheek, her lips.

Imagine what she tastes: the blood on those fingertips, a sweet ambrosial wine that soothes all pain and lulls her into a deeper sleep in which she feels more wide awake than she ever has been.

Imagine what she hears: "Knowing that you would find your way to Me, I have been waiting for you. Although you were unaware of it, you have always longed for Me but, taken hostage and deceived by the flesh, your spirit was led astray first by pain and then by pleasure. Pity the flesh that shall pass away like a wind and come not ever again. The spirit, set free from the body, is impervious to pain and cannot perish. Trust that so long as you love Me, I shall remain in you, deep inside of you, pleasing you so constantly, satisfying you so entirely, that you shall desire no other pleasure than communion with Me. And when the day comes for you to cast off the flesh, we will be as one, perfectly united in life everlasting. When you awaken you will no longer be the victim of worldly desires and fears, cleansed and sanctified by the joyous communion of your soul with Me. By grace of your love for Me and Mine for you, you are absolved of your sins forever and ever. You are forgiven. When you awaken you will be without sin. Cleansed by love, you will awaken in joy. . . . Wake up, wake up and open your eyes. Yes, open your eyes."

Yes, let's open our eyes.

THE LISTENER'S TALE

Story is an exceptionally versatile device in hypnotherapy. It can be a strong, effective part of induction, deepening, or therapy. We employ story alone, a story within a story, two or more alternating stories, and story without an ending. The story with no ending stimulates an immediate unconscious search, the discovery of which may be evident at the next session. Or we may encourage unconscious search in a guided fashion. At the completion of the story with no ending, we ask the client to provide an ending.

GEORGE GAFNER AND SONJA BENSON, *HANDBOOK OF HYPNOTIC INDUC-TIONS* (2000)

Opening their eyes, your listener and mine sit up and, in awakening, become reader and writer, you and me, once more. They pass the book back to us and we read aloud:

Based on what has been suggested, the writer leaves it up to us to imagine more of the tale of Abbé Faria. And how does it end?

As the reader of, or listener to, any story, we enter into a relationship with the characters in that story, a relationship demanding some degree of rapport and empathy with those characters as well as some degree of rapport and complicity with the writer. It would an abrogation of our responsibilities, as imposed by that relationship, not to imagine an ending to the tale. It would be a betrayal of the abbé, the Marquise de Somme, Seraphine Goéland, and any other characters who may have been brought to life by hypnotic suggestion and faculties of imagination and concentration.

"So, how does it end?" I, the writer and reader ask to then fall silent and vanish into the emptiness of the remaining blankness in the narrative. The void below is yours to fill:

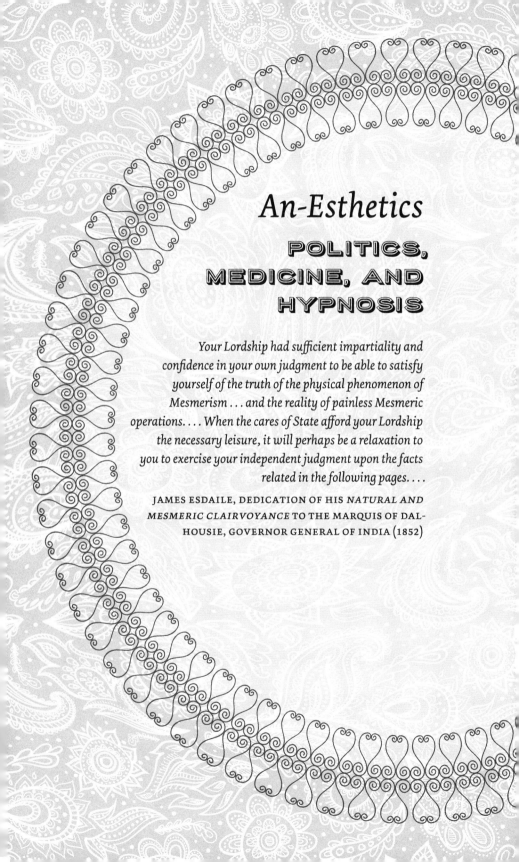

An-Esthetics

POLITICS, MEDICINE, AND HYPNOSIS

Your Lordship had sufficient impartiality and confidence in your own judgment to be able to satisfy yourself of the truth of the physical phenomenon of Mesmerism . . . and the reality of painless Mesmeric operations. . . . When the cares of State afford your Lordship the necessary leisure, it will perhaps be a relaxation to you to exercise your independent judgment upon the facts related in the following pages. . . .

JAMES ESDAILE, DEDICATION OF HIS *NATURAL AND MESMERIC CLAIRVOYANCE* TO THE MARQUIS OF DAL-HOUSIE, GOVERNOR GENERAL OF INDIA (1852)

part one

FOR THE READER

Two Stories to be Read Silently

No matter how well rested I am, every
time I sit down to read, I fall asleep after a
few paragraphs. This is a very frustrating
problem. I am a writer and have always been
an avid reader. This issue has gotten out of
control. It's almost as if I was hypnotized
and told to fall asleep whenever I try to
read. I fight it, shake my head, slap my
face, nothing helps. Can you help?

NUNZIO, "FALLING ASLEEP WHILE READING,"
A USER-SUBMITTED QUESTION ON THE SLEEP
APNEA GUIDE WEBSITE (2011)

THE SURGEON'S STORY

ESDAILE, JAMES (1808–1859), surgeon and mesmerist, obtained a medical appointment in the service of the East India Company and reached Calcutta in July 1831. To use his own words, "I detested the climate, the country, and all its ways, from the moment I first set foot in it." He was put in charge of the hospital at Hooghly where he began to experiment with the use of mesmerism to produce complete insensibility to pain during the most severe operations in 1845. After the first year of this mesmeric practice he had accumulated more than a hundred cases of these anæsthetic operations. . . . The natives had much regard for him. . . . In his domestic life he had many troubles.

DICTIONARY OF NATIONAL BIOGRAPHY (1889)

Arriving in Calcutta on my first visit to India some forty years ago, I was overwhelmed, appalled, and yet strangely thrilled; repulsed and yet somehow enticed; terrified and yet uncannily lured to the brink of surrender.

It was not the city it is now. No, in 1974, rural victims of a famine in West Bengal and refugees from a war of liberation in Bangladesh had thronged by the many thousands into a city of dreadful night in hopes of finding any intimation of refuge. Calcutta was infernally hot and humid, fuming, sticky, and squalid, a funereal phantasmagoria of chaotic streets, lanes, and alleyways, all rotting and reeking with waste and forming a deformed labyrinth of misery, a putrid black hole in the center of a tenebrous bedlam in which the destitute could not conceal their dire penury and myriad afflictions.

It amazed me at the time that, amidst the pervasive squalor, all the Bengalis I met were somehow able to be wholeheartedly sanguine and even cheerful. I did and still do envy such stunning optimism and merriment. It was as if they had been mesmerically anesthetized against the painfulness of looking around them, and that, in some sort of mass hypnotic trance, they were able to vividly envision their beloved city in the splendid light of an imaginary past and future grandeur.

"Welcome to Calcutta," the deskman at the Great Eastern Hotel said with a smile and a mirthful wag of the head. "Calcutta, home of the Nobel Prize–winning poet and philosopher Rabindranath Tagore and so many other great writers and artists, countless great musicians, dancers, and what-have-yous, not to mention our exceptionally renowned delicious cuisine, and undoubtedly the most heavenly sweets on earth. Yes, as such my Calcutta is the Paris of India. Yes, yes, just like Paris in every way, yes every way except, of course, no Eiffel Tower yet."

The Great Eastern, like so many of the other moldering British edifices, seemed to me haunted with the ghosts of prodigal rajas and flamboyant babus, European merchants and British dignitaries, officers and administrators with their demure wives or enchanting bibis. In the louche bar where once upon a time the elect gathered to drink French champagne, snack on English canapés, smoke Burma cheroots, exchange international news and local gossip, banter, report a tragedy, or tell a joke, I sat alone, imagining faint echoes of their distant voices, drinking warm beer under a motionless ceiling fan. The electricity was out but, by the odorous light and flicker of several kerosene lamps, I inspected faded photographs of Calcutta beneath the dusty glass of their old frames: a cityscape, the port on the Hooghly where the ship that brought Esdaile from Scotland must have docked, magisterial monuments, Eden Gardens where the physician might have strolled with colleagues, and portraits of the people he might have known—a Bengali raja in full regalia surrounded by his immense family in ornate traditional garb, a British dignitary with his only wife and two children in formal wear, a tiger hunt, a government parade, a platoon of soldiers at attention, members of the Calcutta Cricket Club lolling on a lawn, and the Great Eastern Hotel as it so grandly was at its opening in 1840.

I now picture in that bar British residents of Calcutta at the time those photographs were taken as Esdaile characterized them in his *Letters from the Red Sea, Egypt, and the Continent* (1839): "They are of a half-caste mind in which Indian indolence, sensuality, and laxity of moral ideas are grafted upon European honour, hardihood, and activity making a singular compound in which the baser part often predominates glad of any excitement if it dispel the *tædium vitæ* which generally oppress the idle and objectless Anglo-Indian."

Trying now to imagine Dr. James Esdaile arriving in Calcutta from Scotland almost a century and a half before me, I close my eyes to situate him in that bar that in my memory I imagined as it might once have been. Esdaile did, in fact, often stay at the Great Eastern during his visits to Calcutta, perhaps in the same room, I'd like to suppose, to

which the merry desk clerk assigned me long ago. The crackled mirror in which I saw myself in that room could have been there a hundred and fifty years before my arrival. It is possible that it once contained his face just as it once did mine.

A surviving calotype print portrait of him allows me to see that face. While the eyes seem inquisitive and sensual, the mouth suggests reserve and temperance to me. And while the high broad forehead intimates keen intelligence, the slumping shoulders insinuate a weakness of some sort.

Knowing as I do now that his seventeen-year-old bride hd died during the long passage from Edinburgh to Calcutta makes me aware that he is grieving and so much lonelier than I was in that bar. Perhaps he met his second wife there. After all, parties at the Great Eastern Hotel and Spence's were venues for husband-hunting unmarried women in what was then the capital of British East India. I imagine her vaguely resembling my listener, with her fair hair and light complexion, a sweet smile and languid eyes. She dotes on her husband with tender grace, unaware that she is soon to succumb to a tropical illness and die in Hooghly, never to return home to Britain.

I imagine introducing myself to them, shaking the surgeon's steady hand, being cordially invited to be seated at their table, and there being enthusiastically informed about Dr. Esdaile's controversial experiments with mesmerism in his Hooghly Imambara Charity Hospital. I inform him that I am indeed very interested in mesmeric practices in India. "In fact, I am currently writing a book about it."

"In that case," I imagine the physician emphatically saying with a rhotic Scottish accent, rolling each of the four r's in "you must read my book, *Mesmerism in India and its Practical Application in Surgery and Medicine.*"

And I have done so. It is a record and defense of his experiments with the use of mesmerism as the anesthesia for surgery in India in 1845–1846.

EXPERIMENT ONE: *A Hog Dealer*

James Esdaile was not sure what he was doing, how to do it, or if it would work when he hypnotized Madhab Kaura, a hog dealer condemned for assault to seven years of hard labor in irons. According to Esdaile's report, the convict, suffering from a double testicular hydrocele, had, in April of 1845, been brought for surgical treatment from his prison cell to the operating room in the Charity Hospital in Hooghly, "a wretched and obscure village" some thirty miles to the north of Calcutta where Dr. Esdaile had, much to his discontent, been posted as a surgeon for the East India Company.

While the Indian cleric Abbé Faria, imagining that women were more susceptible to hypnotic induction than men, most often chose young aristocratic and bourgeois Parisian *belles femmes* to be the subjects of his experiments with *le sommeil lucide*, the Scottish surgeon James Esdaile, imagining that "the natives of Bengal were more peculiarly sensitive to the Mesmeric power" than Europeans, experimented with mesmeric anesthesia primarily on destitute Bengalis, mostly males—rickshaw wallahs, washermen, gardeners, barbers, peasant farmers, beggars, and inmates of the Hooghly prison.

When the surgeon inserted the drainage needle into the hog dealer's grossly engorged scrotum, the patient threw his head back, thrashed his limbs about, writhed, groaned, and shrieked.

"Seeing him suffering in this way," Esdaile, who at the time had no more knowledge of hypnosis than what he had haphazardly gleaned from a few "scraps from the newspapers," turned to Budden Crunder Chowdaree, his subassistant surgeon, to ask if he had ever witnessed mesmerism. Chowdaree avowed that, yes, as a student at Calcutta Medical College, he had watched one of his professors attempt to mesmerize a patient. But it had not been successful.

While neither the Scottish surgeon nor his Bengali assistant had much hope that mesmeric passes would genuinely desensitize the felon, it seemed, given the pitiful patient's agony, worth a try.

Commanding the hog dealer to be quiet and still, Esdaile began to wave his hands over the grimacing face, then up and down the harrowed body, and around and around the clenched stomach. The surgeon understood that, with just such gestures, Franz Anton Mesmer had alleviated pain and, in some cases, even cured diseases in Vienna and Paris. It is likely that Esdaile would have been aware of the widely publicized accounts of the surgical removal of the breast of a Parisian granddame suffering from cancer in 1829. Her medical advisor, a disciple of Mesmer, who had successfully hypnotized her on several occasions, suggested to the eminent surgeon and anatomist Jules Cloquet (1790–1883) that he perform the surgery on the patient in a state of magnetic sleep. It was reported in British and Continental medical publications that she had been able to freely converse during the painful procedure without registering the slightest bit of discomfort.

After almost an hour of making mesmeric passes over Madhab Kaura, Esdaile was on the verge of giving up when his patient began to complain that the room was filling up with smoke. The hallucination encouraged the surgeon to persevere, to continue waving his hands over the patient's face, blow softly his forehead, and intermittently press gently on his stomach until finally the criminal's "countenance showed the most perfect repose."

To test the depth of mesmeric trance, Esdaile pinched the patient's cheek, pushed a needle into his gut, and squeezed the tender scrotum. Madhab Kaura displayed no signs of distress.

Thrilled by the results of his experiment, Esdaile, leaving his cataleptic subject with his Bengali assistant, went to fetch several British officials, notably Judge F. W. Russell and a district collector aptly named Mr. Money, that they might bear witness to the extraordinary phenomenon and test the hog dealer's insensibility for themselves.

Russell and Money took turns poking him with pins, touching his knees with a burning coal, and shouting in his ear. Kaura did not respond. Then, just to make certain that the wily felon was not faking catalepsy, Esdaile offered him a cup of ammonia which, under the sway of Esdaile's suggestions, he "drank like milk and gaped for more."

Leaving his somnambulistic patient on a pile of hay on the floor, Esdaile celebrated his mesmeric success at a luncheon with the judge and collector. He was vexed upon his return to the clinic to discover that the prison doctor, Kureem Ali Khan, had, in Esdaile's absence, come to the hospital, awakened the entranced prisoner by pouring buckets of water on his face, and taken him back to his cell.

When visited there by Esdaile, Madhab Kaura had no recollection of drinking ammonia or being pierced with pins, and he had no inkling as to what had caused the blisters on his knees.

Although the experiment with mesmerism had been successful, the surgery itself had not yet been undertaken. Esdaile postponed it to give himself time to convene the most respectable and credible of witnesses for his scrotal surgery under mesmeric anesthesia. The audience for the sensational demonstration included the governor of Chandernagore, the district magistrate, the principal of Hooghly College, the headmaster of the Lower School, and several physicians, Bengali as well as British.

The rehypnotized patient lay still, silent, at ease, and oblivious as the physician again drove a drainage needle deep into his turgid scrotum. Then, after slicing it open, he dissected out the sacs and scraped away adhesions to the encrusted testes. The hog dealer felt nothing.

"I believe," Mr. Money, who had marveled at the operation, subsequently wrote to Esdaile in testimony, "that if you had cut his leg off, he would not have felt it."

Esdaile did, in fact, soon use analgesic mesmerism to amputate a leg, as well as an arm, a thumb, a breast, and two penises.

Upon awakening, several hours after the operation to discover that his hydrocele was gone, Madhab Kaura looked up at Esdaile and put his hands together in the customarily reverential anjali-mudra to declare, "You are my father and my mother for you have given me life again."

Several days after the operation, the patient began to run a high fever. His pulse was excessively rapid, he had diarrhea, and his scrotum, swelling up again, had become so tender that "the lightest touch caused great pain." The complication afforded Esdaile the opportunity to repeat the experiment and to invite doctors and medical students, both foreign and native, to watch the performance.

Informing the Bengalis present that he was using "*Belattee muntar,* European magic," to sedate the patient, Esdaile replicated his mesmeric induction and, in less than an hour, the convict was comatose. The doctors were cordially invited to prod, poke, and pinch the inflamed scrotum with as much force as they wished. They were pleased to do so.

Continuing to experiment on Madhab Kaura, Esdaile discovered that, with each successive induction, the man he would later characterize as "the very worst specimen of humanity" fell all the more obediently, rapidly, and profoundly into mesmeric stupefaction. "If I point my fingers at him for a few seconds his eyelids droop, his arms fall to their sides; his whole body begins to tremble owing to the incipient loss of command over the musculature system."

In that state, the surgeon declared and demonstrated, the ignoble convict could be commanded to make his body rigid and then be positioned "like a buttress" at an acute angle with his feet on the floor and his forehead against the wall, and the Bengali native would remain in that "inconvenient and grotesque position" until the Scottish physician gave him permission to return to normal consciousness.

The spectacle of an Indian human buttress must surely have impressed and stimulated the colonial imaginations of the governor, magistrate, judge, collector, and other British administrators of the East India Company.

EXPERIMENT TWO: *A Shopkeeper et al.*

Scrotal hypertrophic tumors, symptomatic of elephantiasis and hydrocele and aggravated by syphilis, were rife in nineteenth-century Bengal, abounding there, in Esdaile's opinion, on account of it being a hot, moist, filthy, putrid, malarious land inhabited by an ill-fed and ill-clothed, ignorant and indifferent native population content to "eat, drink, and breathe perpetual infection." Of all the procedures performed under mesmeric anesthesia, the surgical removal of these particular tumors was the most frequently undertaken of Esdaile's operations. Case after case after case of his success with mesmeric analgesia for surgeries for "*hyptrophia scroti*" were reported in *The Zoist*, a quarterly *Journal of Cerebral Physiology and Mesmerism*: "Every month I have more operations of this kind than take place in the native hospital in Calcutta in a year, and more than I had for the six years previous [to using a mesmeric analgesia]." His patients, he imagined, would go to others afflicted with scrotal tumors to promote the operation. "Look at me: I have got rid of my burthen, am restored to the use of my body. This, I assure you, the doctor Sahib did when I was a sleep and I knew nothing about it."

Esdaile maintained that the indigenous doctors' procedures for treating these densely fibrous tumors caused "vexatious complications" and an "irritation that only accelerates the disease." His mission was to demonstrate to those Indian healers the superiority of European medical methodologies and to instruct them in the practice of mesmeric surgery.

The publication in London of lurid photographs of grotesquely gigantic inguinal growths, reputed to be rampantly endemic to Bengal, gave substantial credence to the conviction that British medicine was needed in India no less than British law. If we are to imagine that the relationship between the hypnotist-surgeon and the hypnotized-patient is analogous to and representative of the relationship between a foreign sovereign and its colonized subjects, the fact that the majority of Esdaile's operations were performed on the monstrously swollen and utterly useless reproductive organs of low-caste Indian men, has significant political implications. Each surgery was an affirmation of the value of British governance. The success of colonial domination depended on something akin to what Esdaile explained as requisite for deep mesmeric induction: "passive obedience in the patient and a determined attention on the part of the operator."

The most spectacularly monstrous of all the tumors treated by Esdaile was an eighty-pound growth that had rendered Gooroochuan Shah, a forty-year-old shopkeeper, immobile. "Its great weight and having used it for a writing desk for many years," had, the surgeon recorded, "pressed it into its present shape."

Esdaile's trained assistants took turns attempting to render the shopkeeper comatose. "He became insensible on the fourth day of Mesmerizing, and was drawn with the mattress to the end of the bed (my usual mode of proceeding)." When two attendants, lifting and supporting the huge tumorous growth in a canvas sheet, then pulled it forward to stretch out the base, Esdaile made a swift circular incision. "The rush of venous blood was great."

Surviving the surgery and released from the hospital a month later, Gooroochuan Shah was able to boast to his family and customers that his tumor was "the largest ever removed from the human body."

Although testicles had to be excised during these surgeries on scrotal tumors if there was substantial adhesion, and in some cases it was necessary to sacrifice the penis as well, none of Esdaile's patients with scrotal elephantiasis died on the operating table, and all of those patients, at least according to his account, were profoundly grateful and beholden to the East India Company surgeon. "Brahma is above all, and you are next to him," one of them typically proclaimed. Another bowed and "blessed me, and hoped that God would give me a golden palanqueen and a golden chariot."

The British physician attributed his success "to my patients being the simple, unsophisticated children of nature; neither thinking, questioning, nor remonstrating, but passively submitting to my pleasure, without in the smallest degree understanding my object or intentions. The people of Bengal, a feeble, ill-nourished race, seem to be peculiarly sensitive to the Mesmeric power."

EXPERIMENT THREE: *A Sorcerer*

Babu Essanchunder Ghosaul, the Hooghly deputy magistrate, introduced Esdaile to "one of the most famous magicians in Bengal" as "a brother magician who has studied the art of magic in different parts of the world."

With Ghosaul translating, the Scottish surgeon informed the Bengali magician-hypnotist (whom I shall call Shambaraswami) that he wished to determine if the respective means of inducing trance of the "hakeems of Europe" and "fuqueers of the East" were the same or different and, if different, which was the most potent. "I proposed," Esdaile recounted, "that we should show each other our respective charms, and, after much persuasion, he agreed to show me his process for assuaging pain."

Seated cross-legged at arm's length from yet another inmate of the Hooghly prison with yet another painful scrotal tumor, Shambaraswami, muttering monotonic mantras, slowly waved a leaf-tipped branch before the convict's eyes. After flicking droplets of water from a brass pot onto the subject's face, the spellbinder began to rhythmically stroke the man's body from head to toe with the branch.

Once the patient appeared to be in trance, Esdaile complimented the magician on his "charm" and then, offering to demonstrate the European version of it, insisted that he perform it on the sorcerer himself.

After cajoling the nervous and resistant Shambaraswami into lying down, Esdaile's induction began with a condescending parody of the magician's recitation of a mantra: "I chanted the chorus of 'King of the Cannibal Islands'": Ogaba, ogaba, ogaba, ogaba, ogaba, ogaba, oh!

Shortly thereafter the Bengali charmer jumped up, complained of disagreeably unusual sensations, and tried to flee. With Esdaile blocking the exit from his surgery, Deputy Magistrate Ghosaul insisted that Shambaraswami lie back down. Again chanting "ogaba, ogaba, ogaba," the Scottish doctor passed his hands over the Bengali magician's body.

Covering his ears with his hands, Shambaraswami, mumbling that he felt queasy and drunk, rose to his feet, recovered his balance, and bolted out of the hospital.

Esdaile was uncertain as to whether or not he had actually induced trance until the following day when the Bengali returned to confess that, "Oh, yes, Sahib, you put me to sleep." The doctor interpreted this seemingly humble confession as an acknowledgement of the superiority of European methods for inducing trance over traditional Indian spells.

A Dr. Mouat, professor of medical jurisprudence at the Calcutta Medical College and eventually one of Esdaile's most skeptical critics, reported on his colleague's experiments and local status in the *Record of Cases Treated in the Mesmeric Hospital from November 1846 to May 1847 with Reports of the Official Visitors*: "Few if any of the inhabitants of the globe are more completely under the control of superstition in its widest sense and in its most absurd forms, than the natives of Bengal. They have the most implicit faith in witchcraft, magic, the power of spirits and demons, and the efficacy of charms and incantations. The patients who resort to Dr. Esdaile's hospital all come to him impressed to the fullest and firmest belief in his supernatural powers; in fact the common name under which the Mesmeric Hospital is known among the lower classes is that of the *house of magic*, or *jadoo* hospital."

Esdaile's observation of the Bengali magician-healer casting his spell on the cross-legged inmate of the Hooghly prison convinced the foreign physician that "the medical practice of the Indian conjurors, or *Jadoowalla*, is only Mesmerism disguised by incantations and mummery," and that, as such, mesmerism had been practiced in India "from time immemorial like every other custom in this immutable society." But the hypnotists of India were, in his estimation, "artfully concealing the secret of their power in order to secure the lucrative secret for themselves and their families."

In *Natural and Mesmeric Clairvoyance*, written a year after his return from India to Scotland in 1852, Esdaile collected accounts of traditional Indian hypnotic practices. A Colonel Bagnold of the Bombay army informed him of witnessing a young Hindu girl cured of epilepsy in 1808 "by performing a religious ceremony of *muntur*." The healer "commenced with the usual Hindu offerings such as burning frankincense, breaking a cocoanut, and invoking some god." With the girl seated on the ground, the sorcerer "took from his long matted hair a string of sandalwood beads which he held up before her eyes and directed her to look at; then he made passes with it from her head downwards, occasionally stopping to breathe upon or lay his hands upon her chest. She soon became drowsy, and appeared to sleep when a handful of wood-ashes were waved over her head, thrown in the air, and the charm was pronounced complete."

To British witnesses of his mesmeric performances, Esdaile had demonstrated the ways in which modern European science could empirically explain, and thereby demystify, phenomena that were considered magical in India. Simultaneously, to his Bengali witnesses and patients, he demonstrated that his magic, his *belattee muntar* and *jadoo*, though fundamentally the same as that of the native sorcerers, was more puissant.

If, as Esdaile imagined, modern medical practices were similar to in principle, but more efficacious in action, than traditional Indian healing procedures, it allowed many of the European spectators of his mesmeric exhibitions to reaffirm their conviction that analogously Raj rule in India was more expedient than more archaic Indian systems of governance. Just as the Indian sorcerer had acknowledged the superiority of the British physician's magic to his own, so the native potentates of the Indian provinces should have been willing to acknowledge the political expedience of British suzerainty.

EXPERIMENT FOUR: *A Barber*

In June of 1845, two months after operating on Madhab Kaura, Esdaile, coming upon a crowd gathered in front of the Hooghly bazaar police station, was informed that a barber had just then been arrested for abducting a young boy. Esdaile went in to investigate and was told by the boy that he had gone that morning to a field near his house. A stranger had approached him there and, while passing his hand to and fro in front of the child's face, had recited mantras. This, the boy divulged, made him feel uncannily out of control of himself and strangely compelled him to obey and follow the man. An informant who was acquainted with the boy had become wary upon seeing him trailing behind the stranger. Pursuing them and noticing that the boy appeared deranged, he asked the suspicious character, a barber, what he was doing with the child. The alleged kidnapper and suspected pedophile fled the scene but was soon apprehended by the police.

Esdaile was skeptical of the barber's claim that he had been merely trying to help the boy who seemed to him to have lost his way. "Barbers," the doctor maintained, "all over the world, are a shrewd, observing race; their occupation brings them into close contact with the surfaces most sensitive to the Mesmeric influence; and they are, therefore, very likely to have become possessed of the secret of Mesmerism at an early period, and perhaps it has descended to them as a mystery of their craft."

Indian barbers, Esdaile elaborated, were particularly noted for their scurrilous applications of mesmeric charms to bring people, "usually women," under their control, a statement that insinuates prurient motives for the barber's alleged criminal use of mesmerism to kidnap the child.

Appearing in the magistrate's court as a witness for the prosecution, Esdaile demonstrated how hypnotism could have served the kidnapper. Three of his former patients, including the hog dealer Madhab Kaura, were brought into the courthouse and hypnotized by Esdaile. They were made to walk out of the building and down the street and then to return as Esdaile commanded. Upon being wakened, they claimed to have no memory of ever leaving the bench. Madhab Kaura "was so deeply affected that all motive power was nearly extinguished, and I had to push him from behind with my finger to make him walk: he walked a few yards with difficulty, and then becoming suddenly rigid from head to foot, a slight push sent him down headlong on the floor in a most alarming manner."

Assured as he had been by his encounter with the Bengali sorcerer that mesmeric practices were well known in India, he became further convinced by the case of the barber that those practices often served nefarious ends: "I suspect that they [the native charmers] know the evil as well as the good of Mesmerism, and practice it for the most villainous purposes."

The barber was sentenced to nine years of labor in irons and confinement in the same Hooghly prison where Madhab Kaura was incarcerated. Several months later, however, the superior court, considering the defense's appeal, which was based on the argument that Esdaile's mesmeric spectacle had unduly made a prejudicial impression on the court, reversed the verdict and pardoned the barber.

There were accusations that Madhab Kaura and other of Esdaile's patients from the Hooghly prison had faked mesmeric trance in hopes that by their cooperation with the government surgeon they too might be shown leniency and set free.

Further skeptical appraisals of Esdaile's demonstrations of mesmerism posited that "it is the taste of the coolies of Bengal to have themselves cut to pieces, and to have corrosive acids and red hot pokers applied to their sores without showing a sign of life; or that, knowing my hobby, they come from all quarters to be silently tormented in order to please my Honour; or that passive endurance of pain is no sign of the absence of it . . . and the Indian Fuqueer voluntarily torments himself."

Others suspected Esdaile of drugging his patients with opium, bhang, toddy, or datura, or paying them to act as if they felt nothing when pierced with needles, burned with hot coals, or lacerated with scalpels. The assumptions were that Bengalis were prone to alcohol and drug addiction and that they would be willing and able to undergo excruciating pain for the sake of a few paisa.

In order to dispel such accusations, Esdaile performed two operations on a peasant woman named Lokee, one with mesmeric anesthesia and one without. In the first instance, the entranced patient showed no sign of discomfort as Esdaile removed a large ulcerated tumor from her leg: "She awoke three hours after the operation; felt no pain on waking and asked me who cut off the tumor?" Several months later when the tumor had grown back, Lokee returned to Esdaile's hospital and the surgeon operated on her again without inducing analgesic trance: "The poor old woman screamed miserably the whole time, crying that I was murdering her; and she continued in the greatest pain for hours afterward. If the old woman shammed insensibility on the first occasion, why did she not do so on the second?"

EXPERIMENT FIVE: *A Coolie*

Mesmerism was theater from the very beginning. The set for an early and definitive performance of the magnetic spectacle was a softly lit and opulently furnished room in the Hôtel Bullion in Paris in 1778. The tiled floors were strewn with plush Oriental rugs, the darkly paneled mahogany walls adorned with silvery full-length mirrors and decorated with astrological symbols and occult diagrams, and the oriel windows draped with burgundy velvet. Enchanting melodies wafted from a glass armonica and calmed the audience, gently trance-forming them from spectators into participating performers. Seated around an oakwood baquet with eight iron rods set into its brightly burnished lid, they anxiously awaited the star of the show and hero of the drama—Franz Anton Mesmer. Elegantly if not foppishly costumed in an embroidered lavender silk waistcoat, trimmed with sequins and pearls, with golden slippers on his feet, he made his entrance, slowly circling the room, stopping now and then to fix his penetrating gaze and point an index finger or aim a gleaming metal rod at this lady or that gentleman.

While Abbé Faria eschewed Mesmer's science and debunked his theories, he was profoundly influenced by the animal magnetist's dramaturgy. Faria was no less a showman than the pioneer of hypnosis during his popular weekly demonstrations of le sommeil lucide in the studio on the rue de Clichy.

No doubt inspired by both Mesmer and Faria and impressed by the substantial public appeal of their demonstrations and the revenues garnered from those performances, an actor from a theatrical family, Charles Lafontaine (1803–1892), introduced to mesmerism by Baron Jules Dupotet de Sennevoy, became an itinerant hypnotist, staging his show in the major European capitals and fascinating audiences with demonstrations of the wonders of phrenomesmerism, animal magnetism, electrobiology, and mesmeric clairvoyance. It was after attending one of Lafontaine's performances in Manchester, England, in 1841 that Esdaile's fellow Scottish surgeon, James Braid, began to experiment with the endeavor he would call "hypnosis."

Another peripatetic performer, the Danish hypnotist Carl Hansen (1833–1897), codified what was to become the conventional hypnotic stage show. Subsequent to his verbal and gestural suggestions, volunteers from his audiences would lose sufficient consciousness of themselves—and the inhibitions sponsored by that self-consciousness—to quack like ducks or bark like dogs, sing racy ditties, recite naughty verses, or dance silly jigs, flap imaginary wings, or drink imaginary wine. They would cheerfully endure needles inserted into their skin, feeling no more pain than Faria's blue-blooded Parisian demoiselles or Esdaile's downtrodden Bengali patients.

By the beginning of the twentieth century, hypnotic demonstrations became allied with stage magic, particularly in acts like that of Handy-Bandy and Nadia-Naidyr, in which India was evoked as an exotic and mysterious land where hypnotic enchantments had been practiced by adepts for millennia.

In an effort to distance and distinguish himself from the likes of such hypnotic showmen and establish himself as an empirically sci-

entific medical mesmerizer, Esdaile adamantly claimed in *Mesmerism in India* to be averse to public demonstrations of mesmerism because "all performers in public are not unnaturally suspected to take insurances from Art in the event of Nature failing them." He was, however, "at length requested from a high quarter to gratify some of the inhabitants of Government House with an especial Mesmeric *Séance*. This I could have hardly refused without appearing churlish and it would have been said that I shunned the light because my proceedings would not bare inspection."

Steamships were chartered to bring spectators for the performance from Calcutta and Barrackpur to Hooghly on July 30, 1845. A letter from "A Mesmeric Observer" published in *The Englishman*, described the spectacle: the audience watched in amazement as, from the other side of a wall separating the hypnotist from his subject, Esdaile was able with mesmeric passes to make a native "lady philosopher" nod, blink, fall into a bed and become there entirely cataleptic; after a second Bengali woman was mesmerized from a distance, a local peon took the stage and was rapidly entranced.

"Repeat whatever I say," Esdaile commanded, and "Repeat whatever I say," repeated the mesmerized subject. The menial Bengali then sang whatever Esdaile sang, first "Ye Mariners of England," and then "God Save the Queen." I would imagine that it must have delighted the British audience to hear a dark-skinned native of East India sing the hymn to Queen Victoria: "God save our gracious Queen! / Long live our noble Queen . . . / Send her victorious, / Happy and glorious / Long to reign . . . / O Lord our God arise, / Scatter her enemies / And make them fall / Confound their politics / Frustrate their knavish tricks . . . ."

And then there was a comic interlude in which the humble servant of the Raj chanted "Hey diddle diddle, the cat and the fiddle, the cow jumped over the moon."

"The spectators could not restrain their laughter, in which the singer joined in full chorus," the English visitor from Calcutta reported, "and some said, 'He can't help laughing at himself.' Upon which Dr. Esdaile stopped his performance and pointed out that they were laboring under a mistake who supposed he was laughing." No, he was not really laughing but only imitating the sound of the mesmerizer's laughter. And that realization caused the audience to laugh even more at the behavior of the childlike Indian coolie.

"The farce was nearly turned to tragedy," the report in *The Englishman* continued, when, upon being commanded to show the spectators in pantomime how the natives of Bengal fight with sticks, the coolie, "on bending forward to make a blow, pitched head foremost into Dr. E's breast and both rolled upon the floor. The actor's powers were clearly exhausted and he was in an intense trance on the floor."

Esdaile, to whom the visitor referred as both "the doctor" and "the entertainer," then invited volunteers to drink mesmerized water. "Four out of eight were found to be cataleptic and several were converted into somnambulists."

Such mesmeric demonstrations, fostering as they did the voyeuristic pleasure of witnessing suspensions of inhibition, became a popular diversion at teas and festive soirees at the Great Eastern Hotel and Spence's, as well as at lawn parties on the suburban estates of the prosperous European residents of Calcutta.

Despite avowals of his antipathy to such mesmeric divertissements, Esdaile's operating theater was open to the public. Reports published in the *Bengal Hurkaru* and *India Gazette* in 1846 by Dr. Allan Webb, professor of military surgery at the Calcutta Medical College in 1846, described Esdaile's Hooghly hospital compound as frequently crowded with the carriages that brought physicians, clergymen, judges, magistrates, government administrators, military men, merchants, and students from Calcutta Medical College, as well as distinguished Bengali rajahs and cosmopolitan babus, to witness Esdaile's dramatic surgeries on afflicted natives made insensible to pain by means of mesmerism.

The set for these miracle plays was lined with charpoys, upon which lay patients awaiting surgery. Attending to each of those patients there was a native assistant. Noting that inducing mesmeric trance could be tediously arduous, taking hours or even days to instigate, and that it was thus both a waste of his valuable time and detrimental to his health, Esdaile had trained young Hindu and Muslim assistants to perform the inductions. They would be costumed for the demonstrations in white turbans and robes, their charges wrapped in well-worn muslin sheets.

Tormentor curtains would prevent the spectators from seeing the cots in the wings upon which patients rested in various stages of recovery from their surgeries.

In the center of the stage there would be a wooden operating table with decorative brass handles used to adjust the backrest, and by it a table for the portentous props for the grand-guignolesque drama: an electro-magnetic machine, knives, saws, scalpels and scoops, hooks, forceps, tongs, drills, probes, pins and needles, catlins, bistouries, and gorgets, sutures, bandages, tourniquets, and sponges, dishes for extracted tissue, and pans for avulsed organs.

Act One

- -

[Bending over each prospective patient, a native ATTENDANT, waving his hands rhythmically round and round, up and down a suffering body, occasionally lightly blowing on a sickling's face.]

ATTENDANT: [whispering] *Ekhon ghumao, ekhon ghumao.* Sleep now, now sleep.

[Enter the SURGEON, wearing oilskin trousers, fisherman's boots, and, over his white linen smock, a butcher's apron. He circles the stage, consulting each attendant in order to select the patient most deeply entranced. Once a PATIENT has been chosen and carried by hospital CHAKARS from his cot to the operating table, his sheet is thrown back to display a scrotal tumor larger than the man's head. The SURGEON tests the degree of the PATIENT's insensibility: he pinches the engorged tumor (no response) and then applies a rod from the electromagnetic machine to the suffering servant's abdomen (no response).]

SURGEON: [turning to the spectators] Mr. Reverend Fisher, if you would be so kind, and Dr. Moat, and . . . hmmm . . . let me see, yes, yes, you sir, Babu Kaleedash Chatterjee, please do approach the patient and join me in determining the degree of catalepsy.

[DR. MOAT claps his hands loudly by each of the coolie's ears; REVEREND FISHER pinches and twists each of his nipples; BABU CHATTERJEE, after taking a deep puff on his cheroot, presses the burning end of it onto the center of the patient's forehead.]

REVEREND FISHER: This poor nokar is no more sensitive to pain than a corpse.

DR. MOAT: Or damn good at not showing it.

BABU CHATTERJEE: [taking another puff on his cigar] Permit me, honored ladies and gentlemen, on this marvelous and momentous occasion to aptly invoke the sublime words of Britannia's mellifluous Avonian bard: "They say miracles are past, and we have our philosophical persons, to make modern and familiar, things supernatural and causeless."

[The gentlemen return to their places as the spectators applaud].

Act Two

[The cathartic operation begins: a bistoury, inserted into the prepuce, is yanked back in a quick and forceful outward slice to expose the ulcerous and inflamed penis. An incision is made from the root of it across the spermatic cords, and down to the perineum. As the base of the festering tumor is carved, there is an explosive gush of blood. The jetting vessels are pinched and tied off by an ATTENDANT as the SURGEON digs his fingers deep into the tumor to dissect out the parts. The PATIENT begins to moan as the twitch and writhing of his arms and legs suggest that he is waking up. The ATTENDANT waves his hands over the PATIENT's face and breathes on his forehead again and again until the PATIENT descends back into deep trance. The SURGEON resumes the operation. Due to adhesion and encrustation, the testicles are sacrificed and discarded into a bell-metal pan. Loose flaps of scrotal skin are stitched back together, bandages wrapped, and the SURGEON, stepping back from the operating table, wipes the blood from his hands and face, removes his apron, and covers the lower body of the PATIENT with a sheet.]

Act Three

[The denouement: CHAKARS, on their hands and knees, wipe up the blood from the floor with sponges and rags.]

SURGEON: [waving a bottle of smelling salts under the PATIENT's nose, then dribbling water from a cup onto his face, then blowing into his ear, then slapping his cheek] *Utho! Utho!* Open your eyes! *Utho!* Wake up!

PATIENT: [opening his eyes, bewildered, sitting up slowly and seemingly woefully] When will Doctor-Saheeb perform the operation?

SURGEON: It has already been done.

PATIENT: [reaching down to feel his groin and then crying out with amazement, delight, and reverence] You have restored me to life, Lord Mastar! *Dhonnobad! Dhonnobad!* You are my savior, second in power only to Brahm, second in my heart only to Ram. But second to no man on earth. Ishor upnar! You are greatest magician of all! *Jai Eshdaile-Sahib! Jai Britannia! Jai! Jai!*

Curtain

During the six years he remained and practiced medicine in Bengal after the success of his first experiment with mesmerism as the surgical anesthesia, Dr. James Esdaile, proclaiming himself "the Apostle of Mesmerism in India," performed two hundred and sixty surgeries on hypnotically sedated patients. Although not all of the operations were successful, at least the patients who died on the table felt no pain under the knife.

THE ANESTHESIOLOGIST'S STORY

The history of Anæsthesia in India can be written beginning with Susruta in the pre-ether era when in 500 BC operations were performed using opium, wine, Indian Hemp and of course by tying up! There is a mention in 527 AD in Bhoj Prabandh of a cranial operation on Raja Bhoj himself using "Sammohini" (hypnosis) for induction and "Sanjivani" for recovery! Later alcohol was used for unconsciousness during the Muslim period. In 1843 [sic], James Esdaile started mesmerism at the Imambarah Hospital Hooghly, Calcutta and published 216 operations, however a government report says it was not universally nor uniformly successful.

DIVEKAR NAIK, "EVOLUTION OF ANÆSTHESIA IN INDIA" (2001)

"Over a hundred years ago, Dr. James Esdaile, a British physician in India, was anesthetizing Bengali patients for surgery," the senior house officer training in anesthesiology at the Radcliffe Infirmary in Oxford declared with a sly grin during a conversation in the Turf Tavern in 1974, "and now I, Dr. Subhash Chatterjee, a Bengali physician in England, am anesthetizing British patients for surgery." The ironic grin gave way to a perverse chuckle: "I wonder—is India repaying Britain for its colonial medical services through me? Or is India having her revenge?"

I had met Chatterjee the previous afternoon at a college garden party in Oxford, where I was a postgraduate student in the Faculty of Oriental Studies. Because I was preparing to go to Calcutta to do field research, a mutual friend introduced me to him. "I'm sure he'll be able to give you some practical advice, where to stay in Calcutta, what to see and do, and maybe even how to have some fun in that Black Hole."

At the party, the Bengali doctor had been costumed in a white dhoti of spun cotton tied at the waist and passing through his legs, matched by a loosely fitted ochre Punjabi top, and silver embroidered khussa slippers. For our meeting at the pub, he wore jeans and a casual corduroy blazer.

Recently, while reading James Esdaile's *Mesmerism in India*, I could not help but imagine that Esdaile's subassistant surgeon, Budden Crunder Chowdaree, looked rather like Subhash Chatterjee, a handsomely swarthy and robustly husky Bengali with a trimmed mustache, playfully sparkling eyes, and irrepressibly smiling full lips. I could hear what I remember as Chatterjee's richly resonant and strongly Anglicized Bengali accent as I read that Chowdaree had reported to Esdaile that, as a medical student at the Calcutta Medical College, he had witnessed mesmerism unsuccessfully attempted.

Dr. Chatterjee did not seem particularly interested in meeting me. The introduction interrupted a cocktail party oration he was delivering to an attractive young French woman with a smile of amusement on her lips and a coup of champagne in her hands.

"Parties in England just aren't what they used to be," the anesthesiology resident continued without pausing for so much as a "pleased to meet you" or any other such cordiality. "By the end of the eighteenth century, laughing gas soirees were all the rage in British upper-class circles. Benjamin Franklin became quite an aficionado of nitrous oxide as a guest at such parties in London. Yes, back then, as an anesthesiologist, I would have been the life of the party, offering each and everyone here a few big whiffs of nitrous. Wouldn't it be amusing to see a few of these straight-laced Englishmen and their demure ladies lose control, to hear a few proper Basils and prim Fionas stuporously giggle? Of course, as an Oriental I wouldn't have been invited to the party unless

I was some sort of maharaja, potentate, or diplomat. And in that case, I would probably be offering you a bit of Indian opium or hashish. Or I might offer to hypnotize you. Hypnosis, no less than happy gas, was another popular party *passé-temps* for the leisured elite. Charles Dickens, you know, was an amateur mesmerist and would often entertain guests at parties like this with demonstrations of it. Imagine him hypnotizing Lady Dedlock and then making her dance a jig, blow a raspberry, or raise up her skirts!"

"I'd like to be hypnotized," the enthralled mademoiselle exclaimed, "as long as you promise not to make me do anything naughty."

"Contrary to popular misconceptions," the physician assured her, "the hypnotist cannot weaken his subject's moral code or make her do something she doesn't want to do. So you can't blame me if, under hypnosis, you happen to raise your skirts."

Before leading his eager subject off in search of a place suitable for a hypnotic induction, he finally turned to look at me and extend a hand: "So sorry, I didn't catch the name."

"Lee Siegel," I said and, as we shook hands, our mutual friend explained that I was studying Sanskrit and that I was leaving soon to do thesis research in Calcutta. "It'll be his first trip to India."

"Well then, we must get together," Dr. Chatterjee responded with what seemed to be sincerity. "I'll make a list of things you must see in my wonderful, exciting city and I'll give you my parents' address. You must drop in on them. They're very hospitable, as is typical of Bengalis, and so they'll probably invite you to stay in our home. However, since it's your first time in India, you should probably decline the invitation and stay at the Great Eastern Hotel, because there you will have the sort of toilet to which you are undoubtedly more accustomed, not to mention the toilet tissue to which you're probably attached. Shall we meet tomorrow? Let's say at around six? At the Turf?"

The first round of double gin and tonics, paid for by me, fueled the Bengali's proud approbations of the city of his birth. "You will love Calcutta, beautiful, unforgettable, enchanted and enchanting Calcutta, the artistic and intellectual capital of India...."

During the second round of cocktails, again paid for by me, the physician brought up the subject of hypnosis. "Although practiced mostly in secret, hypnosis has always been well-known in Bengal, where we call it *shammohan* or *shambeshan.*" He seemed to genuinely believe that it had been used by Ayurvedic doctors in ancient India both to alleviate pain and cure diseases.

"At the same time as doctors at Calcutta Medical College, the first medical school in Asia and, incidentally, my alma mater, were experimenting with both ether and chloroform as surgical analgesics, a Scottish surgeon named James Esdaile, posted in Calcutta, was experimenting with hypnoanesthesia. That's what I'd like to do here in Oxford, to investigate instances in which hypnosis might be preferable to chemoanesthesia or at least useful as a supplement to it. Well, of course, pharmacological anesthesia is preferred by the medical establishment over hypnosis because of the ease of administration and predictability of results. But hypnosis could be used to alleviate preoperative fear and anxiety, facilitate the inhalation of anesthetic gas, and reduce postoperative stress. Hypnosis also has obviously significant value in pain management and a definite advantage over potentially addictive analgesic drugs. My professors at the Radcliff have, I'm sorry to say, been dismissive of my research interests in this area. But, despite their conservative opinions, I've been attending weekly Wednesday night meetings of a hypnosis training workshop organized by the British Society of Hypnotherapists in London. And this summer, when I go home to visit my parents, I'm going to consult with traditional Bengali healers to better acquaint myself with the ancient Indian methods and applications of hypnosis."

When I mentioned that I had done an eighth-grade elementary school science project called "Hypnosis East and West, Past and Present," Dr. Chatterjee, without showing any interest in hearing any of the details about it or about me for that matter, exclaimed, "That proves it—we were destined to meet!"

During the third round of drinks, again paid for by me, Chatterjee talked specifically about James Esdaile, maintaining that the British colonial surgeon had learned hypnosis from a Bengali magician but had concealed his indebtedness as an embarrassing acknowledgement of the sophistication of traditional Indian healing practices and a recognition of the superiority of those practices over the procedures employed by the medical officers of the East India Company. "I have such a strong impression and sense of Esdaile, at once an identification and a loathing, a loathing and disregard for the hegemonic surgeon who experimented on subjects he considered primitive, ignorant, and simpleminded, and, at the same time, an identification and sympathy with him as a foreign physician, a man out of place and struggling to understand what's going on beneath the surfaces of the strange world in which he finds himself. James Esdaile! You know, it once fancifully occurred to me that perhaps I might be Esdaile reincarnated. That would explain my interest in medical hypnosis. I don't actually believe it, of course, but it's amusing to imagine it."

Over the fourth double gin and tonics, finally paid for by Dr. Chatterjee, he confessed the real reason he had been willing and eager to meet with me. "I have a favor to ask of you. I'm writing an article for the *British Journal of Anæsthesia* on the history of the analgesic uses of hypnosis in India from ancient times until the present. And there is a sixth-century Sanskrit text that documents the use of hypnoanesthesia in ancient Indian neurosurgery. I'd really like to get my hands on a copy of the original Sanskrit text. And I'd like to have a literal translation of it and any commentaries on it. Since you're a Sanskrit scholar working at the Oriental Institute Library and the Bodleian, I would imagine that you could help me with that. It's called *Bhojaprabandha*. It's the biography of Raja Bhoja, the king of Malwa, who as a young man suffered from severe headaches caused by a brain tumor. After every known painkiller and treatment had been tried without success, two Bengali healers, one a magician-hypnotist, the other a barber-surgeon, were summoned to his court. Upon examining the patient, the magician announced that the king would soon die if the tumor were not immediately removed. Granted permission to proceed, he administered the anesthetic known as sammohana—hypnotism. And then the barber trepanned the king's skull and painlessly excised the malignant tumor. King Bhoja was free from migraines for the rest of his life. I would really appreciate it if you could get a copy of the Sanskrit text for me and go over the translation of it. It's an important source of evidence for the rather provocative argument I hope to make in my journal article."

After the fifth round of drinks, again paid for by Chatterjee, as we rose to leave the pub, staggering because of the strong drinks and stooping because of the low ceiling beams, Dr. Chatterjee slurred an avowal that, if I found the text for him, he would return the favor. "Yes, I'll help you. I'll hypnotize you and use hypnosis to make you stop smoking."

A week later I telephoned Dr. Chatterjee: "I found it. The text. The *Bhojaprabandha* of Ballaladeva. Chapter ninety-one."

In his excitement over the news he insisted on coming immediately over to my flat in Wolfson College.

"The story is not exactly as you reported it," I warned him. "And, by the way, Bhoja lived in the eleventh, not the sixth, century, and the text wasn't actually composed until the fifteenth century."

"The precise dating of books, people, and events in India is always vague and hard to determine with any precision," Chatterjee observed. "We are not as obsessed with time in India as you are in the West."

"Okay, that's fine," I conceded and, opening the book I had checked out of the Oriental Institute Library, continued: "According to Ballala, King Bhoja went to bathe in a pool where, and I quote, 'he washed out his skull'—whatever that means—'as he had been accustomed to doing since childhood.'"

"Yes, yes," the doctor was quick to explain, "he irrigated his ear canals and nasal passages. This is, and has been since ancient times, quite a common practice in India. We have always been quite conscious of hygiene, particularly when it comes to the bodily orifices."

"Okay," I continued. "As King Bhoja was doing this, the text announces that 'some fish got into his skull.' Naturally that caused his head to ache."

"Fish," Chatterjee informed me, "are no doubt metaphorical for his pain. It felt like fish were in his brain. Also, you must realize that certain fish contain large amounts of tyramine, a chemical compound that commonly triggers migraine headaches. It's likely that the ancient Indian healers knew about tyramine in fish long before your Western neurologists. They certainly knew about cysticercosis, a disease caused by the ingestion of the larvae of the pork tapeworm found in contaminated water. These larvae migrate to the brain where they form cysts that cause headaches as an inflammatory reaction. Perhaps the Bengali barber-surgeon removed these worms from the king's brain and observers mistook them for little fish."

I continued my literal rendition of the hagiography. "The royal physicians prescribed every drug in their pharmacopeia, but none of the medicines alleviated the king's pain. After a year of suffering, King Bhoja became so disillusioned with doctors and drugs that he decreed that every physician be banished from his kingdom and ordered that all medicines be thrown into a river."

"Yes, and that is why the Bengali healer resorted to hypnosis, rather than drugs, as the analgesic for the surgery. This is excellent."

"According to the text, those Bengalis of yours were actually the heavenly Ashvins, the physicians to the gods, the sons of Lord Indra. In order to preserve the practice of the medical sciences on earth, Indra directed them to disguise themselves as human doctors and cure King Bhoja so that he would have a higher opinion of drugs and greater respect for physicians."

"Of course, of course," the doctor insisted, "That is a poetic way of saying that these Bengali healers were so accomplished that they were like gods, like the Ashvins. In India it is common to praise someone's extraordinary accomplishment by saying 'you are like a god' or 'you are a god to me.'"

"Okay, but gods or not, they did not, according to this text, use hypnosis to sedate the king. The passage in question explicitly states that they administered '*moha-cūrna*' for that. *Cūrna* means 'powder' and moha means 'stupefaction.' So they used some kind of drug to render the king unconscious and then, the passage continues, they 'removed the top of his skull and retrieved the fish.' After gluing the top of his skull back on, they revived him to consciousness with an antidote to *moha-cūrna*, a drug called *sanjīvani*.

"There is," I repeated, "no mention of hypnosis. So, I'm sorry to have to tell you, you won't be able to allude to the tale of this surgery in your article on hypnotism for the medical journal."

"Well," the undaunted physician retorted, "that's one version of the story, but there are others in which it clearly states that *sammohana*, which is to say 'hypnosis,' was used on King Bhoja as the anesthesia for the surgery. That the text you have translated is, according to you, from the sixteenth century, explains the mistake—it is no doubt a fanciful retelling of the original sixth-century historical account using poetic license to transform a factual story into a literary tale. No, that's not the version of the account I am looking for. But I am sure you'll be able to find the original text in the manuscript archive of the Calcutta Sanskrit College, the oldest institute of higher learning in India. I'd really be pleased and indebted if you could do that for me. In anticipation of repaying you for your generosity, let me reaffirm my offer to hypnotize you and to use hypnosis to make you stop smoking. Let's do it! What better time than right now?"

While I tried to get out of it, insisting that I was easily distracted and incapable of prolonged concentration and was thus not particularly susceptible to hypnotic suggestion, he insisted: "Please, Lee—may I call you Lee? You must call me Subhash, after all we have become friends by now—so please, I ask you as a friend, let me try to hypnotize you. You have nothing to lose, and so much to gain by giving up cigarettes. If not for yourself, do it for me. I attended the BSH seminars in London on smoking cessation but have not yet had the opportunity to test what I learned on anyone. So please, let's give it a try."

There was no way out of it.

"Now get as comfortable as you can, my friend," the hypnoanesthesiologist began. "Comfortable and relaxed, resting your head on the back of the chair and fix your eyes directly above you at a spot on the ceiling. Keep your eyes focused on that spot and as you do you'll soon notice that your eyes begin to get tired, very tired, and as your eyelids get heavier and heavier, you are becoming more and more relaxed. Calm, peaceful, and relaxed. Breathe deeply in and slowly let it out and with each breath you become more calm, comfortable, and relaxed. And if you wish to go into a deeper state of relaxation all you have to do now is let your eyes close, close tightly, tighter and tighter together. You are paying attention only to the sound of my voice, sinking further and further down, deeper and deeper asleep. That's good, Lee, very good. You are resting calm and comfortable in a deep hypnotic sleep. Now listen to me. You have made up your mind to stop smoking, Lee. Yes, Lee, you are a nonsmoker. If you were ever to puff on a cigarette again the terrible taste of it will nauseate you and make you vomit. Lee, you are a nonsmoker because you know that cigarettes are poisonous. You hate the taste and smell of them, and even the sight of them. Every time you see a cigarette you will grab it, break it in half, and throw it away because, Lee, you are now a nonsmoker."

Once Subhash had brought me out of what he imagined to have

been a deep hypnotic trance, I took the pack of Dunhills out of my pocket, slowly removed one of the cigarettes from it, and inspected it. I considered breaking it in half in order to please my new friend but, after reconsidering the impulse, I lit it instead.

"What are you doing?" Subhash asked.

"Testing," I answered and, taking a puff deeply in and slowly letting it out, gazing at the lovely cloud of white smoke, and again deeply in and slowly out, with each puff I became all the more calm, comfortable and relaxed. "I love the way it smells and tastes and the way in which it makes me feel calm and relaxed. I guess that means that, as I suspected, I'm not very susceptible."

Subhash asked for one of my cigarettes, took it, lit up, inhaled, hesitated, exhaled, and then assured me that "everyone is susceptible to hypnotic induction to some degree."

Chatterjee agreed with Esdaile that Indians, and particularly Bengalis, were more susceptible than Europeans or Americans—not, as Esdaile imagined, because they were more simple and credulous than Westerners, but rather because Indians, and particularly Bengalis, have keener imaginations and a greater ability to vividly visualize what they imagine than Europeans. He also agreed with Faria that women are more susceptible than men—not, as Faria imagined, because of the thinness of their blood, but because "deep down women want to surrender, to be dominated, and controlled."

Dr. Subhash Chatterjee took another puff on the cigarette, smiled, and said, "You wouldn't be smoking right now if only you were a Bengali woman."

part two

Two Tales to be Read Aloud

If you feel sleepy a few pages into your book, you may want to read aloud. Yes, it sounds silly, but reading aloud triggers a different section of your brain. If you don't have someone to read to, try reading the book aloud to yourself in a mirror and it will be impossible for you to fall asleep.

EHOW WEBSITE, "HOW TO STOP FALLING ASLEEP WHILE READING" (2012)

THE PATIENT'S TALE

সম্মোহিতি

Hypnotic the sound of Mohan-Krishna's flute
    enchanting milkmaids,
    and blossoms spill from disheveled locks of nodding heads;
Hypnotic the sight of trembling peacock feathers in his crown
    infatuating milkmaids,
    and gaze-fixed doe-eyes love-languid close;
Hypnotic the taste of nectars trickling from his mouth
    intoxicating milkmaids,
    and ruddy love-ravenous moist lips open;
Hypnotic the fragrance of sandal powder on his chest
    bewitching milkmaids,
    and breathing in and crying out is love's pranayama;
Hypnotic the feel of blue lotus hands upon their bodies
    enrapturing milkmaids,
    and limbs tremble, breasts swell, as in this love-spell
    each girl imagines God embraces her alone.

BENGALI FOLK SONG, TRANSLATED BY LEE SIEGEL WITH SUBHASH
CHATTERJEE

"James Esdaile, a Scottish physician for the East India Company posted at a charity hospital in a town north of Calcutta," the writer informs his listener to prepare her for the reading of this tale, "began to experiment in 1845 with mesmerism as a surgical anesthesia."

Telling her about that first experiment on a hog dealer who was serving a seven-year prison sentence, he explains that the surgeon didn't know very much about the theory or methods of mesmerism when he decided to try it as the analgesia for the painful operation on the convict's scrotal tumor. "Most of Esdaile's patients were abject Bengalis—peasants, laborers, peons, porters, scavengers, beggars, and a few fakirs. The physician would invite guests to the surgeries—members of the medical profession, British administrators, military officers, clergymen, and distinguished Bengalis. As with Mesmer, Faria, and other hypnotists, Esdaile's demonstrations of hypnosis had a spectacular theatrical quality. Mesmeric surgery had dramatic appeal.

"Let's imagine," the writer continues as his listener gets comfortable and ready for another hypnotic tale, "that we've been invited to a demonstration of hypnosis. Take a few relaxing deep breaths and, as you listen to my account of an operation performed by Esdaile on a Bengali dairymaid, allow yourself to pretend that we are witnessing it."

Focus your eyes on a spot on the ceiling again and, now that you're accustomed to these readings, to listening, imagining and concentrating on what you imagine, you may notice that the spot soon becomes hazy or faint, perhaps changing shape or size and, as you continue to gaze at it, your eyes will blink as your eyelids begin to feel heavy . . . heavier . . . and heavier. Take in a few more deep, relaxing breaths, deep and comforting. . . . With each inhalation feel a calmness filling your lungs . . . with each exhalation feel tension released, flowing out of you and allowing you to feel all the more comfortable and relaxed. . . . As your eyelids become heavier and heavier still, feel yourself slowly slowing down, breathing slowing . . . pulse slowing . . . thought processes slowing, slowly, calmly, comfortably . . . thinking of nothing . . . doing nothing . . . just relaxing, breathing, drifting . . . just listening to my voice as I begin to read the milkmaid's tale. You can, if you wish, close your eyes to listen and to see.

The tale takes place in West Bengal in the mid-nineteenth century. Try to picture it as you allow yourself to play along with the story and imagine we're there, pretending that we're standing outside a dilapidated Victorian gothic building looking at an inscription over the entryway: Hooghly Imambarah Native Charity Hospital.

Picture a row of a dozen or so faux-marble pillars imposed over the once white whitewash of the building's moldering facade and out of proportion to the more modest dimensions of the structure. The pillars seem a fanciful colonial gesture designating the hospital an official station of the East India Company. The incongruous shape of the windows and the carved ornamentation on their sandstone frames suggest that they may have been brought here during construction from a Moghul ruin. Torrential monsoons past and present neglect have left the walls stained and cracked in places. Chipped and disintegrated patches of the edifice's dirty white plaster skin reveal the dark red-brick dermis of the aged and ailing architectural body.

The brazen heat at this time of year, the season's enervating omnipresent sultriness, seems to have sedated all living things, causing the leaves of kadamba trees to listlessly droop, their red flowers to turn brown, wither, and fall from the branches. Cows drowsily graze on parched grass and slowly, so slowly, weary women bring water from the well in the clay pots balanced on their heads. Imagine the slumberousness duly induced by the flagrant heat of a languorous Bengal.

Although the sky is cloudless and the air breezeless, the humidity augurs the immanent arrival of seasonal rains. Let yourself imagine the heat and, as you take in another deep breath, you can feel the soporific sultriness of India in your lungs.

Taking refuge from the merciless midday sun, let's go through the open wood doors into the hospital. Because your pupils are still constricted by the bright sunlight, the vestibule seems dark, but slowly, as those pupils begin to dilate, a man takes shape in the shadows. Gradually he emerges, comes into focus, and is stranding in front of you. He's not as tall as you, thinner and more pale. Imagine his eyes looking into yours inquisitively, if not judgmentally, and notice that the right eye is curiously wider open than the left. Picture the high forehead, its hairline receding, graying side-whiskers, a rather delicate nose, and an almost lipless mouth. He's wearing oilskin work trousers, fisherman's boots, and, over his white linen smock with rolled-up sleeves, a canvas apron stained with dark blotches of dry blood. As he reaches to shake your hand, notice the long, thin, steady fingers that will do the surgeon's work.

Let me introduce you to him, Dr. James Esdaile, and, as you imagine shaking hands with him, tell him your name. Yes, say it out loud. . . .

He gestures for us to follow him from the reception room, down a dark hall slowly, cautiously up a small flight of stairs, onto a shady landing, and then through a curtained doorway into the operating theater, suddenly bright with sunlight blazing in through tall windows wide open.

Cushioned pews are arranged around the room to form a center stage set with a deodar wood operating table with brass fittings. Fatigued by the heat, let's take a seat, here, yes right here, and now look up to see the wooden frames suspended from the ceiling in which linen-covered fan blades slowly wave, wave to and fro, rhythmically flapping, flap-flapping back and forth, lazily sweeping the air with each tug to and fro of hemp ropes in the hands of the tired punkah-wallahs posted in the shadowy back recesses of this surgical chamber.

Fix your gaze on those wagging fans, and breathe in the balmy air they stir, breathe in again and out, in and out again, and, with each repeated wave and swish and breath, the operating room in Bengal so long ago gradually becomes more and more present in place and time, more and more vivid, more audibly real (hear the murmurs of the other guests), more tactilely real (feel the softness of the cushions upon which we sit, resting, comfortable and calm), more olfactorily real (smell the salty soap, coconut oil, faint fumes of wood vinegar lightly laced with ammonia and sulfur), more and more visibly real (see the attendants in their white lungis draping the operating table with a thick black blanket, then covering it with several layers of heavy cotton sheeting).

Imagine an adjoining table set with Esdaile's equipment and in-struments: scalpels, retractors, calipers, forceps, catheters, bistouries, pans, sutures, and a brass speculum with ivory handles, and notice another table for sheets, towels, sponges, and bandages and a small stand for the mesmerist's electromagnetic machine with its coils, cyl-inders, wires, dials, and knobs.

Let me point out a few of other guests to you and, as I do, fashion them out of imagination and memory, allowing yourself to picture them one by one, establishing them here and now: there are the phy-sicians from Calcutta Medical College—Doctors Moat, Webb, and Blalock—and seated next to them the collector, Mr. Money, then the missionary Reverend Small (who suspects that mesmerism is Satanic magic), Mr. Sassoon (an opium merchant just back from China), Mr. Siegel (who is writing a book about hypnosis in India), and over there, on the other side of the room, the Bengalis seated together—Babu Kaleedash Chatterjee (a poet and playwright wearing a dhoti incon-gruous with his double-breasted frock coat imported from Paris), Raja Ram Ramkissen Bahadoor (a patron of the hospital), and on his right is Babu Essanchunder Ghosaul, deputy magistrate of Hooghly (here to translate Bengali into English for the surgeon and for us, and English into Bengali for the patient, her husband, the hospital attendants, and the magician Shambaraswami).

Remember Shambaraswami—his matted beard of serpentine tresses, his face and chest smeared with crematory ash, a scarlet tilak on his forehead, the peacock feather in his hand, and around his neck a string of rudraksha beads and the sloughed skin of a cobra? He has been invited here so that Esdaile can demonstrate to him the superiority of British medical practices over Indian procedures for healing.

And there's the patient, a girl named Kamala, over there, on that low charpoy, covered with a sheet. The man attending to her in a white robe and turban is Budden Crunder Chowdaree, Esdaile's native assistant. Listen to the soft voice with which he deepens trance. *"Ekhon ghumao,"* he whispers. Sleep now. *"Ekhon, ekhon ghumao. . . . Ghum peyechhe?"* he asks. Are you feeling sleepy? *"Ekhon ghumao,"* he repeats again and again. *"Eta shobar samay."* This is the time to sleep.

He blows gently on her forehead and begins to make hypnotic passes with both hands. As you imagine those hands, concentrate on the rhythmic movement of their rotation around and around her face, now in circles over her breast, then down her belly, now around and around over her pelvis, then up and down her legs, and, continuing to keep your eyes on those hands, listen to the soothing hypnotic voice again, the calming whisper, counting slowly, slowly back from ten to one, *"dash, noy, aat,"* pausing between numbers to repeat, *"Ekhon ghumao, ghumao . . . shat, soy, panch . . . ghumao . . . char, tin, dui, ayak. Ekhon ghumao."* Sleep, yes sleep, deep in deep soft sleep.

Over this repetitious verbal deepening of hypnotic trance, Esdaile tells us about the patient. Imagine the Scottish rolling of his r's, as slowly, calmly, confidently he speaks: "My patient today is Kamala, a twenty-four-year-old milkmaid from Kenduli village in the Birbhum district, the third wife of Balbhad Dass, a forty-eight-year-old dairyman upon whom I recently, successfully, and painlessly operated for a scrotal tumor using mesmerism as the analgesia. Kamala has been married to Balbhad for twelve years and has three surviving daughters. Her problems began last spring when a fourth child, a hydrocephalic boy, was stillborn. Her husband brought her here several weeks ago and informed me of her symptoms—persistent vaginal bleeding, acute inguinal pain, and severe burning of the vulva. He divulged that, without his consent and against his good judgment, she had turned for treatment to Shambaraswami, the Hindu healer seated over there, a magician who enjoys a high reputation among the natives of Bengal particularly for his successful treatments of hysteria. His diagnosis of Kamala's condition was that the spirit of her stillborn child remains in her womb, refusing to come out and causing great disturbances there. In vain, Shambaraswami attempted to cure her with mantras that he believed had the power to lure the malevolent ghost of the boy out of her. It was because of the failure of that treatment that Balbhad was able, albeit with some difficulty, to convince her to come here. She was terribly frightened of me. 'She does not want the operation,' he divulged, 'but she understands that she must do whatever her husband commands.' He had, I surmised from the bruise on her cheek, beaten that understanding into her.

"Balbhad has had great faith and complete confidence in me ever since I operated on him several months ago for a scrotal tumor, an affliction rife in Bengal. His right leg was affected with elephantiasis, and he was suffering from progressively frequent inflammation accompanied by periodic high fevers. We induced a mesmeric trance that enabled the dairyman to become so completely passive and insensible to pain that he bore the knife with all of the steadfastness and silence of a cadaver during autopsy. Waking up from his trance only to discover that, much to his astonishment, his tumor was gone, he declared me the eleventh avatar of his god Vishnu, that almighty being mercifully descended to earth as me in order to teach the doctors of India the magic by which they too can perform painless surgeries.

"I do not personally suppose that the native doctors, though certainly unaware of the pioneering work of Franz Anton Mesmer, are necessarily ignorant of mesmeric practices. I must, in fact, confess to having considerable respect for Shambaraswami, believing as I do that he has ample skill as a naturally intuitive mesmerizer. I suspect that if Kamala's somatic symptoms were psychologically based, as so many gynecological complaints inevitably are, his treatment would probably have been effective. Given his failure, however, I performed a pelvic examination, which indicated a uterine cancer immediately requiring a perilously painful surgical hysterectomy. While such surgeries have an approximately 80 percent mortality rate here, I maintain—and firmly believe—that with mesmeric anesthesia I can so sedate the patient today as to lower blood loss, agitation, exhaustion, and shock to the nervous system to the degree that we can expect to reverse those odds and give her at least an eighty percent chance of survival.

"In preparation for the procedure, my subassistants have been mesmerizing the girl every day for the last fortnight, each of those daily sessions lasting for at least two hours, and each showing an exponentially progressive susceptibility and depth of trance. We have monitored that depth with this galvanomagnetic apparatus. During each mesmeric session, Kamala has been made to hold in her hands these two copper cylinders. With each successive mesmerization, she has been able to endure greater and greater voltages of electrical current without showing the slightest signs of discomfort. Our little Mother India," Esdaile concludes with a satisfied smile, "is now ready for surgery."

With that, two subassistants lift the cataleptic girl from the charpoy and carry her to the operating table. As Esdaile uncovers Kamala, we see the prettily fine-featured face with a bruised cheek, russet skin, acorn nipples on flaccid breasts sloping down her sides, and delicate limbs, lithe and limp. Her hair has been wrapped in a black shawl, her pubis shaved, and all ornaments removed.

After positioning a copper cylinder attached with wires to the electromagnetic machine in her flaccid hand and squeezing that hand into a tight grip around it, Budden Chowdaree switches on the apparatus. Imagine the electrical crackle and buzz, louder and louder, as Esdaile turns the dial that increases the voltage, higher and higher, and the milkmaid remains as still and silent as a corpse.

Turning the girl over, the attendants raise her buttocks and bend her knees, tucking them under her in the lithotomy position. With her head lowered, her forehead and palms flat upon the surgical table, she could be some splendid naked Muslim houri bowing in heavenly prayer.

At the head of the operating table, Chowdaree continues magnetic passes over and around Kamala's face to maintain the trance; at the foot, Esdaile lubricates a four-bladed, ivory-handled brass speculum with clarified butter. On each side of the table, a subassistant pulls on a cheek of the girl's buttocks to expose, open, and expand the vaginal canal.

As the surgeon slowly inserts the speculum, Kamala softly moans, prompting Chowdaree to whisper, "*Ekhon ghumao . . . ekhon ghumao, Kamala . . . ekhon ghumao. . . .*" Sleep Kamala, sleep, deep in deep sleep, soft and sweet, deeper and deeper, sleep . . . .

And in deep sleep dark and sweet with dreams
a refuge from her fear and fearful pain
A world of pure pleasure or so it seems
as mohana-raga's rapturous refrain
From Krishna's enchanting golden flute peals
beckoning her with all the love he feels
Awakened entranced suddenly she flees
deeper deeper into a darkness where
Her soundly sleeping husband dreams he sees
Kamala naked on a table there

As the surgeon squeezes the ivory handles of the brass speculum, the blades dilate the vaginal canal for inspection. The uterus is curetted and irrigated and, as a retractor is introduced to expose the cervix, and another to elevate the bladder, the patient remains still, seemingly impervious to the discomfort of the procedure and "*Ghumao*," Chowdaree whispers, "*Ghumao, shundor Kamala.*"

In radiant darkness eyes open wide
and she breathes in the fragrance of the night
And tastes its succulence so sweet inside
and feels the soothing softness of dim light
Hears in it amorous murmurs calling
as silently and secretly she's crawling
To fetch her wedding sari and her shawl
red diaphanous and black as night
"*Edike eso*" the flute seems to call
"come here Kamala come into my sight"
Drawn by the music the sway of its spell
she sneaks out of her hut down to the well
To bathe adorn prepare for her lover
by light of a moon shining above her

The cervix is pulled forward with traction forceps and incised with a scalpel. Uterine ligaments are clamped, cut, and suture-ligated. The bladder is catheterized and a sponge is pushed into the vaginal cavity to displace the ovaries, tubes, and bowel. Esdaile's fingers explore the crevasse before incising the vaginal mucosa. "Don't stop, Chowdaree," the surgeon commands. "Continue the magnetic passes. Don't stop!"

> She daubs vermillion on swollen lips
>   black kohl on her eyes is stippled with care
> Breasts saffron anointed attar on hips
>   fresh jasmine sprays braided into her hair
> Lush loins aching ardent fervent and wet
>   pulsing tumescent all ready and set
> Rapt in black shawl its darkness her cover
>   unafraid of beasts or ghosts of the night
> She hurries to him runs to her lover
>   as her husband wakes up to the sight
> Of his wife disappeared gone from his bed
>   to that of her lover his arms instead

Bleeding vessels are urgently tied off, restraining fibers snipped away with steel scissors, and the uterus is tugged into the vagina. The surgeon clamps the fundus and then uses forceps to grasp and pull on the cervix. It's incised with a long bistoury and ligaments are clamped, cut, and sealed with sutures. "Don't stop, Chowdaree."

> Entranced by a sweet sandal-scented breeze
>   night blooming jasmine and songs of night birds
> Herons and shelldrakes singing lovelorn pleas
>   Krishna's flute music suggesting his words
> "Come to me Kamala come face to face
>   dissolve into me melt in our embrace"

As the surgeon bisects the uterus, attendants wipe the blood purling down the girl's inner thighs, and Chowdaree persists with word, gesture, and breath in an effort to maintain the girl's trance. Shambaraswami mutters mantras to himself and Reverend Small whispers a prayer to his God.

> Imagine now the dark-blue deity
>   appearing to the transported milkmaid
> Yellow clad flute in hand eyes gleaming gaiety

> all surrendering her boundaries fade
> Not to an idol worshipped in a shrine
>   but to a man who makes her flesh divine
> When adoring at his feet she bows down
>   Krishna then lifts her up and delights her
> Waving a peacock feather from his crown
>   scratches and squeezes kisses and bites her
> Transforming her in his amorous ways
>   with his passing hands and entrancing gaze

The surgeon inserts retractor blades and chooses another, longer, bistoury to detach the uterus, the cervix, fallopian tubes, ovaries, and tumor. Then, as he tugs on them with forceps, Chowdaree strokes the girl's feverishly sweating forehead, whispering, "Kamala, Kamala."

> "Kamala" Kamala hears him repeat
>   as her dark shawl and sari slip away
> Anklet bells jingle on her trembling feet
>   as in love the lovers begin to play
> By ornaments her nakedness is enhanced
>   and by it her entrancer is entranced
> And his hands spread apart the tumid thighs,
>   gently, slowly, deeply, entering her
> Opening her wide and closing her eyes
>   knowing not who they are or where they were

The perineum is retracted and then the uterus together with its appendages is delivered through the stretched, gaping, bleeding vagina. Gauze pads with long strings attached are pushed into the cavity and then removed. Examining each ligature, the surgeon replaces several loose ones, then cauterizes raw membranes as the patient begins to shiver, murmur, and moan. "*Arama, arama, Kamala*," Chowdaree urges, "relax, be at ease, calm and comfortable, Kamala." And the surgeon begins the final suturing and cleansing of lacerated flesh. "*Arama.*"

> And "*arama*" Krishna echoes as clinging
>   to him loving Kamala holds on tight
> To him around and within her singing
>   darkness obliterated by his light

> Losing herself in him deeper, deeper
>   her divine lover her lord and keeper
> So deep the pleasure he deigns to give her
>   two merge into one no longer apart
> Pain of their pleasure making her shiver
>   never to end and forever to start
> Moaning with their bliss ecstatic she screams
>   with a fear of waking from such sweet dreams

The scream in the operating theater is alarming, the silence following it full of dramatic suspense. Has the patient died under the knife? It's natural for us to wonder and worry until finally, the surgeon, seemingly exhausted by the procedure, ambles away from the table and toward us to assure us that, yes, Kamala has survived. "It's done," he says, as he removes his blood-splattered apron and hands it to an attendant. "It has gone well, very well. The girl will be fine. She'll be able to return to her village in a few days and she will recall nothing of the surgery. She will not remember feeling even the slightest bit of pain. May God bless her."

When the attendants turn her over onto her back, Chowdaree conceals her nakedness with a fresh sheet that she imagines is Krishna's golden yellow shawl, imagines that it is Krishna's breath as Chowdaree blows upon her face to awaken her, that it is Krishna's fingertips as Chowdaree strokes her cheek, that it is Krishna's voice when Chowdaree beckons her out the mesmeric dream: "*Jaga, jaga,*" that voice commands, "Wake up and open your eyes."

Yes, open your eyes. Wake up for the end of the story. Yes, wake up now, open your eyes, and I'll read to you what the writer told his listener.

Once the dairymaid had been awakened and was sitting up with her eyes open, Esdaile asked Babu Ghosaul to inform her in Bengali that the operation was over and had been successful. "Tell her she has been cured."

"*Ami besh bhalo bodh korchhi,*" the girl responded and then elaborated with Ghosaul translating. "She says that, yes, she knows she has been cured, that, yes, she feels fine. But she tells me that she knows you are lying to her, that you did not perform an operation. She imagines that last night while everyone here was sleeping, she heard the call of Krishna's flute and snuck out of the hospital to go to him. She believes that Krishna cured her last night in a bower in a palm grove."

"Let her believe whatever she wants to believe," Esdaile remarked with a subtle mixture of amusement, condescension, and self-satisfaction. "The rest of us, having witnessed the power of mesmerism, know the truth."

"She also believes," Ghosaul added, "that God's great love will continue to sustain her in this life until it finally delivers her from this world into a life of eternal bliss in Goloka, Krishna's heavenly abode."

A month or so later, hearing from Chowdaree the sad news that Kamala had died of sepsis, Babu Ghosaul tried to imagine that what the girl had told him about the power of God's love might somehow, in some way, actually be the truth.

"Ah yes," he sighed, "I wish I could believe that she is with Krishna in Gokula right now. Don't you?"

THE MESMERIST'S TALE

The method I decided to try for markedly increasing rapport was to have two S[ubject]s simultaneously fill the roles of both hypnotist and hypnotized S[ubject], what I will call mutual hypnosis. That is, I would have A hypnotize B, and when B was hypnotized he would then hypnotize A; then A would deepen B's hypnotic state, then B would deepen A's hypnotic state, and so on. . . .

CHARLES T. TART, "PSYCHEDELIC EXPERIENCES ASSOCIATED WITH A NOVEL HYPNOTIC PROCEDURE, MUTUAL HYPNOSIS" (1969)

In preinductional preparation for the final hypnotic tale, the writer reads to his listener from James Esdaile's *Mesmerism in India:* "I had to-day the honour of being introduced to one of the most famous magicians in Bengal. Baboo Essanchunder Ghosaul, deputy magistrate of Hooghly, at my request introduced me to him as a brother magician. I proposed that we should show each other our respective charms, and after much persuasion, he agreed to show me his process for assuaging pain."

After the sorcerer, whom I've called Shambaraswami, had effectively hypnotized one of Esdaile's patients by traditional means, the British surgeon, confessing that he was amply "convinced of the great efficacy of his charm," proposed that he "would now show him mine; but that he would understand it better if performed on his own person. After some difficulty, we got him to lie down and give due solemnity to my proceedings."

Having successfully mesmerized the Indian sorcerer, the British physician concluded, and concurred with his Bengali subject, that, although the rhetoric and gestures of the scientific European and magical Indian inductions differed, the results were phenomenologically the same.

"It seems to me," the writer continues as his listener begins, as she has become accustomed to doing, to make herself comfortable for the last reading from this book, "that Shambaraswami should have insisted that Esdaile, his 'brother magician,' would likewise understand the traditional Indian charm 'better if performed on his own person.' He ought to have demanded that, to be fair and make a comparison valid, Esdaile have done unto him what he had done unto another.

"I've tried to imagine it. And now, let me read the story I've written about it so that you might imagine it as well."

Are you comfortable and ready?

As you listen to this final tale, allow your body to relax again, just as you've done for the previous stories, again taking a few deep, comforting, relaxing breaths . . . again . . . and again noticing that your eyes, and particularly your eyelids, may begin to feel drowsy, heavy, sleepy . . . and as soon as they begin to blink they'll become heavier still, yes, heavier and heavier . . . hard to keep open . . . and as they close you'll be able to feel a sensation of total relaxation . . . simply listening to another tale, doing nothing else, just letting the sound of my voice take you deeper and deeper into a state of calm concentration in which it is natural and easy for you to imagine that we are in Bengal again, long ago, once more in the Hooghly Imambarah Native Charity Hospital, where we watched the surgical operation on the young dairymaid named Kamala. Remember?

The operating table, surgical instruments, and electromagnetic apparatus have been moved to the far side of the room and in their place today are two cane chairs facing one another. Sitting in one of them is James Esdaile. Remember the surgeon? Picture him here again today, this time dressed, despite the heat of Bengal, in a black broadcloth Victorian frock coat, striped gray trousers, high-collared white shirt, and a wide-cut black cravat.

Across from him is Shambaraswami in a loincloth. Remember the magician—his matted beard of serpentine tresses, his face and chest smeared with holy ash, a scarlet tilak on his forehead, the peacock feather in his hand, and around his neck a string of rudraksha beads and the sloughed skin of a cobra?

The pews are now empty, the punkah fans still, the windows curtained, the room dim. We're the only ones here to watch the two hypnotists demonstrating for one another their respective methods for trance induction. Each of them imagines that his procedure is more effective than the other's.

Picture them sitting quietly across from one another, staring intently into the eyes of the other.

The agon begins as Shambaraswami breaks the silence with a soft muttering of a spellbinding mantra, *om na-mo ma-ya-vat-yai sva-ha sva-ha*, and, hearing it, Esdaile starts to slowly rotate his hands in a rhythmic motion in front of his opponent's face, around and around, around and around, to which the magician responds with a peacock feather, waving it back and forth, back and forth. Picture it—the feather moving to and fro as the hands move around and around— and listen to the hypnotic syllables, *om na-mo ma-ya-vat-yai sva-ha sva-ha* and now to the whispers of the mesmerizer *sleep-sleep deep-deep in-deep-sleep*, a repeated utterance the magician understands no more than the physician understands the monotonous mantra, but the effect does not seem to require comprehension, just listening. *Sleep sleep om na-mo ma-ya-vat-yai sleep sva-ha sleep dee-per and dee-per in deep-sleep sva-ha....*

Struggling to resist the magnetic forces he imagines radiating from Shambaraswami's deep dark eyes as they peer through the metronomic waving of the peacock feather, Esdaile, persistently making mesmeric passes, strives not to succumb, to keep his own eyes wide open, straining to do so with such force that his eyelids begin to tire from the endeavor, to grow heavy and heavier. The harder he tries to keep his eyes open, the more they blink, blink, and finally close.

Still repeating the magic formula, *om na-mo ma-ya-vat-yai sva-ha sva-ha*, still hearing *sleep-sleep deep-deep in-deep-sleep*, still watching Esdaile's rotating hands, Shambaraswami sets down his peacock feather and cannot restrain a yawn. In an effort to ward off the magic power of the surgeon's hands, the magician closes his eyes, and then cannot help yawning again, and again as he imagines that the physician is deeply entranced and entirely under his control.

In Bengali, Shambaraswami tells Esdaile that he will hear everything he's told as if it were spoken in English. "Under my spell you will understand my language as your own . . . my will as your own. . . . Understanding as I do how difficult life in Bengal is for you, how hard it is to be so far from home, in this heat, amidst the squalor and chaos of this land, responsible for the care of so many afflicted people, I will take you to a realm of refuge, the most beautiful, comfortable, peaceful, enchanting place imaginable. Come with me. Follow me out of this stuffy room, down the dark corridor, darker and darker, so dark that you've never noticed this flight of stairs. Take hold of the hand rail to guide you and let's begin the climb, counting the stairs as we do: one . . . two . . . three and up to four . . . five . . . higher and higher . . . and you'll notice how, with each step, the stairwell seems to slowly becomes lighter and lighter . . . six . . . seven, lighter . . . eight . . . and notice that with each step your body becomes lighter and lighter . . . nine . . . ten . . . and you've become so light that you begin to float up the stairs, eleven . . . twelve . . . lighter, yes, lighter . . . thirteen . . . floating higher and higher . . . continue counting to yourself, floating higher and higher with each number and soon you'll be there. . . ."

Shambaraswami opens his eyes, stares at Esdaile, and remains silent until he sees the surgeon's head fall forward, his jaw become loose, his breathing deep and rhythmic, his limbs limp. And then, "You're here," he whispers, "here in Krishna's paradise, Gokula. Imagine it."

The entranced physician sees golden cows meandering in meadows lush with field flowers, primrose, purslane, and periwinkle in bright pastel purple and blue bloom. He smells honeysuckle, jasmine, and wild rose, hears the love songs of skylarks, orioles, and shama birds, feels the rejuvenating coolness of the gently flowing waters of a crystalline stream as he dips his cupped hand into it and then tastes it.

Hearing the soft melodic voice of a girl welcoming him to Gokula, he turns to see Kamala, the milkmaid, standing behind him, her cheek no longer bruised, her sumptuous silken black hair hanging long and loose over bare breasts. Her eyes glisten with forgiveness.

When she kneels down next to him by the stream, he dips his hand again into the water so that she might drink and, as she does so, he feels the warm graze of her lips on his palm. He wants to never leave her.

"I am going to count backward now from ten to one," Shambaraswami says, "and when I reach one, you will open your eyes and see me sitting across from you. When you wake up you will realize that I entranced you with sammohana. Ten . . . nine . . . eight . . ."

At the sound of "one" the physician opens his eyes, sees the magician and hears him ask: "Did I not enchant you, Doctor-sahib? Did I not take you in trance to Gokula? Has it not been demonstrated that my sammohana is more powerful than your mesmerism? Have I not won the contest?"

"Yes, you have," Esdaile answers, "and yet, no, you have not. For as you were entrancing me, I was mesmerizing you, and, in doing so, I was able to bring your mind so completely under my control that, in my trance, I was able to cause you to imagine that you caused me to imagine that I was transported to Gokula. And although I may still be under your spell, you too remain under mine. Let me, if you dare, my brother, take you deeper. Yes, let's go deeper."

In their mutual trance, Shambaraswami understands Esdaile's English suggestions as if they are spoken in Bengali: "Feel the magnetic forces emanating from my hands as I wave them around you, engulfing you, taking you deeper into sleep . . . sleep . . . sleep-deep in-deep-deep sleep. . . .

Repeating that mantra again and again, the physician continues to make hypnotic passes until, seeing the magician's eyes close, his head fall to the side, his breathing deepen, and his arms fall loose and limp at his sides, he imagines he has complete control over the sorcerer.

"Listen to me, Shambaraswami, my Bengali brother," Esdaile orders. "Listen carefully. You must reveal the secrets of your magic to me, divulge the traditional native methods by which you enchant your subjects. You must teach me the Indian practice of sammohana. Speak to me, Shambaraswami, my brother. Speak."

The magician obeys somnambulistically. "I was initiated into the mysteries of sammohana and vashikarana by the goddess Mayavati in her shrine in Hardwar. She taught me her secret knowledge on the condition that I would never in my life reveal the teaching to anyone. To break that solemn vow would be to lose the power with which she entrusted me. I do not dare to teach you."

Continuing to rhythmically rotate his hands in trance-deepening mesmeric passes, Esdaile insists. "Listen, listen. Your god, Lord Krishna, commands you to confide in me so that, by incorporating the methods of your magic into my own, I might more effectively assuage the pain experienced by my Bengali patients. It is to help your own countrymen, your suffering brothers and sisters, that you will reveal all to me. Brahm, Shiv, Ram, Durga—all of them, no less than Krishna, beseech you to teach me."

Yielding to the mesmerist's suggestions, the magician recites for him the arcane syllables and draws for him the occult diagrams, the mantra and yantra by means of which he had in yogic trance, under Mayavati's guidance, attained the power that rendered him entirely self-controlled, impervious to all stimuli beyond those generated by his own mind according to his own will.

That done, Shambaraswami reveals that Mayavati had guided him to the cremation grounds and taught him there, amidst smoldering cadavers and ravenous scavengers, her inviolate sadhana. She commanded him to remain there meditating on the nature of the relationship between illusion and reality until the charnel stench of rotting flesh smelled as sweet as sandal, the harrowing screams of vultures sounded as dulcet as the songs of nightingales, and the rabid fights of snarling jackals over skeletal bones looked as graceful as the dances of temple girls.

"She offered me five gifts," Shambaraswami continued: "the skull of a child, a yantra drawn with tiger blood upon a strip of desiccated human skin, a leather pouch containing the crematory ashes of a Brahmin priest, this, the peacock feather with which I entranced you today, and an initiatory name—Shambaraswami.

"Because I have broken my vow to Mayavati, revealing to you her secrets, as demanded of me by Lord Krishna, I must pass these things on to you. I am no longer entitled to her gifts and the power with which they have endowed me.

"With that power I have been able in self-induced yogic trance to traverse time and space, incarnating my spirit in various bodies both in the past and in the future. In the body of a Bengali physician I used her power to entrance Raja Bhoja of Malwa so that he felt no discomfort when a surgeon opened his skull to remove a malignant tumor from his brain. In the body of a poet I used her power to so enchant the Raja of Kashi with tales of love that, while listening to me read them, he imagined he was Pururavas holding the heavenly nymph Urvashi in his arms. In the body of an ascetic mendicant residing in a cremation ground, I used her power to cause a nasty old crone and a feeble-minded merchant to fall so passionately in love that the hideous hag imagined that the bumbling bumpkin was more noble than Pururavas, and he believed that she was more beautiful than Urvashi. In the body of a Goan Christian cleric I used her power in Europe to demonstrate the superiority of my sammohana over your mesmerism. I have used her power to foresee that in a body yet to be, I will meet a foreigner, an English speaker like yourself and as eager as you to learn the secrets of sammohana. What will his story be?"

Let's imagine it.

Conducting field research for a book about hypnosis in India, an American writer will ask an Indian hypnotherapist he has interviewed if he might be able to introduce him to a practitioner of traditional methods of hypnosis. Dismissive of the indigenous practitioners of vashikarana as quacks and disapproving of them as charlatans taking financial advantage of superstitious people, the hypnotherapist will be resistant to the idea and only finally give in as a favor to the writer, who insists that a story about meeting such a person would be crucial to the completion of his book.

Asking various vendors in the local market if they happen to know of any mantravadis in the area, the hypnotherapist will eventually be informed by a vegetable seller that, yes, there is a vashikaran residing in a rice-farming village some twenty kilometers away. The man will claim that the magician has cured his wife's malaria with his charms.

The hypnotherapist will reluctantly agree to drive the writer to the village and translate for him there.

Surrounded by groves of coco palms and verdant stretches of paddy, the village will be a jumbled conglomeration of whitewashed huts with brightly colored cotton curtains in their doorways, windows wide open, and palm thatch roofs. Cows will graze, dogs will laze, and brahmany kites will roost in the majestic pipal tree at the center of the village where the writer and the hypnotherapist will be offered tea by the leader of the village panchayat and told to be seated to wait for a man named Shambu who, the villager will report, once enjoyed a great reputation throughout the region as an itinerant vashikaran. "But now," the fellow will add, "being quite old and, if the truth be told, a bit senile, he has settled down and is not doing much of anything."

Hoping for a character with matted locks and holy ash on his face and chest, wearing a loincloth and amulets around his neck, the writer will be somewhat disappointed that the magician-hypnotist will be a rather ordinary looking bald and bent-over old man wearing a rumpled white dhoti, thick glasses, and rubber chapels. He will at least, however, have a vermillion sectarian tilak on his forehead and, most promising of all, he will carry a peacock feather in his hand. A young woman in a homespun blue cotton work sari will hold him by the arm to help him make his way to the pipal tree.

Other than a few key words and phrases—*vashikarana, sammohana-vidya, jadu, indrajal, siddhi, mantra, yantra, tantra*—the writer will understand very little of the long conversation between the old man and the hypnotherapist who will eventually smile as if finally succumbing to the old man's charm.

"The fellow has reluctantly consented to show you how he hypnotizes patients," the hypnotherapist will explain, "but he insists that you will only understand what he is doing if he performs it on you."

The writer will then ask his translator to tell the vashikaran that he is not a very susceptible subject, that he has tried at various times to be hypnotized but never with any significant results.

"No," the hypnotherapist will answer with a frown, "No, I must not tell him that. It doesn't matter whether he is able to hypnotize you or not. At least for the sake of politeness, you must play along with it, even if you have to pretend that you are hypnotized so that he doesn't feel we are wasting his time or making fun of him. Just try to imagine he is hypnotizing you. Even if his spell has no effect, you will, for the sake of your book, be learning how he does what he does."

The writer will not be surprised when the attempted induction begins with a mantra (*Om na-mo Ma-ya-vat-yai pher-ing-ghee mam vash-yam ku-ru ku-ru sva-ha*) and a peacock feather waved back and forth.

Although there will be no verbal suggestions—no your-eyelids-are-becoming-heavys nor commands to relax or take deep breaths—the heat of the afternoon will begin to so tire the writer that his eyes will blink, blink again, and then finally close. And then he'll recline.

Imagine it—an American writer, wearing jeans and a khurta, lying on his side on a straw mat with his eyes closed beneath a pipal tree in a village in India, next to him an elderly man in a dhoti waving a peacock feather and muttering meaningless syllables, an Indian hypnotherapist, wearing a striped sports shirt and khaki trousers, standing by them, and not too far away, curious villagers trying to suppress their laughter over the spectacle of a strange looking foreigner submitting to the spells of a senile old magician.

As on and on the vashikaran chants, the writer, feeling more bored than hypnotized, will let his mind drift, *Om na-mo Ma-ya-vat-yai pher-ing-ghee mam vash-yam ku-ru ku-ru sva-ha*, drift, drifting, feeling drowsy, feeling light, lighter, *Om na-mo Ma-ya-vat-yai*, seemingly asleep, yes sleeping in deeply dreamy sleep and imagining there that he is reading a story about the British mesmerist James Esdaile and an Indian magician named Shambaraswami.

He reads it aloud to a listener: "Picture them sitting quietly across from one another, staring intently into the eyes of the other. Shambaraswami breaks the silence with a soft muttering of a spellbinding mantra, *om na-mo ma-ya-vat-yai sva-ha sva-ha*," and, hearing it, the listener's mind begins to drift, drifting drifting in a trance in which she imagines that someone is reading this story aloud to another listener—you.

Yes, she imagines that you are listening to this right now and that, just as she is able to picture you, so you, as you listen to these words, should be able to imagine her.

Imagine that she hears this voice reading this to you right now, the voice of your reader asking her and you to wake up, telling you that when you open your eyes James Esdaile, Shambaraswami, the old village magician, the villagers, the hypnotherapist, and the writer will disappear. But each of them will leave some of their remains in your memory.

When you open your eyes she too will disappear, turning into you, and leaving you and your reader alone together, awake, and more really real than anyone in any story or tale, written or read, told or heard.

So wake up, yes, wake up, and open your eyes.

BIBLIOGRAPHY
History, Fiction, and Hypnosis

IN[TRO]DUCTION: *Reading, Listening, and Hypnosis*

Barber, Theodore Xenophon. *Hypnosis: A Scientific Approach.* New York: Van Nostrand Reinhold, 1969.

Bergson, Henri. *Time and Free Will, an Essay on the Immediate Data of Consciousness.* Translated by Frank Lubecki Pogson. London: S. Sonnenschein & Company, 1910.

Ferenczi, Sándor. *Sex in Psychoanalysis.* 1916. Reprint, New York: Basic, 1950.

Freud, Sigmund. "A Case of Successful Treatment by Hypnotism" (1893), in *Sigmund Freud: Therapy and Technique,* edited by Philip Rieff, 41–54. New York: Macmillan, 1963.

———. *Group Psychology and the Analysis of the Ego.* Vol. 18 of *The Standard Edition of the Complete Psychological Works of Sigmund Freud,* edited by James Strachey, 67–143. London: Hogarth Press, 1956–1974

———. "Hypnotism and Suggestion" (1888), in *Sigmund Freud: Therapy and Technique,* edited by Philip Rieff, 27–39. New York: Macmillan, 1963.

Gafner, George, and Sonja Benson. *Handbook of Hypnotic Inductions.* New York: W. W. Norton, 2000.

Gauld, Alan. *A History of Hypnotism.* Cambridge: Cambridge University Press, 1992.

"How to Stop Falling Asleep While Reading." *eHow,* December 24, 2008. Accessed June 1, 2013. http://www.ehow.com/how_4690480_stop-falling-asleep-reading.html.

Hypnotic Eye. DVD. Directed by George Blair. 1960; Hacienda Heights, CA: Allied Artists, 2010.

Kroger, William. *Clinical and Experimental Hypnosis in Medicine, Dentistry and Psychology.* Philadelphia, PA: J. B. Lippincott, 1963.

Nunzio. "Falling Asleep While Reading." *Sleep Apnea Guide.* Accessed June 1, 2013. http://www.sleep-apnea-guide.com.

Orne, Martin T. *The Nature of Hypnosis; Selected Basic Readings.* New York: Holt, Rinehart and Winston, 1965.

Pavlov, Ivan Petrovich. *Lectures on Conditioned Reflexes; Twenty-five Years of Objective Study of the Higher Nervous Activity (Behavior) of Animals.* New York: Liveright, 1928.

Poe, Edgar Allan. "The Case of Mr Valdemar," in Poe, *The Complete Tales and Poems of Edgar Allan Poe,* 99–106.

———. *The Complete Tales and Poems of Edgar Allan Poe.* New York: Modern Library, 1938.

————. "Dream within a Dream," in Poe, *The Complete Tales and Poems of Edgar Allan Poe*, 639.

————. "Mesmeric Revelation," in Poe, *The Complete Tales and Poems of Edgar Allan Poe*, 41–48.

————. "A Tale of the Ragged Mountain," in Poe, *The Complete Tales and Poems of Edgar Allan Poe*, 601–8.

Romanyshyn, Robert D. *Technology as Symptom and Dream*. London: Routledge, 1989.

Shor, R. E. "The Three-Factor Theory of Hypnosis as Applied to the Book-Reading Fantasy and to the Concept of Suggestion." *International Journal of Clinical and Experimental Hypnosis* 18 (1970): 89–98.

Tart, Charles T., "Psychedelic Experiences Associated with a Novel Hypnotic Procedure, Mutual Hypnosis," in *Altered States of Consciousness; a Book of Readings*, 291–308. New York: Wiley, 1969.

Tatar, Maria. *Spellbound: Studies on Mesmerism and Literature*. Princeton, NJ: Princeton University Press, 1978.

Tinterow, Maurice M. *Foundations of Hypnosis, from Mesmer to Freud*. Springfield, IL: C. C. Thomas, 1970.

Wambach, Helen. *Reliving Past Lives: The Evidence under Hypnosis*. New York: Harper & Row, 1978.

Yapko, Michael D. *Essentials of Hypnosis*. New York: Brunner/Mazel, 1995.

MAYAVATI'S SPELL: *India, Stories, and Hypnosis*

Abbot and Costello Meet the Killer. In *The Best of Abbot and Costello, Vol. 3*. DVD. Directed by Charles Barton. 1949; Hollywood, CA: Universal Pictures, 2004.

Allen, Grant. *Kalee's Shrine*. New York: New Amsterdam Books, 1879.

Anangaranga of Kalyānamalla. Edited by Vishnuprasada Bhandari. Benares, India: Chaukhamba Sanskrit Series, 1973.

Bhagavadgītā. Edited with the commentary of Śankarācārya by Dinkar Vishnu Gokhale. Pune, India: Oriental Book Agency, 1950.

Blavatsky, H. P. *A Modern Panarion: A Collection of Fugitive Fragments from the Pen of H.P. Blavatsky*. London: Theosophical Pub. Society, 1895.

Braid, James. *Magic, Witchcraft, Animal Magnetism, Hypnotism, and Electro-Biology*. London: John Churchill, 1844.

————. *Observations on Trance: Or Human Hibernation*. London: John Churchill, 1850.

Caycedo, L.A. *Letters of Silence: A Selection from the Correspondence between Dr. Alfonso Caycedo, M.D., and Great Yogis and Scholars in India*. New Delhi: Bhawani, 1966.

Claflin, Edward, and Jeff Sheridan. *Street Magic: An Illustrated History of Wandering Magicians and Their Conjuring Arts*. Garden City, NY: Doubleday, 1977.

Chandu the Magician. DVD. Directed by Cameron Menzies and Marcel Varnel.

Fox Film Corporation, 1932; Los Angeles: 20th Century Fox Cinema Classics Collection, 2008.

Chowdhary, Shitika, and Jini K Gopinath. "Understanding the Trance State in Patanjali Yoga Sutras and Its Similarities with the Trance State in Hypnosis." *Indian Streams Research Journal* 2, no. 9 (2012): 1–10.

Frost, Thomas. *The Lives of the Conjurers*. London: Tinsley Brothers, 1876.

Goudriaan, Teun. *Maya Human and Divine*. Delhi: Motilal Banarsi Das, 1978.

Gupta, Ashum. "Hypnosis: Facts and Misconceptions." *Indian Journal of Psychological Medicine* 12, no. 2 (1989): 79–82.

Harshavardhana. *Ratnāvalī*. Edited with an English translation by M. R. Kale. Bombay: Booksellers' Publishing Company, 1964.

Hergé. *The Blue Lotus*. Boston: Little, Brown, 1984.

———. *Cigars of the Pharaoh*. Boston: Little, Brown, 1975.

Ibn Battūta. *Voyages*. 3 vols. French translation from the Arabic by C. Defremery and B. R. Sanguinetti. 1895. Reprint, Paris: François Maspero, 1982.

Kabir. *The Bījak of Kabir*. Translated by Linda Hess and Shukdev Singh. San Francisco: North Point Press, 1983.

Kipling, Rudyard. *The Collected Works of Rudyard Kipling*. New York: AMS, 1970.

Knowles, Elmer E. "Oriental Hypnotism, Telepathy, Concentration, Magnetic Healing Magic, and Wonders of the Orient." Branch Six of *Prof. Elmer E. Knowles' Complete System of Personal Influence and Healing*. London: National Institute of Sciences, 1914.

Kumar, Sadhu Satish, *Oriental Methods of Hypnotism*. Calcutta: Castle Courses, 1958.

Laurence, L.W. de, ed. *India's Hood Unveiled: South Indian Mysteries "by a Native Hindu of South India."* Chicago: The de Laurence Company, 1910.

McGill, Ormand, *Hypnotism and Mysticism of India*. Los Angeles: Westwood Publishing Company, 1979.

Rājaśekhara, *Karpūramañjarī*. Edited by Sten Konow, translated by Charles Rockwell Lanman. Harvard Oriental Series, no. 4. Cambridge, MA: Harvard University Press, 1901.

Roth, Leopold. "Hypnotic Magic and Sexual Seduction in *Kāmaśāstra*." *Journal of the History of Sexuality* 12, no. 2 (2000): 69–96.

Schrenck-Notzing, Albert von. "Ueber den Yoga-Schlaf." *Zeitschrift für Hypnotismus* 3 (1894–95): 69–75.

Siegel, Lee. *Love and Other Games of Chance: A Novelty*. New York: Viking, 2003.

———. *Net of Magic: Wonders and Deceptions in India*. Chicago: University of Chicago Press, 1991.

Sorcar, P. C. *History of Magic*. Calcutta: Indrajal Publications, 1970.

Srivastaya, C. M. *Vashikaran siddhiyan sadhna avam Prayog*. Delhi: Manoj Publications, 2007.

Temptress. Film. Directed by Lawrence Lanoff. Los Angeles: Playboy Enterprises, 1995.

"The Unknown Terror." *Ramar of the Jungle.* DVD. Arrow Productions and ITC Entertainment, June 13, 1953; West Conshohocken, PA: Alpha Home Entertainment, 2008.

Vyas, Bhaskar, and Rajni Vyas, ed. *The Indian Handbook of Clinical Hypnosis.* Calcutta: New Central Book Agency, 2006.

Yogavāśishtha. Edited by V. L. S. Pansikar. Bombay: Nirnaya-Sagara Press, 1937.

Yva, Yvon. *Les Fakirs et leurs secrets.* Paris: Gallimard, 1963.

LE SOMMEIL LUCIDE: *Religion, Sex, and Hypnosis*

Abbé Faria (website). http://www.abbefaria.com.

Bernheim, Hippolyte. *De la Suggestion et de son Application à la Thérapeutique.* 1886. Reprint, Paris: Harmattan, 2005.

Buyanov, Mikhail. *Child Psychiatry and You.* Moscow: Mir Publishers, 1989.

Carrer, Laurent. *Jose Custodio de Faria: Hypnotist, Priest and Revolutionary.* Victoria, BC: Trafford Publishing, 2006.

Chateaubriand, François René de. *Mémoires d'outre-tombe, Deuxième partie, Livre II.* Paris: Penaud frères, 1849.

Currimbhoy, Asif. *Goa and Abbe Faria.* Bombay: Soraya Publishers, 1964.

Dalgado, D. *Mémoire sur la vie de l'abbé de Faria.* Paris: Jouve, 1906.

Darnton, Robert. *Mesmerism and the End of the Enlightenment in France.* Cambridge, MA: Harvard University Press, 1968.

Dumas, Alexandre, *Le Comte De Monte-Cristo.* Paris: Garnier, 1962.

Dupotet, Jules-Denis Sennevoy, *Manuel de l'étudiant magnétiseur.* Paris; Baillière, 1851.

———. *Traité complet de magnétisme animal:cours en douze leçons.* Paris, Baillière, 1882.

Faria, Jose Custodio de. *De la cause du sommeil lucide ou étude de la nature de l'homme.* Paris: H. Jouve, 1906.

Figuier, Louis. *Histoire du merveilleux dans les temps modern.* Paris: L. Hachette, 1861.

Fernandes, Diogo Mesana. *Abbe Faria: The Master Hypnotist Who Charmed Napoleon.* New Delhi: Ritana Books, 2006.

Fustier, l'Abbé de. *Le Mystère des magnetiseurs et des somnambules.* Paris: Chez Legrand, 1815.

In Search of Abbe Faria: The Hypnotic Vision of a Goan Pioneer. DVD. Directed by Isabel Vas. Panjim, Goa, 2006.

Jouy, Victor-Joseph Etienne de. *L'Hermite de la Chaussée d'Antin, ou observations sur les mœurs et les usages français au commencement du xixᵉ siècle.* 5 vols. Paris : Chez Fillet Ainé, 1812–1814.

Mello, Alfredo de. "Memoirs of Goa." *The Goan Forum.* August 15, 1999. http://www.colaco.net.

Moniz, A. Egas, *O Padre Faria na história do hipnotismo.* Lisbon: Faculdade de Medicina de Lisboa, 1925.

Noizet, François Joseph. *Mémoire sur le somnambulisme et le magnetism animal.* Paris: Plon frères, 1854.

Perry, Campbell. "The Abbé Faria: A Neglected Figure in the History of Hypnosis." In *Hypnosis at Its Bicentennial: Selected Papers from the 7ᵗʰ International Congress of Hypnosis and Psychosomatic Medicine*, edted by F. H. Frankel and H. S. Zamansky, 37–45. New York: Plenus Press, 1978.

S. du M. "Des séances publiques de magnetism, qui ont lieu chez M. l'abbé Faria." *Annales du magnétsme animal* 5 (1816): 186–91.

Santos-Stubbe, Chirly dos. "Abade Faria (1756–1819) in Scientific and Fine Arts Literature." In *Goa and Portugal: History and Development*, edited by Charles J. Borges and Hannes Stubbe, 336–48. Presented at the 2nd conference, "Goa and Portugal: History and Development," Goa, India, September 6–9, 1999.

Sharma, Shridhar. "Abbé de Faria: First to Explain Hypnotism." *Indian Journal of Psychiatry.* 16 (1974):307–11.

Stubbe, Hannes. "José Custodio de Faria, the School of Nancy, and Sigmund Freud: An unknown Goan source for Psychoanalysis." In *Goa and Portugal: History and Development*, edited by Charles J. Borges and Hannes Stubbe, 326–35. Presented at the 2nd conference, "Goa and Portugal: History and Development," Goa, India, September 6–9, 1999.

Vas, Luis S. R. *Abbe Faria: On the Life of a Pioneer Indian Hypnotist and His Contribution to Hypnosis.* Panjim, India: Broadway Book Center, 2008.

Vernet, Jules. *La Magnetismomanie, Comedie-Folie.* Paris: Chez Fages, 1816.

AN-ESTHETICS: *Politics, Medicine, and Hypnosis*

Arnold, David. *Colonizing the Body: State Medicine and Epidemic Disease in Nineteenth-century India.* Berkeley: University of California Press, 1993.

Baber, Zaheer. *The Science of Empire: Scientific Knowledge, Civilization, and Colonial Rule in India.* Albany: State University of New York Press, 1996.

Bala, Poonam. *Imperialism and Medicine in Bengal: A Socio-historical Perspective.* New Delhi: Sage, 1991.

Dingwall, Eric. *Abnormal Hypnotic Phenomena: A Survey of Nineteenth-Century Cases.* 4 vols. London: Churchill, 1967–1968.

Divekar V. M., and L. D. Naik. "Evolution of Anaesthesia in India." *Journal of Postgraduate Medicine* 47 (2001): 47–149.

Eliotson, John. *The Zoist: A Journal of Cerebral Physiology and Mesmerism and their applications to Human Welfare* Vol. 6, no. 22 (Hypollite Bailiere, 1843–1848).

Ernst, Waltraud. "Colonial Psychiatry, Magic, and Religion: The Case of Mesmerism in British India." *History of Psychiatry* 15 (2004): 57–71

———. "Under the Influence in British India: James Esdaile's Mesmeric Hospital in Calcutta and its critics." *Psychological Medicine* 25 (1995): 113–23.

Esdaile, James. *The Introduction of Mesmerism into the Public Hospitals of India.* London: W. Kent. 1852.

————. *Letters from the Red Sea, Egypt, and the Continent.* Calcutta: S. L. Hyder, Medical Journal Press, 1839.

————. *Mesmerism in India, and Its Practical Applications in Surgery and Medicine.* London: Longmans, 1846.

Kumar, Anil. *Medicine and the Raj: British Medical Policy in India, 1835–1911.* New Delhi: Sage, 1998.

Mouat, Frederick J. *Record of Cases Treated in the Mesmeric Hospital from November 1846 to May 1847 with Reports of the Official Visitors.* Calcutta: W. Ridsdale, Military Orphan Press, 1847.

Prakash, Gyan. "Science 'gone native' in Colonial India." *Representations* 40 (1992): 153–78.

Pulos, L. "Mesmerism Revisited: The Effectiveness of Esdaile's Techniques in the Production of Deep Hypnosis and Total Body Hypnoanesthesia." *American Journal of Clinical Hypnosis* 22 (1979–1980): 206–11.

Gupta, Giri Raj. *The Social and Cultural Context of Medicine in India.* New Delhi: Vikas Pub. House, 1981.

Winter, Alison. *Mesmerised: Powers of Mind in Victorian Britain.* Chicago: University of Chicago Press, 1998.